AMMA JI AND ME
(My mother and me)

Zahir H. Kazmi

www.Amma-Ji-and-me.com
Please post your comments on the website.

PUBLISHED BY:
ZHK & Associates, Ltd.
210 W 22nd Street, Suite 115
Oak Brook, IL 60523
Tel: 630-575-0404
Fax: 630-575-0050
Email: zkazmi@zhkcpa.com

ISBN: 1460995635
ISBN-13: 9781460995631
Library of Congress Control Number: 2011904188

To the woman with whom I share my life: my loving wife Bernadette. This book would not have been possible without her encouragement and faith in me to take on this project. It was she who thought that my mother's story is worth sharing.

❦

Also to the hundreds of thousands of women who had to struggle to give better life to their families and face human beings brutality in the aftermath of independence of India and Pakistan.

FAMILY TREE

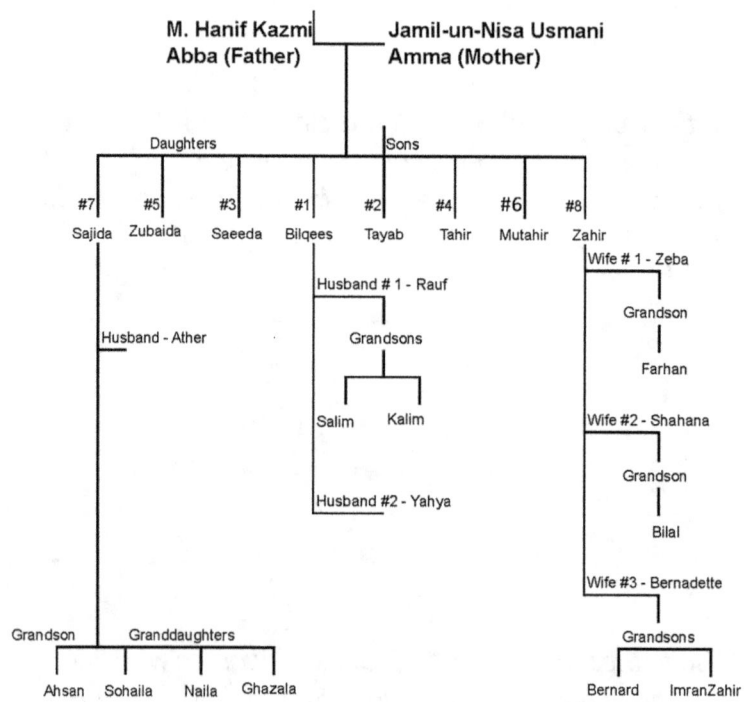

Due to space limitation, only those family members
mentioned in the book are included in the family tree.

CONTENTS

INTRODUCTION

My mother was the single most influential person in my life. It has always been that way, from the days when I was a child who depended on her for everything to the time when our roles reversed and she had to rely on her children. My mother died on August 31, 1998, yet to this day her love and wisdom continue to guide and shape my life. She reminds me of this each morning when I open my office door. My office suite number, 115, printed in bold just above the door lock, is the same number as my mother's gravesite. I cannot help but think that my Amma had something to do with those three digits on my door.

I still miss her, and I will never tire of telling people what an amazing woman she was, especially considering the times in which she lived. I have recalled the stories about my mother's life to my wife, Bernadette (Bernie); so many times that she knows them all by heart. Bernie never stops me or says she has heard them all before. Whether the stories make me laugh or cry, the telling never fails to give me joy. Bernie loves hearing them because she also loved *Amma Ji* (mother dear). We are all lucky to have known her. I am proud to say I am her son. She went well beyond the call of motherly duty, sacrificing to ensure that her children received the education, support, and love we needed. A few of us may claim to be self-made, but we would not make such a claim if our mother had not provided the tools.

Amma Ji was a woman without formal education, and she was born to a conservative family in a small farming community in India at the turn of the last century. The only book she was taught to read was the holy Quran, and even as a young girl she was not trained to understand it. She was born in a place and time marked by the accepted belief that educating girls was a waste of money and effort. From the moment she could speak, she was taught to understand that her role in life was to be an obedient wife to her husband, to bear his children, and to do the required household chores.

Each time I told my mother's stories, my wife responded, "You should put all this in writing." I didn't think I was up to the task, but Bernie insisted. I was very close to Amma Ji, and because of this, my wife believed that I was the only one who would be able to take on the work and the only one who possessed the sufficient knowledge. "Who else can tell it better?" Bernie insisted. "Just write her story the same way you tell it to me." With Bernie's encouragement, I decided to give it a try. This book is the result.

The story is not only my mother's but also mine. Amma Ji was my constant companion for much of my life. When I was a small boy, she took me with her everywhere she traveled, not because she needed my company, but because she worried that if she left me home with my older siblings, we might get into fights. (I was the youngest and was likely to lose.) I liked my mother's company, and so we continued to spend a lot of our days together, even after I was big enough to stand up to my siblings. Spending so much time with Amma gave me a chance to witness her struggles and to see how she dealt with those challenges. It also gave me the opportunity to listen to her wisdom and sometimes to hear stories of the life she lived before I was born.

My mother was a pioneer in many ways. In a society that enforced the belief that the only place for a woman was in the home, she became the first woman in her entire extended family to start a business. She was the first woman among them to travel by train, ship, or airplane, and she was the first woman in her family to make the holy pilgrimage to Makkah.

Though my mother received no formal education, she recognized the importance of literacy. In her midforties, with a little help from her children, she taught herself to read and write. She realized that her life and our childhood would have been easier had she and her husband been formally schooled. In many ways, this is what motivated her, and she insisted that all her children, both the boys and the girls, received the education their parents had missed. Our family often found it terribly difficult to make ends meet, but no matter what, Amma made sure that there was enough money for school. Thanks to her, most of her children and grandchildren earned postgraduate degrees and went into professional careers.

Amma Ji did more than help with our schooling. She gave us a value system without which success would be meaningless. I have my mother to thank for every blessing in my life.

She was one of a kind.

"Amma Ji with youngest grandson, Imran."

ALVIDA

I sat with my wife, Bernadette, and our three youngest sons, Bilal, Bernard, and Imran, in the departure hall of American Airlines at John Wayne Airport in Santa Ana, California. We were waiting for the boarding call for our flight home to Chicago. My family sat clustered around me, but they seemed far away, as I lost myself in memories. I knew this airport all too well. For many months, I shuttled between Chicago and Los Angeles while my mother wavered between life and death. Sitting by my Amma's hospital bed in Los Angeles, holding her hand, I experienced the exact moment when her heart gave up and allowed her soul to escape, leaving her tiny and frail beautiful frame behind.

After that, everything became a blur. There were the unexpected details of funeral preparations, the Islamic religious ceremonies, and the dozens of family members and friends, circling like friendly bees arriving to drink the final nectar of a cut flower. The sweetness of her love still lingered among us, giving us peace as we kissed her white-shrouded face and lowered her body into its final resting place.

I spent so much time running around that sitting still and silent amid the chaos of the buzzing airport announcements and whining jet engines allowed me to consider what had really happened. She was gone. The source of my life, the teacher of my mind, the conscience of my soul—my Amma was no longer here. I spent hours sitting among muttering, listless, impatient passengers over the past months, and the time gave me almost too much space to grieve and let go. After the constant visits to Los Angeles came to a close, once we had buried her, once I had completed my responsibilities as a son, I found myself holding on for just a moment longer—not to cling, but to remember all the hours of a life lived completely. My mother knew no other way to live, and the memories of that life, both the parts I witnessed and those she only told me of, were her final gift to me.

Jamila Kazmi was not just my mother but also a daughter, a sister, a grandmother, and a mother to many. Mostly she was herself, a strong woman with an independent mind in a time when women were not known for either.

Her life began in obscurity in the little north Indian town of Pur Qazi. All her life, she was a brave voyager, traveling to big cities in India, Pakistan, and across an ocean to America. She had a big heart and put family before everything else. She also had an able mind that insisted on education for all her children. She was born at the turn of the last century and lived to see the new millennium. I can only dwell for so long on how she died, but her life was a series of vivid pictures worth recounting in detail.

I am the youngest of her eight children, which is probably why I was closest to her. My earliest memory of my mother is of my fist wrapped firmly around her index finger, as I hopped after her down the streets of Sialkot, Pakistan. In those early moments with her, I felt safer than I ever have since. I had no worries in the world, and I felt proud as I tagged along, seeing myself as her escort, her taking me and me taking her here, there, and everywhere as we walked along those dusty streets. No one else but me knew her beautiful, loving face. She was wrapped in a *burqa* from head to toe, and her face was hidden behind a net veil. She was invisible to everyone else, but in my eyes, she was everything, and the memory of those happy walks makes me smile even now.

The vivid mental picture gives way to one of an event that happened before I was born. Even though I was not there, I have heard about it so many times that I can see it clearly. She was standing proud and angry in the *angun*, or courtyard, of our first house in Pur Qazi, India, defending her rights. Another family jointly owned the house, but they refused to equally share it until she staged an invasion, commanding my older siblings to take over the household territory that was rightfully theirs.

When I was six, I did not understand why we left my *Abba* (father) behind in Pur Qazi, India, to move to Sialkot, Pakistan. When India gained its independence, the country's leaders divided it in two, and my two older brothers moved to the new country of Pakistan. By then, Amma was middle aged, yet it was she who decided to take the three youngest children by train to join my brothers in a new and unfamiliar country. No other woman of her day would think of taking such a journey with small children and without an adult male relative by her side.

More images follow, like photographs in a camera. The click, click, click of years go by as all of Amma's children moved to different corners of the world, experiencing its pleasures and pains but still guided by her wisdom; it is a continuous thread that binds us like patches in a quilt. We have grown older, things have changed, but Amma remains constant, spreading her comfort over us like the broad shadow of a *pepal* (oak) tree on a 100-degree day.

She lived her life to the fullest, a fierce love and good-humored fight, well into her nineties. When the time came for her to die, I first thought there was little to be sad about. When she had difficulty breathing and seemed to be struggling to hold on, I held her hand in mine and whispered, "Amma, as you know, we all have to leave this world one day. The time has probably come for you to leave us. I know how much you love us and how much you must be worrying about our well-being, but you know you have raised us well and taught us to be strong, and you can trust us to carry on in this journey of life. Please go in peace, and wait for us to join you and Abba. You know when the time comes, we will follow your path, and we will all be reunited in the eternal world."

I meant those words when I said them, but they now feel empty.

As my family and I sat waiting for our flight, my heart dropped, and a great void in my body opened. She wouldn't be there for Imran's graduation or Bilal's wedding. I tried to tell myself that this was not true, that she would always be here, that her spirit would protect us no matter where we were, but the void remained.

I am a stoic man and do not often give in to my emotions, but at this moment I felt overwhelmed by the urge to cry, just as Bernie and my sister Sajida did at Amma Ji's funeral. The airport was hardly the place. A voice announced our flight. I took a deep breath, picked up my heavy briefcase, and stepped in line behind my wife and sons.

As our plane rose into the sky, I looked down at the expanse of Los Angeles, and the vision came to me. I saw her face floating above the flat urban landscape, shining like the morning sun. I smiled and whispered, "Alvida (goodbye), Amma. Allah Hafiz (God be with you)." Before her face dissolved into the rooftops of Los Angeles, I saw her smiling back at me as she replied,. *"Alvida*, my son, goodbye."

-2-

JAMILA

Amma Ji crawled out from under a veil and made a life for herself and for her children. It took strength to do this; the veil was heavy. It took passion to do this, something the veil could not repress.

Education was not available to most girls in rural India, or to many boys, but if a girl lives behind walls surrounded by mango trees, the mouth-watering smell of ripe fruit fills the air with temptation. If no one rolls a mango into her home so that women hidden within can try a taste of it, how long do you think it will be before one woman finally ventures out to pluck one for herself? In her family, Amma Ji was that one.

When she was a girl, the holy Quran was the only book taught in the home. At first, Amma Ji did not understand the Quran, but she later learned to love and revere it. Throughout her life, she would yearn to know more words.

Amma Ji was never sure of the exact date of her birth, but it was long before the Industrial Revolution reached India. She guessed the year to be 1905. She was given the name Jamila and born into a palatial family compound in the small farming village of Pur Qazi, District Muzaffarnagar, in the Indian state of Uttar Pradesh. The region is known for its fertile land, particularly for sugarcane and mango groves. Her earliest memories were of two primary smells: the earthy perfume of the blushing mango groves outside the walls of her home and the pungent, gray-green herbs of her father's medical practice within. Her father, Sheikh Ahmed, was a *hakeem*, or herbal physician, and his daughter learned to associate the smell of drying plants with the love and security of home.

Sheikh Ahmed adored Jamila, the eldest daughter of his second wife. When she was beginning to walk, her chubby legs wobbling toward the cut flowers on his desk, perhaps he pictured her walking into a courtyard full of flowers where she would meet the only man not of her blood who would ever lift her veil. Maybe she would even marry a *zamindar*, a feudal lord of Uttar Pradesh. Then again, he would be happy if she simply married an educated man, maybe a hakeem like him.

Jamila was a smart little thing, and she was better at reading the Quran than any of his other children. If she had been a boy, her father would have sent her to school, following in his profession, but he believed, as did the men of his time, that education was wasted on women. Instead of learning the plants of healing from her father, Jamila learned the spices of good cooking from her mother. It didn't occur to her to be angry because she did not attend school like her brothers but stayed home and learned domestic responsibilities. So far, her life had been good, and there was enough life to fulfill her within the family walls.

The home consisted of a large residential quarter with many rooms, a medical clinic with a patient visiting area, a wing for manufacturing and storing medicine and medical supplies, a stable for horses and other animals, a carriage house, and extensive grounds.

Jamila's mother observed *purdah*, meaning that she spent most of her time confined within the walls of her husband's compound. Purdah comes from the Hindu word for "curtain" or "veil." It refers to the practice of shielding women from men outside their immediate family. Sometimes Jamila's mother donned a soft and elegant two-piece burqa, a type worn by well-to-do women, and stepped into a curtained wooden palanquin called a dolly—this usually meant that she was going to visit relatives. The dolly would shield her from the eyes of men along the way, and the burqa would take over that role once she got there. When she stepped out of the palanquin, her only view of the world would appear to her in little crosshatched squares as she looked through the netting that covered her eyes.

A few times, Jamila went with her mother on those visits. For her, stepping into the darkness of the dolly must have felt like stepping inside a magical box that transported them to another world. Hidden inside, in the dark, feeling only the bouncing footsteps of the carriers, she likely witnessed the same tension between joyful secrecy and the fear of discovery she experienced when she played hide and seek with her brothers, sisters, and cousins. Stepping out into an unfamiliar house was a special adventure, but until she was eleven, Jamila was most content when she was safe in her own home.

She did not know that the winds of change were coming and that they would start not outside the family walls but within them.

WINDS OF CHANGE

Though Jamila was born into wealth, her affluence only lasted long enough to give a dream-like quality to her memories of early childhood. When Jamila was eleven, her easy life gave way to struggle. It started with a devastating loss. That was the year her father died, one of the most dangerous events that could happen to an Indian girl.

At first, Jamila only knew that she had lost someone precious to her. After her father's death, when condolences came pouring in, she recognized that her community, and many towns far and wide, had lost a healer who had dedicated much of his life in service to the health and well-being of his fellow man. Jamila had little time to grieve his death before she was forced to suffer the consequences. Her once-happy family split into two camps that were at war with each other.

The first camp was made up of the three children from her father's first marriage to a woman named Fatima. Taqi Ahmad, the eldest boy, became the head of that family. After Fatima's death, Sheikh Ahmed married Aisha, who was the head of what became Ahmed's second family. Jamila was the eldest of Aisha's two children, and Aisha was pregnant with a third. As in most wars, the victor would receive the spoils, and the victor could not possibly be a girl.

Jamila's father left plenty of property and assets behind, but her mother did not have control of her late husband's estate. Jamila's older half-brother, Taqi, took control of the inheritance.

Years later, Jamila understood just how much her father's death put her own future in jeopardy. She was no longer a bright flower in the eyes of a protective male who doted on her. As a girl on the cusp of womanhood, having no male benefactor was a precarious state of affairs. Her fate would be left to an older half-brother whose primary concern was his father's first family, not his second.

Although Jamila's mother, Aisha, was technically the head of her husband's second family, she had no real protection from the law. She was a second-class citizen, both in effect and in fact. At that time, Muslim and Hindu women were totally dependent on men to provide for them. In India's agricultural society, few men had access to education or jobs, but women had no access at all. Women could not inherit ancestral lands, a practice that continues in India to this day. A widow like Aisha was forced to depend on the mercy of whatever men remained in her family.

Like her daughter, Aisha had been taught to read the Quran but wasn't taught what the words meant. She only learned to make the Arabic sounds on its pages, and her language was Urdu.

Aisha had relied on the example of her own mother to understand her duties as a wife and mother, but no one had shown her how to be a widow. There was no frame of reference.

She was no match for her wily stepson, who now had control of all that her husband once shared with her. He had an enormous advantage over her simply by being a man. He not only had control of the estate, but he also had education, the ability to move freely outside the home, the shrewd and worldly ways one develops in so doing, and the power to enter into contracts and agreements outside the family sphere. Aisha had no education, no legal rights, no freedom of movement, and no worldly experience, and she retained the girlish naiveté that went along with all of this.

Aisha didn't have enough worldly knowledge to understand how to maneuver through the politics brewing over her late husband's household. Instead of standing her ground when she argued with her stepson over how to divide the estate, she fled in anger and fear. She retreated to her parent's house with her two young children in tow and a third child in her belly. By vacating the premises, she gave Taqi free reign to take complete control of the property. He did not hesitate to do this and left my grandmother and her children penniless.

As a woman brought up to serve an educated, well-to-do husband, Aisha had only learned one skill considered useful in her world: obedience to tradition. When Jamila turned thirteen, Aisha became impatient to marry off her daughter, even though thirteen was barely old enough for marriage, even in Indian Society in those days.

Aisha began searching a prospective son-in-law. My *Nani* (grandmother) was not only obeying the rules of tradition but also acting in panicked self-preservation. The sooner Jamila married, the sooner she would be someone else's responsibility. It never occurred to Aisha that she might be doing her daughter a disservice. She believed that once her daughter was married, she would have a husband to provide for her. This was the greatest service a mother could do for her daughter—to give her some semblance of the security that Aisha herself no longer possessed.

Although Taqi had taken over the family estate and finances, he was not done trying to exert power over his father's second family. When he found out his stepmother was seeking a husband for Jamila, he went to her and asked her not to rush. "Jamila is my sister and I think it is only right, since I am the man of this family, I have a say in who she marries," Taqi said. "She is young enough, so there is no need to rush. I think we can take our time and find her a husband who is well established, who has the resources to take good care of my little sister." Taqi was young and prone to self-interest. However, in this case, I like to think he really did have Jamila's best interest at heart.

Arranged marriages were the accepted norm of the time for both Muslims and Hindus. Love did not factor into the decision. Instead, the prospective couple's parents considered all the other factors that would likely lead to a mutually beneficial relationship: religion, family background, language, values, age, height, color, education, wealth, and social standing. According to Islamic law, marriage requires consent of the bride and groom, so parents often went through the formality of asking their children to consent to a match. However, obedient children were expected to go along with their parents' choice. If they did not, the consequences could be severe. Their family could financially or emotionally cut them off, or they could find themselves shut out of social circles. The reasoning behind arranged marriages was simple. Parents were not only older but believed to be wiser about life's experiences, positioning them to make better choices on an appropriate spouse for their child. If a wise, well-considered, long-term choice was the goal of an arranged marriage, then Taqi's suggestion to wait and weigh all the options was certainly the one more likely to benefit his sister in the long run.

However, after Taqi's betrayal of her side of the family, Aisha found it safest to assume he was her enemy in all affairs. She believed no matter what he suggested, it would probably be better for her family if she chose the opposite. But I like to think maybe it was because there was a little twinkle of feminine rebellion hiding in my Nani. She reminded him this was one area where she did not have to follow what the man of the house said. "In this case, Taqi, I do not have to listen to you. It is a girl's parents, and her parents alone, who decide on a proper husband for their daughter. If her father was still here, he would have the final say. But he isn't. So, as her mother, it's up to me, not you."

She was right. Jamila's future husband was a decision that would be made by her mother, and her mother alone - a woman of no education or worldly experience.

Jamila was an intelligent girl, as even Taqi had been heard to remark. If anyone had asked Jamila's opinion in the matter, she likely would have agreed to the wisdom of her half-brother's suggestion. But no one was about to ask a young girl for her consent to something as important as her marriage. Tradition demanded that she marry whomever her mother told her to marry. Anything to the contrary would have brought shame and disrepute to the family. Because she was not only intelligent, but also obedient, she went along with her mother's wishes.

Later, Amma would tell us, "Someone would take more time and care to look closely while buying a cow or goat than my mother took in selecting the man with whom I was to spend the rest of my life."

Even today, there are an overwhelming majority of weddings in India arranged by the couple's parents. There are few love marriages, despite several Bollywood musicals to the contrary. Sometimes couples from arranged marriages grow into love. But, at least for my

Amma, falling in love before marriage would have been impossible. As a Muslim girl, she was hidden behind the veil of purdah and never had the opportunity to meet a young man outside the family, much less fall in love with one. Even if that had not been the case, at thirteen what chance did she has to understand what romantic love really was?

As my mother later told me, her mother settled on a bridegroom with utmost speed. Mohammad Hanif Kazmi came from a family of Pur Qazi that was just as respectable as Jamila's. Unfortunately, he was also just as poor as she was. The bridegroom was not a landowner or a man of letters, as her father might once have dreamed. But at least he was not a man twice her age, as Jamila had feared.

Hanif was in his late teens, just a few years older than his bride. There were striking similarities in their family fortunes. His father had died just a few years before, the land holdings he left behind were being managed by Hanif's older brother, and the older brother had transferred all the property to his name and sold the rest. Hanif had no education that might help make up for his lack of family fortune and no skills to enable him to find a decent job to provide a living for himself and Jamila. Ironically, his lack of wherewithal to support Jamila formed the grounds on which Taqi opposed the marriage.

Taqi was also concerned the marriage would put his family, his primary family, at a political disadvantage. The young groom's first cousin was Abdul Hai, the most powerful zamindar of the area. Taqi feared his stepmother would use her relationship with her new son-in-law to forge an alliance with Abdul Hai. If she had such an ally in her corner, Taqi might yet be forced to give his stepmother and his half-siblings a share of their father's estate.

Though the mother had final say in her daughter's marriage, Indian culture still gave deference to the male head of household, so Taqi decided to press his case. He changed from brotherly affection to patriarchal declaration. "Under no circumstances will I allow this marriage to take place!" he said.

As determined as Aisha was to avoid confrontation with him, she was equally determined not to let him get the best of her. In her day, subterfuge and manipulation were the only tools women had to gain access to power. So she conspired with the bridegroom's brothers and sisters to arrange her daughter's wedding in total secrecy. Taqi's family and the rest of the community did not find out about the marriage until after the deed was done.

Taqi was hopping mad. "You clearly have no respect for me and my family. You treat us like we do not exist."

"If you no longer wish to treat us like family, Stepmother, then have it your way. We are no longer your family," said Taqi. "Jamila, I expected better from you! You know your father would never have approved of this secret wedding. Do not expect for you or your husband to ever be invited to our home, since I never approved of this marriage." Of course, he knew his sister had no say about whom she would marry, or when, or how. She remained silent, but she gave Taqi a measuring look, her mind busy calculating how to deal with him.

Jamila appeared soft on the surface, but even at thirteen she had a steely inner strength. It was not the kind of strength that fights wars, but the kind that wages a relentless peace. She may have worn a visible veil to hide her face from men, but she also wore a veil of patience over her weapons of compassion, understanding, and compromise.

Within days of Taqi's proclamation, she told her husband, "I think as a newlywed couple, you and I should pay our respects to my half-brother and his family."

"Even though he has forbidden us to come?"

"Especially because he has forbidden us to come. We must be the ones to make the gesture of apology. If we do not have harmony in our families, you and I will never know any peace."

I can almost see Hanif's lips spreading in the slow smile I would come to know so well. "My bride is young, but she is wise."

With that my mother and father became a team. For the first time since her wedding, Jamila donned her burqa, a simple one-piece garment of white cotton, the kind the poorest peasants wore. It was all her mother could afford for her dowry. Then she and her husband walked to the house where she used to live until just two years before. As they made their slow march through the village, perspiration would certainly have spread over her skin from nervousness as much as the heat. The burqa protected her from the sun, but it was also stifling. I picture this young girl, worrying her sweat would make the cotton outfit cling to her in an unseemly way, trying to hurry her steps, then reminding herself she was a woman now, and slowing her pace. I see her taking a deep breath and looking at the netted world around her as if she has never seen it before.

It was true, she had only seen her own neighborhood on rare occasions, spending most of her time in the confines of one family compound or another, moving from living quarters, to courtyard, to kitchen, and back again. But she had seen glimpses of it all before. There were the whitewashed homes, the mango trees, the dirt roads, the goats and cows. The difference now was she was a married woman, no matter how much her legs twitched with the urge to run like a girl. She would have been glad her eyes weren't easy to read behind their filmy curtain with so many feelings bubbling inside her, and her struggling to get them under control.

Her husband would surely have stared straight ahead and said nothing; though his eyes occasionally rolled to the side to make sure she was at his heels. He gripped a basket in both hands, their humble peace offering. I can see him also sweating, small telltale trickles tracing fear across his taut forehead.

When they arrived at her childhood home, Jamila stood discreetly behind Hanif. When a servant called on her brother Taqi to come to the towering double doors, Jamila had to suppress the urge to laugh at her half-brother's look of surprise. She sucked in her breath and waited.

"Mr. Kazmi, I did not expect to see you here." Jamila suspected he felt some of the shame that she had hoped he would.

"My wife and I wanted to apologize for not inviting you to our wedding. We brought a small peace offering to make it up to you. Some dates." Hanif handed the basket of dried fruit to his brother-in-law.

Taqi reached out for the basket, his hands slow and reluctant, while his eyes darted fast and wary around the front drive. "I do not usually like dates, as Jamila knows, but thank you."

"May we come in?" Hanif asked.

"I suppose it would be rude to leave you here," Taqi said. "So since you have come, we will invite you in." By this, Jamila knew she had a chance to win her way back into this family.

She stepped in, smiled, and went about the task of repairing ties she had no part in breaking. That first visit might not have started with the warmest of welcomes, but Taqi's family could only maintain the tension for so long.

Jamila not only took on the role of peacemaker with her father's first family, but also with her husband's family, who struggled with similar issues. Everyone wanted a piece of the family pie and there were limits on how much there was to go around. They certainly did not want to share with this newcomer, Hanif's young wife. Some of the family members were outright nasty to her. They could not directly disobey the tradition that had obliged their brother to find a wife, but if they must add another woman to the household, then they were determined it would be to their advantage. And no one was more determined to stake her claim to advantage in that house than the wife of Hanif's oldest brother.

Since Hanif's mother was dead, his oldest brother's wife became the female head of the household. As such, she took on the role of Jamila's mother-in-law. It was traditional for a daughter-in-law to be obedient and helpful to her mother-in-law, and the older woman pushed their roles to the hilt.

Either way, Jamila was in for a tough time. In a home shared by in-laws, the kitchen was a battlefield, and despite being either noisy or silent, the women on that battleground were always at war.

- 4 -

SURVIVAL

While Jamila fought a family cold war on two fronts, there was a more immediate issue requiring the thirteen-year-olds attention: survival. It could have taken years to win over her families. Meantime, her husband had no job and neither of them had any money to live on. Whether the families accepted them or not in the long run, they could not rely on these people to support them financially in the present. Resources were limited and those not lucky enough to inherit a father's estate had to pull their own weight.

For a young family without education or resources, moving away from their network of family support was not an option, however minimal the support might be. Pur Qazi was a small town, so Hanif's options were few, but he had two skills that were more important than they might seem at first sight. He was trustworthy and he was willing to work hard, and he had one connection his wife advised him could become the key to his future.

"You should ask your cousin, Abdul Hai, for a job," she said.

"I don't want to beg him for a job. It's too embarrassing. He'll hire me, why? Just because I'm his cousin?" Hanif answered.

"Yes. That's what family is for, to support each other. But it's not just because you are his cousin. It is because you are a cousin he can trust to be a reliable employee. That's more than many people can offer, cousins or not."

It was hard to argue with her. It was their only option.

Hanif went to work for his cousin, Abdul Hai; the zamindar that Taqi had feared would come to the aid of his stepmother's family. Abdul needed someone to work as his personal assistant, and his young cousin was one of the few people he believed could do the job.

The pay was too humble to launch young Mohammad Hanif Kazmi into an independent life. He and his bride had no choice but to continue living in his childhood home, which had once seemed spacious and comfortable but now was crowded with the jealous, suspicious, competitive families of his older brothers. She knew her struggle to reunite the family was not enough to change that imbalance. She would also have to increase her financial power. In her day the only way to do that was through her husband.

Although Hanif supported his wife's dealings with their families, it is not to say they were of one mind on everything. Instead, they were of two very different minds. One was passive and the other aggressive. One was easygoing and the other ambitious. By nature, Hanif was content with his small portion in life, a simple person with no big future plans. He was always reluctant to embrace change and eager to point out the potential downside of any new venture his wife suggested. He was a follower, not a leader.

Unlike her mild-mannered husband, Jamila was not satisfied with their circumstances. She had higher goals for herself and her family. She had seen better times, times not of dissipation, but of contentment and family joy, and she was determined to find a way to achieve that again. Plus, she wanted one thing for her children that she never had: education. She knew achieving all this would require climbing up above their current circumstances. That meant shrewd saving, investing, and planning. She was prepared to grow and change to make these things happen, and to ask her husband to grow and change with her.

These differences ultimately worked quite well for the couple. They were a duo, working in tandem, balancing each other's natures. If they had both been leaders, they would have been in competition with each other. Jamila pushed them to new endeavors, while Hanif often put on the brakes to prevent them from doing anything too impulsive. That's not to say they worked together easily. Their partnership was successful because of dynamic tension, two opposing forces working together toward a greater result. There was friction and sparks often flew when Jamila passionately tossed her ideas out for discussion and her husband resisted.

You might say Jamila blindsided Hanif with her ambition. He was content to turn over all his earnings to her and trusted her to keep the household accounts. What's more, he was glad to have a prudent, thrifty wife who always set aside part of his meager pay for their future. But he did not know what she planned for that future. At first, neither did she. She only knew someday they would invest their savings in something that would carry them to greater success. She did not yet know exactly what that investment would be. This would evolve in time as she learned more about the secret strengths of her outwardly docile husband and the strengths she was just beginning to discover within herself.

Jamila was young. Time was on her side. As she waited for the money and the ideas to come, each night she listened to her husband talk about the work he performed for the zamindar. She noticed very quickly how her husband had an ability to make people like and trust him, and he knew how to determine a need and fulfill it without being told. He was not necessarily a man of action, but he was certainly a man who knew how to anticipate. These were good qualities in a businessman. So, after just two years, she advised her husband to stop working for his cousin and venture into business for himself.

Hanif was stunned by this announcement and immediately declared it a ridiculous idea. "Am I not a good husband to you? We have a roof over our head, food to eat, and money saved for the future. Someday we may need that money for our children. Why risk losing it on some business venture? We know nothing about business."

"You're right. Someday we will have children. We cannot stay in this crowded house forever, but on your salary we will never be able to afford to move. If we have children, what will they inherit? Your brother owns this house, this property. We have nothing. If we do not take the risk, we will never have anything more than we have now. There is no future here."

"Someday my cousin will promote me, give me more responsibility. Then I'll make more money. If I go into business for myself, I could lose everything."

"If you work for your cousin, you can only go so far. Yet if you work for yourself, his connections could help you go even farther."

"And with what will I start this business? I do not make a lot of money."

She took him by surprise when she pulled out the money she had saved, a respectable stack of bills and coins.

"This still is not enough to launch a whole business."

She explained this was where the relationships her husband had been building in the community as he ran errands for his cousin would finally pay off. He would seek loans from his new contacts in the community.

It would take her several more weeks to convince him. But through nagging - the time-honored method of ambitious wives without power - Hanif simply grew tired of arguing with her. In the end he had to admit it was not a bad idea.

Her business idea? Agriculture. It was what was familiar to them. More specifically, she stuck to the arena in which her husband had gained knowledge while working for his cousin.

"Haven't you told me many times what a bother it is that farmers have to travel so far out of town to buy their oxen, cows, and goats?" Jamila said.

With the instinct of a born entrepreneur, Jamila identified a niche no one else was filling. Her husband would travel to the trade center where livestock was bought and sold, buy multiple animals at wholesale prices, and bring them back to sell to local farmers.

Jamila also suggested they bring another business tactic into play, credit. It was a practice not unheard of but rarely used in their tiny town. Many of their neighbors did not have enough savings to buy the livestock they needed. Yet if they had oxen to help them plow and sow their crops, they would increase their chances of making more money at harvest time. Jamila realized that if credit was extended to farmers to buy livestock at planting time, they were investing in a bigger return at harvest time. The farmers, grateful for their improved fortunes, would pass on the good word and would also become return customers.

At first, Hanif balked at the idea of extending credit. However, working for his cousin had given him a chance to get to know many local farmers and learned which ones he could rely on to repays their debts. Those he believed to be unreliable had to provide proof they had other financial backing or he wouldn't extend them credit. Meanwhile, his close relationship with the zamindar, the local feudal lord, gave him muscle to enforce any financial contract. Not that Hanif wanted to strong-arm anyone, but since local farmers knew he had a powerful cousin they were likely to pay their debts to him before their other bills. They feared the kind of pressure they might experience if they did not.

In the end, some of Hanif's fears came to fruition. A few customers could not pay when the time came. But Jamila's hopes also proved correct. The couple made more money than they lost and slowly and steadily their business grew.

Jamila regularly set aside a portion of their income. And again, when they accumulated enough funds, she suggested they invest in a new venture.

"Really?" Hanif said, raising an eyebrow, "and what is that?" He was sure it would be more than he wanted to take on. But he also knew his wife's power of persuasion. Her next words would likely hold his new fate.

"Mangoes," she said her voice firm and certain. "Our community is known for having the finest mango groves in the region."

"But the local farmers already work as a group to sell their mangoes and they already have buyers."

"Yes, but you know more people than they do and you're already making the trip to the market. You can bargain for a better price. Then when it's time to make the trip, you will leave town with mangoes and come back with livestock. Since you already have to make the trip, it will be more productive. You will make money going both ways. It will be more convenient and profitable for everyone, including you."

Of course Hanif made a few more arguments. It was his nature. But he was already smiling and shaking his head, knowing the young wife had already won the argument before they started. After a few weeks, he was convinced to move forward with her ideas. He pictured himself leading a caravan of carts to the city, strong oxen pulling piles of ripe mangoes, all of which he had bargained for. He pictured himself building Jamila a house like the one her stepfamily had taken over, a house like the one his father had.

It was not a bad idea at all.

THE FIFTY PERCENT HOUSE

A t home, Jamila continued to wage her campaign for peace with her two extended families. She brought the same skills to this task as she did on her personal financial goals for herself and her husband: persistent patience, tempered with a determination to stand up for her right to a place in the world.

Her half-brother Taqi continued to be rude every time she visited, but she kept coming back. It took months to get them to be civil to her, but her efforts paid off. Taqi was impressed by her persistence. She was not just a worthy adversary, but a truly generous girl who was sweet to his children and continued to offer assistance to his wife no matter how many times she was rebuffed. He began to treat her with growing respect, even warmth, and the other brother followed his lead. Soon, those who did not know of the rift between the two halves of their family would have been stunned to hear of it.

Although Jamila did not choose her husband, she was lucky. He stood behind her choice to patiently re-weave the torn relationships of her family. By working together to solve this first problem, they created a strong foundation for their own marriage. Their mutually supportive partnership worked magic on those around them. They met rudeness with dual pillars of kindness, humbling her family to display their better sides. And they met the world as a united front, inspiring their family, friends, and neighbors to seek more harmonious relationships in their own lives. Hanif's patient efforts to restore family unity earned him so much respect with his wife's extended family that they began to bring their problems to him and seek his advice. A young man of no education had become a man of stature in their eyes.

Jamila was not just seeking to patch things up in her family. She went beyond repairing relationships to build strong bridges between herself and all those around her. No matter what resistance she encountered, she patiently drove in the pylons, tightened each bolt, and erected each girder until she was part of a strong interlocking framework of mutual support that would not fall. When she determined the right course of action, she had the courage to stand behind her decision. If someone told her she was wrong, she would not let that person stop her, yet she would also hold her temper. She simply moved forward until the force of her conviction carried that person along with her.

All this was done in the face of opposition from her own mother, who still saw half of their family as the enemy.

Jamila understood something her mother failed to grasp. It was not only a family she was trying to strengthen, but in those days in India, a family was a community system. A family did not just include the immediate circle of husband, wife, and children. It extended outward in a large spiral, including uncles, aunts, and cousins of multiple generations. Such an expanded idea of family was an unavoidable necessity in the agricultural society into which Jamila was born. Even in a wealthy family, particularly in a wealthy family, it was critical to maintain these ties because it was the only way to keep family fortunes intact. Those fortunes, big or small, were typically made of one thing: land. Landholdings were passed down from one generation to the next and each generation held the land in joint tenancy. If they wanted a stake in the land they were forced to deal with each other, whether they liked it or not. Instead of fostering closeness and sharing, this interdependency often created inter-family tension and conflict. That was not good enough for Jamila.

Because she understood how small actions in the present could create a ripple effect of consequences well into the future, Jamila became the calm eye of the family storm. And because the family saw this in her, they dragged her into the middle of every jealous squabble and ultimately every major power struggle. She sought to shift her family from the philosophy of "every man for himself" to "all-for-one and one-for all." And she took on this job at the age of thirteen.

Meanwhile, among her in-laws, the war dragged on. The older brother's wife continued to order Jamila around and the others followed suit. Jamila politely did as she was asked when she could, but she always made it clear she did it out of kindness and respect. She had enough courage to draw a line, to sometimes declare, "No, I'm sorry, I have other chores I must finish first, for my husband." Over time, seeing her give selflessly while still holding her head proudly as she balanced her husband's needs with the needs of the larger family, even her in-laws were shamed into treating her with respect.

She became an unspoken leader in her family, though they would not have admitted as much of a woman who was still little more than a girl. She gained a reputation for being good at managing money and at solving disputes. Both her family and her husband's family started seeking her advice. As often happens, her natural leadership continued to bring about envy among the pettier family members. They wanted her to fail and tripped her up as often as possible. The war would never completely end, though she would forge important alliances along the way, including Taqi in one household and her brother-in-law's wife in the other.

As time went on, whenever female relatives from both sides of the family visited her, they would offer to help her prepare meals.

"You do so much for all of us. Today you should let us help you," they would say. That's when Jamila knew her place in the family was secure. Still, there was one more family she would have to fight.

If birth control had been available in Jamila's youth, she might have put off having children. She was, as I have said, a patient girl. She pictured her husband growing a business strong enough so they could build their children a home as comfortable as the one she remembered and a living as secure as she had once believed hers to be before her father died. I am certain Jamila would not have put the cart before the ox. But it is something she never questioned. Married girls became pregnant and it was a blessing. A married woman hoped for healthy children and that was that.

Except in Jamila's case. This woman hoped for healthy, *educated* children.

Jamila had been married for two years when she became pregnant with her first child. She was not quite sixteen when she gave birth to her daughter Bilqees. She did not know how long it would be before her dreams of a comfortable life and an education for her child would be possible. But she knew it was time to take the next step and make another investment. This investment would be of a much different nature than her previous ones.

Hanif was always amazed by the amount of money Jamila was able to save from their earnings, for they always seemed to be reinvesting it. Yet there it was again, a little pile of money sitting on the table between them, his wife's musical voice floating above it.

"Our children need a house, one where their father is the master. I do not want our children to grow up feeling like second-class citizens in their own home, so we must build one." When had his wife's girlish soprano turned into a woman's contralto?

Once again, Hanif's wife wanted him to make a change when he saw no need for change. He looked at her growing belly and turned his eyes away in embarrassment. All right, he thought, change was coming whether he liked it or not. But a new house? It was too much. He stared at the small but impressive stack of money between them. "My dear wife, you know this is not enough money to build a house."

"Not by ourselves, but as you know, many families in need of extra income will sell a share of their house. We will buy half a house."

"Half a house? We live in half a house now."

"Excuse me, but we do not. We live in less than a quarter of a house, and we do not own any part of it. Your brother owns it and your sister-in-law runs it. If we buy into a new house, we will own half and we will be masters of our half. Later, when we have more money, we can sell our half and buy a better house. This is an investment in our future."

As you might have guessed, Jamila won this argument.

Buying a home, whether half a home or all of one, was a much different proposition in rural India in the 1920s than most people today would understand. In fact, even in those days, it was a different proposition than most people elsewhere in the world would have found familiar. In Pur Qazi, the buyer and the seller of a home usually knew each other, or at least knew each other's families, long before the transaction. They entered into a verbal agreement witnessed by community elders. Money changed hands and promises passed from lips to ears without benefit of any written agreement. The only guarantee of follow-through on the terms was the presence of witnesses and the threat of community disapproval if anyone reneged.

Under the agreement, Hanif, Jamila, and their family would move into a portion of the house. But because the house was made for one family, not two, and was not exactly symmetrical, the ownership of each area would be decided when they moved in. The arrangement did not sound promising but it was the best they could do. The other family seemed reasonable and they were certain they could come to some sort of compromise when there were disputes on things like the common area and the kitchen.

When everyone moved in, the family who had sold Jamila and Hanif half of the property immediately started using delaying tactics to put off dividing the house. It started with the use of the angun, or central courtyard. Throughout Pur Qazi, this was traditionally the part of a house a family used as its primary gathering place. In the summer, in the absence of indoor fans, most families used their anguns as sleeping quarters. Since this house was not formally divided, both families were sharing the angun. Under the rules of purdah, it was forbidden for the female members of one family to be seen by the male members of another family, so one family was left without a place to gather throughout the year or to sleep in the heat of summer.

In perfect contradiction to her purpose of taking on this new investment, Jamila found herself once again banished to a corner of someone else's home. I've been told some of what happened next and I can well imagine the details.

One day, shortly after she and her family moved in, the very pregnant Jamila grew hungry for a snack. She left the living quarters and headed across the house, careful to peek into the angun to make sure there were no men from the other family lurking there before she walked across to the kitchen. After she found a snack, perhaps some fruit and yogurt, or chapatti and cheese, she tried to return across the courtyard, but when she peeked out of the doorway she saw one of the men from the other family sitting in a wicker chair, reading the paper. With a gasp, she quickly backed into the kitchen again.

She pulled her small snack tight against her chest, as if fearing it might jump into his line of sight and give her away. She wondered how long the man would remain in the courtyard. Because he was a man not of her family, she did not even remember his name. She thought about the paper he was reading. The baby kicked, startling her, and she addressed a thought to the owner of that small foot.

"I cannot read a newspaper. But someday you will. I'll make sure of it. For now, the important thing is for this man to stop reading his newspaper. I wonder how long it will take."

She thought about retreating all the way into the kitchen and sitting on a chair to wait but then she ran the risk of him walking in on her and catching her unaware. If he saw her, it would bring shame on her husband.

She stood close enough to the door to watch for him to leave and to make sure of the direction he was heading next.

After more than an hour, she became faint. This is not good for the baby, she thought, angrily. She suspected the man knew she was in the kitchen and wanted to make her suffer. Perhaps he and his family hoped this kind of behavior would force her and her family out of the house so his family could keep both the house and her family's investment money.

The man in the angun finally left for another part of the house and Jamila scurried across to the living quarters.

This happened many more times. The *angun* was the axis of the household and often Jamila found herself imprisoned at one end of the house or the other for hours at a stretch. Sometimes the men really did know she was stuck in the kitchen or washroom, a tactic in yet another battle with yet another family. But this family had no long-term hold on her and this time she felt little need to preserve future harmony. Jamila remembered what had happened when her mother had let frustration get the best of her and retreated from her late husband's home. They had lost everything. She would not let that happen again.

Jamila begged her husband to get aggressive.

"You must sit down with them and come to an agreement for dividing the house. You must make it clear how we have paid for half the house and deserve uninterrupted access to half of the home," she said.

"Yes, yes, you're right of course. I'll talk to them," Hanif agreed.

Although he was a hard worker, he was still not a man of action. What Jamila saw as procrastination, he saw as waiting for the most auspicious time to deal with a delicate matter. The truth was he preferred to avoid confrontation at all costs. She was the one who had wanted half a house, not him. Why should he have to argue with these strangers?

It did not have an impact on Hanif's life, since he was out of the house all day. Finding a cool place to sleep in the summer was not a problem for him. He simply spent the nights in the mango groves, snoring among the sweet-scented fruits he had bought in advance to sell in the city later. One of the investments Jamila suggested had become his perfect hiding place where he could remain deaf and dumb to the harassment she now faced inside their latest investment. When the other family saw how Jamila's husband took no steps to intervene, they turned up the heat. And in the height of a Pur Qazi summer, that is saying something.

- 6 -

A MUSLIM BUSINESSMAN

Jamila became the de facto matriarch of her family from the very moment she was married. After her father's death and her stepbrother's ensuing coup, Jamila's mother took on the role of the defeated woman. She seemed to relish the part, taking every opportunity to loudly lick her wounds, lest her family forget.

"When your father died, my life ended, too," she said, as Jamila stood grinding curry paste with mortar and pestle. "Your half-brother made sure of that. Yet you side with him over your own mother."

Jamila sighed. "I don't take sides, Amma. I only try to keep the peace."

"Peace for whom? I have no peace. I have nothing in this world. And now even my own children no longer respect me."

"Of course I respect you, Amma." Jamila changed the subject. "Would you like to help me cut the vegetables?"

"It's nice of you to try to cheer me up, but I know I'd only get in the way."

Jamila sighed again, more heavily this time. Her mother ignored the hint. She did not completely blame her mother for taking the attitude of a martyr. Watching her stepbrother pull her father's house out from under her mother, Jamila had wakened to the precarious foothold women had in her society. Though Aisha made a drama of her changed fortunes, what she said was not entirely false. She had nothing of her own in this world, and it served as a reminder to Jamila that she did not either.

Jamila had taken over one of her mother's responsibilities, the care of her two younger brothers, Jamil and Zaheer. After her half-brother Taqi took all their father's estate, her mother could not afford to take care of her own children. At the time of Jamila's marriage, her brother Jamil was nine years old and Zaheer was two. Though Jamil was only four years younger than she, both he and Zaheer looked on Jamila and her husband as their *amma* and *abba* (mother and father). As hard as Jamila had to work to convince her husband to take on new business ventures, she never even had to ask him to open the door to her family.

Hanif and Jamila always treated the boys as if the two were their children. When Jamil was thirteen, one day when the *angun* was free, he and his adopted parents sat down at the outdoor table to discuss the idea of going away to school.

"Away from you and Abba?" Jamil asked.

Jamila's eyes filled with tears. He was the same age she had been when she married just four years ago, yet he looked so young and vulnerable to her. His face still had traces of the baby roundness that made her want to reach out and pat his cheek, though she refrained, knowing he would not like it. She blinked away the tears and continued.

"Yes, away from Abba and me. I wish you could stay here and go to school. But you know the opportunities are not as good here. This would not be a school for more book learning. We cannot afford that. You would go to a vocational school and learn a trade."

"Can I learn to build houses?"

"Yes, if you like, you can learn to build houses."

"Good. Then maybe someday I can build you and Abba a house of your own so you do not have to be a prisoner in someone else's house."

Jamil grinned. He was repeating the phrase she had so often used. "A new house would be nice. But we'll be proud of you whatever you do, so long as you go to school and study hard."

Jamil sat taller in his chair. "Thank you, *appa* (older sister). I promise I will make you proud."

So, out came another of Jamila's little piles of money and off Jamil went to vocational school in the teeming capital city of Delhi.

Some mothers can send their young out into the wider world, while the mothers still cling to the smaller world they know. Jamila was not one of those women. Although the bother of covering up from head to toe made it a chore to venture far from home, Jamila's love for her family outweighed the burden of a burqa. And, though she would not admit it aloud, so did her curiosity to see the modern wonders her little brother described whenever he would write or come home from the big city.

A woman from her community would never dare travel so far without her husband or another man of her family. It was easy to convince Taqi to take her to see her brother, as he missed the young man, too.

As they stepped off the train in Delhi, Jamila stared unblinking at her netted view of the many-limbed, wheel-turned, box-stacked confusion before her. As a girl she might have thought the outside world a frightening place, but ever since she had discovered, more than once, that the peace and security of home could be stolen from her at any time, the outside world no longer seemed so scary.

Still, it overwhelmed her senses. The cries of vendors ricocheted in her ears and the competing smells of so many different foods made her mouth water with cravings at the same time that she swallowed the urge to vomit. The familiar country smells of fruit and sugarcane and freshly turned earth were replaced by the city smells of grease and dust and the human sweat of thousands. The hands of beggars clawed the damp and sooty air that pressed in on her burqa. She leaned away from their futile fingers and turned wide eyes toward Taqi. But he did not seem to see them. He did not seem to see any of it.

Taqi waved a low arm until a *tanga*, a small horse-drawn buggy, stopped to pick them up. Was this how men developed their power? By ignoring every distraction except whatever fulfilled their immediate needs?

The *tanga* bumped over the rutted roads until it felt as if her head might fly from her neck. No rides in a dolly had ever been this rough or this terrifying. Without a curtain around her, she could see every near-miss with the many buggies and people, cows, and goats that grudgingly shared the road.

When they arrived at Jamil's tiny apartment, she felt guilty, seeing her little brother living like an egg tucked in its slot, lost in a stack of multiple cartons. He offered his sister the only chair. Then he served them tea. This familiar ritual made her feel better, among the rude chaos of the city. They drank their chai in awkward silence for several minutes. Jamila stared into her cup until her brow knitted into a puzzled frown.

"These cups are so much prettier than the ones I have at home. Where did you get them?" she asked.

Jamil gave her a knowing grin. "At the market."

"But Jamil, these look expensive. Are you being careful about how much money you spend?"

"Relax, *appa*," he said. "They didn't cost very much at all. The marketplace is full of wonderful things at very good prices. Would you like to see it? Beware now, you may be tempted to spend money and I know how you hate that."

Jamila gave him a wry smile. She was tired from the long journey and leery of being swindled by big city con artists. But she felt relieved at the idea of getting out of this tiny apartment, which closed in on her like an early grave. Besides, she had been yearning to see a Delhi marketplace.

This time they went on foot, because the market was not far. When they arrived at the first stalls at the end of the maze, Jamila stopped in her tracks. She stared in disbelief down the long wood-and-tarp tunnel that snaked on so long she could not see its end. Even with the slits of open air above, the place was a hothouse of bodies.

"Jamila, don't just stand there. You will get run over!" Taqi grabbed her arm and yanked her to the side. She startled in surprise and turned to look over her shoulder at a couple of men who had almost bumped into her. Then she turned back to stare at the household goods stacked before her. She admired the many copper pots and pans, handmade dishtowels, and colorful, lightweight pottery that looked as pretty to her as a field of flowers.

"Wasn't I right?" Jamil said. "Aren't there more amazing things here than you ever imagined?"

Jamila nodded silently as her fingers glided over all the marvels that a woman could use to make life easier in the kitchen.

She paused to admire a shop full of books. She wished she could buy one of them. But they were expensive. Anyway, she had never read any book besides the Quran. What time did a wife and mother have for reading? Still, she vowed that someday her children would have books like these, the girls as well as the boys. A man of letters would command respect, as her father had. And she had heard of women who went to school. Maybe such a woman would be less likely to get kicked out of her own home as her mother had been.

Jamila commanded her mind to return to the needs of the present and decided to buy a few things she could use at home, like copper pots, lightweight pottery, and soft dishtowels. Jamila was a master haggler who stuck to her bottom line no matter what honeyed ploys the shopkeepers tried.

"I see you're from out of town. So I'm giving you my special visitor price."

"No, thank you. I can just let the air dry my dishes."

"Wait, wait! For you, I will take two pennies off. I assure you that at that price you're practically stealing them from me."

Jamila grinned as she walked away from the marketplace loaded down with bags.

"You see?" Jamil said. "You can buy anything here and it's not too expensive."

"Yes, I'm glad we came," Jamila said.

It was inexpensive, she thought. And that prompted an idea to form in her mind.

As they sat in the train on the way back to Pur Qazi, Taqi said, "I think you were wise to send Jamil away to school. He's really turning into a responsible young man."

Jamila smiled with pride. "Jamil is a good boy," she said. She closed her eyes and began wondering what the women in her village would think of all the cunning little things she had bought for her house. Maybe they would like to have some of their own. Maybe they would pay the "special visitor price" or even a few rupees more.

When Jamila arrived home loaded down with bags, Hanif laughed and asked, "What's all this?"

"This," she said, dropping the bags on their bed, "is my new business."

"Business?! What business?"

"These are modern conveniences we don't have in Pur Qazi. They're inexpensive, and they make life easier and local wives will buy them from me."

"You cannot go into business. You are a woman. Where are you going to set up shop? In the marketplace? No one will buy from you."

"No, I'll sell them here."

"People go shopping at the market. No one will want to shop in Someone's House."

"Of course they will. I think they will like it even more. Then they can relax and enjoy themselves. It will be like a party."

"A party?! And what if I don't want you to throw a party in my house?"

"*Your* house?! It's our house! And home is the territory of women. If the noise bothers you, you can hide where you always do, in the mango groves."

A few days later, Jamila invited all her friends and acquaintances from the village to her house. The back rooms filled with more than a dozen teen wives and mothers who giggled and squealed with delight over the ingenious and pretty objects spread before them. Jamila sold everything in one visit and pocketed a tidy little profit. It would be nearly three decades before American women threw their first Tupperware parties. Jamila was a woman ahead of her time.

"Jamila," one woman said as the pile of goods began to shrink. "I want some of those cute little copper measuring cups, but you're all out. When will you go back to Delhi?"

Jamila grinned. She had no idea. "Next month," she said.

She was in business, and her husband was in the mango groves.

∞

BATTLE FOR THE FIFTY PERCENT HOUSE

When Jamila opened the doors of her home to those women shoppers, she opened a hidden door to a world she had only imagined, a world typically forbidden to women. She still wore her burqa in public, but hidden under that head-to-toe veil, she had secretly entered the world of men.

She began routine trips to Delhi, to buy goods and bring them home to sell. She loved the challenge of trying to figure out what her customers might buy and the reward of seeing her favorite kitchen gadgets fly out the door in bags carried by her neighbors. In those days, as in these, word of mouth alone could provide a powerful marketing campaign. Jamila's clientele grew. For a couple of years, she had the most successful small business her village had ever seen, or rather, not seen.

Invisible behind the walls of her home, at first she did not attract attention. But other vendors became curious, when they realized that the marketplace always seemed to empty around the same day each month. This was when Jamila discovered that word of mouth is a two-edged sword. As women bragged about their clever purchases to their husbands and their husbands mentioned it to one another, ultimately one of the marketplace merchants overheard. As word spread of Jamila's unexpected success at selling goods from Delhi, the merchants did what any smart entrepreneur would do when faced with stiff competition; they started carrying the same products.

Having more years of experience and profit under their belts, more contacts among merchandisers, and greater power to buy wholesale, after a few years they put her out of business.

But Jamila had enjoyed her taste of power and there was no turning back. She was ready to take on anything. The temporary loss of extra income was barely a setback. By then, she had already pushed her husband so far in his business as a supplier of fruit and livestock that she was well on her way to her dream of giving all her children an education.

Jamil's education was already paying off for him. He had learned to build furniture and he had become such a good craftsman that his services were in high demand. Soon he saved enough money to start his own furniture manufacturing and rental business. Like his sister, he understood the importance of finding a need that was not being filled and then filling it. In 1930s India, even in a big city like Delhi, there were still no well-built stadiums for sporting events. For bigger events, managers would offer contracts to whoever could help them create sufficient seating arrangements. At first, Jamil's factory was the only one that made enough chairs and had enough manpower to effectively set-up such large venues. Until the city began building coliseums, his business had an informal monopoly on sporting event contracts in Delhi. Jamila was as proud of her brother as if he had been her son.

Jamila's younger brother, Zaheer, also moved away in his teens to go to school in his ancestral home where their mother now lived. Jamila was sure he, like his brother, would also make her proud. Young Jamila and Hanif were proving to be successful at the job valued most in their community, raising smart and accomplished children even those who were not their own.

But there was still one battle that Jamila had yet to win. It was the one with the people who refused to share her fifty-percent house. Now that she had tasted success—not only as a mother who could look out for her own but as a businesswoman who could compete in the world of men—she was no longer willing to let a domineering family use the rules of purdah to keep her from moving freely in her own house.

Twelve years had passed since they had bought half the house and for twelve years she had asked her husband to confront the head of the other household. I imagine one night she looked in the mirror and thought, "He may be the man of the house but home is the territory of women. It is time to defend your territory." I suspect she hardly slept that night, not because she was afraid, but because she was excited. Once she made up her mind she knew there was no turning back. Tomorrow, she would take her half of the house and just let anyone try to stop her.

I was not born yet, but I am able to form a vivid picture of what likely happened that day, piecing together the stories I knew about Amma and the ones she and my brothers and sisters later told me.

She woke her three children early, shaking them from their beds. "Get up! Up, up up! Today we're moving to our new quarters."

By the time the children were dressed, she had small piles stacked on the beds and in the kitchen. She began pointing, "Bilqees, take those clothes. Tayab take the bed linens. Sayeeda take the towels. Now follow me." The children had no idea what was happening but their mother's serious tone made it clear that now was not the time to ask. She marched through the angun with the children trailing behind her like a line of ducklings, startling one of the adult sons of the second family. He had never even seen Jamila before, no man outside her family ever had, and now here she was with no burqa, just a simple headscarf, marching right past him. She kept her eyes focused straight ahead and did not look at him. Her eldest daughter, Bilqees followed suit. But the younger boy and girl could not help turning their heads to stare at him with wide eyes. Curious, the young man stood and followed them as they continued into the parlor. Walking behind Amma Ji, eleven-year-old Bilqees leaned toward her mother's ear and whispered.

"But Amma, what about purdah?"

"I don't care anymore about burqa or no burqa! I've had enough!" her mother hissed.

When they entered the parlor, Amma Ji started instructing the children where to put their burdens. Her voice was firm, though her body vibrated ever so slightly with fear and perhaps with a little thrill of excitement at her own audacity.

"What are you doing?" the man asked, still more curious than anything.

But Amma Ji ignored him as she and the children returned across the *angun* for more of their belongings.

"Amma!" the young man called to his own mother. A moment later Amma Ji heard voices raised in the kitchen. Her children cast nervous glances at her.

"Don't worry. Just keep moving," she said.

One by one, the other family members began gathering in the courtyard, until they formed a wall of flesh to block her path to their part of the house. Four large men as well as women and children created a blockade. Amma Ji's children were frightened when they saw the towering men lined up to confront their tiny mother. But, as Jamila had said, home is the territory of women and it was the women of the second family who became as feral as dogs in the face of this threat to their territory.

The mother, a middle-aged woman with a severe face, howled, "What do you think you're doing!"

"We own fifty percent of this house and from today we're going to start using what's rightfully ours," Jamila said. "We had an agreement. We've given you twelve years to divide the house, but you haven't lived up to your word. So, if you won't decide which half you want, then I will. I'm taking this half. If you want, you can move into the quarters where you've left my children and me prisoners for the past twelve years!"

"Prisoners?! You have the best part of the house. You have the living quarters, while we must make do with sleeping in the parlor and the *angun*."

"You know that the angun is where people sleep most of the year! And you can hardly call it fair when most of the time we can't get into the kitchen or bathroom. You wouldn't say that eating is a necessary part of living? Or bathing? Or using the toilet?"

Their children burst out laughing at Jamila's passionate outburst over the use of a toilet. Though it was her most dramatic move yet, the women were used to her pestering them about splitting the house and she had always backed down before. They thought this nothing more than an empty gesture of defiance. They knew her husband would not back her up. He never did. They could not believe a tiny young mother with three small children was prepared to take them all on, with or without her husband.

"Come on children!" Jamila said. She then circled around the wall of people, her children trying to follow her, clearly terrified to be left alone with this angry troop of towering grownups.

The older mother ran after the younger mother, grabbed her by the arm and yanked her back into the *angun*. She pulled so hard that Jamila would later find bruises there, like the fat shadows of that woman's fingers. "This will never happen!" the woman said. "You have no right to lord it over us like a queen. Does your husband approve of this outrageous behavior? Running in front of our men without any covering! It's shameful."

"It's you who should be ashamed, treating us like criminals in our own home, bullying me and my children!" Jamila pulled her arm back. Her voice shook as she turned away from the older woman and said, "Come on children, we're still moving!"

The woman followed her into the parlor.

"You can't just take over any part of the house you want, when it's half ours. If you insist on putting your things in our part of the house, then your things are now ours. And we can do whatever we want with them. Razia!" she called to her eldest daughter. "Take these clothes and throw them away."

"Really, Amma?" The girl hesitated.

"Do as I say!"

Jamila stepped in between the girl and the pile of clothes on the couch, "Don't you dare!"

The mother pushed her aside, grabbed the clothes, and threw them to another of her children. "Someone help me!" Half of her family began grabbing boxes and piles, rushing through the house and throwing them out of the front door.

"Stop! You know what you're doing is wrong," Jamila said, her voice shaking.

"I know no such thing. And who's going to stop us? One crying girl and three small children?"

As both women's voices rose in spiraling anger, all the children gathered around them to gape. A couple of the smaller children started to cry.

"Tayab, go get your Abba's cousins to help us!" Jamila said, her eyes wide with the kind of fear that only appears as the twin to resolve. If they wanted to turn this into a matter of physical might, Jamila could also play that game. She and Hanif had plenty of relatives and she had been no fool when she had chosen to spend all those years nurturing even the most difficult of her family relationships. Jamila understood networking before anyone invented the word. If need be, she could call a formidable army of brothers, sisters, cousins, and in-laws to her defense.

Hanif's cousins lived only a few doors away. Once they showed up and saw on one side Jamila with her three children and on the other side four large men and several women, they did not bother to ask for explanations.

One cousin simply turned to Jamila and said, "We'll take care of this." Then he turned to her son, Tayab, and said, "Run to the Mango groves and get your Abba."

Over the years Jamila and Hanif had earned great respect and affection in the community. Jamila had good ideas and organizational skills, and Hanif had a straightforward honesty and humility about him. While their children knew them as Amma and Abba, their neighbors, friends, and cousins called them *Appa* and *Bahi*, the Urdu words for elder sister and elder brother. When people needed her help or advice, Appa's way was not just to serve up tea and sympathy but to offer practical advice and leadership. If there was a family dispute, "Let's ask Appa to settle this," went the refrain. If there was a financial question, "Ask Appa, she's good with money." If there was a question of duty or social propriety, "Appa will know the right thing to do." If she now needed her cousins to return the favor of her wisdom with a little of their muscle, they were more than ready to stand up for her.

Hanif's cousins lined themselves alongside Jamila, face-to-face with the other family with a few faces to spare on Jamila's side. "If you want to pick on one defenseless woman and her small children, you'll have to go through us first," said the eldest, a man in his thirties.

Relieved to finally have a male opponent, whom propriety allowed them to directly address, the men started shouting all at once. One voice rose above the others, "We did not pick on this woman! She invaded our home!"

"Well, and doesn't she live here?"

The men continued to shout.

One of them pointed at her living quarters. "She lives *there*, not here. That is her half. We're supposed to share the house, not just give it all to her!"

Hanif arrived within minutes, panting so hard and with eyes so wild that his wife knew he had just run faster than ever in his life. She smiled at him, her eyes telling him, "I know that I can count on you when things look the worst."

He smiled at her in return and then turned a grim face to the family that he had avoided for twelve years. They explained the situation, while Jamila waited in silence for him to ask her to explain her side of the story. But he did not.

"Well, are you going to call off your impertinent wife?" the head of their house said.

"No, I'm not. You know full well that my wife is right." Hanif said. For once, Jamila was grateful that her husband was a quiet man. The sound of his calm, reasoned voice would surely humble these men into realizing the falseness of their position. "This house should have been divided a long time ago. Either you must sit down with us and divide the house fifty-fifty, as you agreed to do twelve years ago. Or, if you won't keep your word, we'll pick our own fifty percent since we're entitled to half."

"You can't pick just any part of the house you want. We know you'll pick all the best rooms for yourself."

"No, we won't. But if you were worried about that, you should have done something to resolve this before."

Hanif's oldest cousin interrupted, "If you try to stop our cousin from taking what's rightfully his, we'll consider that a declaration of war on our family. In which case, we'll have to move into this house to protect Appa and her children."

The opposing family finally agreed to call in some of the village's most respected elders to resolve the dispute. Soon all that was left in the courtyard was a handful of old men, the opposing family, Hanif, and Jamila who finally put on her burqa out of respect for the elders.

After hearing both sides of the story, the leader of the elders surprised Jamila by turning to her instead of to her husband and asking, "How do you propose to divide the house?"

"I really don't care anymore. You can let them decide. They can have whichever area they choose as long it is fifty-percent of the total area of the house, as we all agreed upon."

This made it easy for the elders to decide. They talked among themselves for only a few minutes before the leader turned to the mother and father of the other family and said, "You must stop being unreasonable and hold up your end of the contract. You can't ask for a better deal than they're offering you. However, if you decide to wait for us to step in and draw the lines, we won't be as generous as Mr. and Mrs. Kazmi."

Seeing that they had no choice, the other family agreed. That very day they divided the house right down the middle of the *angun*. This time, Jamila and Hanif knew better than to only rely on the words of the other family and the ears of the elders. While the elders were still on hand, they drew up a written agreement that they later registered with the village of Pur Qazi.

The second family grumbled among themselves but said nothing more to the Kazmis, as they spent the rest of the afternoon packing their clothes and furnishings and carrying them across the courtyard while the Kazmis did the same. The two families passed each other several times, carrying their loads in silence occasionally muttering a strained "excuse me" or "after you."

Jamila did not care if they never spoke to her again. Her eyes were lit with triumph. In just one day she had ended the feud her husband had left to simmer for twelve years.

"So are you happy now that you finally have your home, Amma?" Abba asked, in all sincerity.

"No thanks to you," she teased. "What took you so long?"

"I ran as fast as I could."

"Twelve years? At that speed, you'll never win any race."

"True. But you must admit I always cross the finish line."

They both laughed.

Over the years, Hanif had learned to accept Jamila's constant scheming to get ahead, pushing him to pursue goals he never had. Meanwhile, she had learned to accept her husband's lack of ambition, forcing her to reign in her ambition to rebuild the lost life her father once gave her. They understood that each of them offered strength that the other did not have. Each showed the other a different side of life and much as they might complain, they each enjoyed that unusual second view of that other world. He was impressed at her talent for making things happen and she yearned for his ability to relax and accept life as it came.

Husbands and wives did not talk about love in those days. Feelings were not a matter for discussion. Jamila would not have even thought to ask herself that question. But, though she did not know her husband when she married him, she now knew him better than anyone. In spite of herself, she admired and appreciated the gentle man who shared her life and felt grateful for the respect he returned. What is that, if not love?

Confident in his wife's affection and satisfied that he had finally risen to the occasion to help her win her long battle for their half of the house, Hanif thought he could finally relax and forget Jamila's schemes for a while. His agricultural businesses had done so well over the years that he had been able to hire extra farmhands and assistants. This allowed him to keep one eye on the mango groves while he played chess with his friends in the village or gossiped with the men in the fields. He was eager to return to his simple routine. But Jamila's battle for her fifty-percent house was not over yet.

- 8 -

BUILDING A HOME

W hen the opposing family in their shared house drew a line down the middle of the *angun*, although it technically gave my parents fifty percent of the house, the decision still left them with a lopsided arrangement. The other family got the main house and the living quarters while Jamila and Hanif's family got the washroom, storage room, kitchen, and half of the courtyard. In some ways it was an improvement except for the obvious question: what would they use for living quarters? After they put up the proper dividers, they could sleep in the *angun* during the long summers, but that did not resolve the question of where they would keep their clothes and personal items, or the problem of where they would sleep when the cold of winter drove them indoors.

In those days, it was common to build a couple of rooms on the side of a house for storing wheat, rice, grain, and other supplies. Hanif suggested that they use the storage rooms as temporary living quarters until they could build larger quarters at some later date.

"Good idea," Jamila said.

Hanif beamed at his wife's praise.

"Maybe we can stay there while we build our new living quarters."

"You mean until we can *afford* a new living quarters?"

"No. We must build new living quarters without delay."

"I know we're doing better now than when we got married, but we still do not have the money to build a home, not when we have three children to feed."

"That's exactly why we need to build more space—because we have three children and may soon have more. There is not enough room for all of us to sleep with the rice and the wheat."

"I understand, Amma. Just be patient a little longer."

"No, no, no! I know what *that* means. By the time your little longer is over, I'll be dead!"

"What do you propose? Selling everything we own? If we want to build, we'll have to borrow. What if we have a bad mango season and can't repay? I'll end up in jail."

Jamila raised her eyebrows at her husband's flair for drama. "Abba, you don't need to worry about the money. I'll take care of it."

"Sometimes you need to learn to take no for an answer," he said and walked out the door.

As she watched his retreating form, she shook her head in defiance and quietly said, "No."

The next day, while her husband played chess in the village, Jamila called her children in from playing outside. "Today, we empty the storage rooms."

"But Amma Ji, we just moved everything the other day!" Bilqees whined. Though all of Jamila's children adored and respected her, Bilqees was approaching twelve, the awkward age when even the best-behaved girls can toy with defiance. Jamila looked at her daughter and realized the girl was only a year younger than she herself had been when she married. How young she had been.

"Would you rather be stored with the food or sleep in a nice bed?" she said to the girl.

"A bed."

"Okay then. Do what I tell you and make a good example for your brothers and sisters. We're moving everything out of the mud rooms."

"Everything?!" Tayab asked.

"You heard Amma Ji," Bilqees said and tapped her brother on the rear, nudging him in the direction of the mudrooms.

"Quickly," Jamila said, urging her children to move in and out of the storage rooms to the kitchen, lugging cartons and sacks.

When the rooms were empty, Amma Ji took a last look, wiping the sweat from her brow with one long sleeve, blowing out a small sigh, and turning to smile at little Sayeeda. "Say goodbye tiny rooms!"

"Goodbye, tiny rooms!" Sayeeda giggled and opened and closed her hand in farewell.

Jamila then asked Tayab to head into the village. "Go to the market, to the place where all the men stand around talking. I want you to find two of them that look strong and tell them I'll hire them as day workers if they can get hold of tools. Remember this, whatever you do, do not go near the sundry shop where your father plays chess. In fact, make sure your father does not see you at all."

"Why not, Amma Ji?"

"Because it's a surprise."

Jamila knew there was only one way to convince her husband to build the home she wanted.

That evening, Jamila looked out the window repeatedly as she cooked dinner, waiting for Hanif to return. She saw him stop just outside the house to stare in disbelief at the pile of crumbled mud next to the kitchen. The storage rooms were completely demolished. He put both his hands up to his face and pressed the heels into his eyes, removed his hands, and stared again. He bent over, put his hands on his knees, and started laughing, the laughter of a prizefighter that realizes he is facing an undefeatable opponent.

He stood, tucked the smile away, and walked toward the house. Jamila scurried away from the window. When he entered the kitchen, she was singing and setting the table for dinner. He stood in the doorway, nodding as the smells of his favorite dishes made his mouth water in spite of himself. He never grew tired of lamb biryani, paratha and yogurt, and mango chutney.

Bilqees stood at the stove, stirring something. She chewed her lip as she turned to look at her father over the sacks, crates, food stores, and clothes that littered the room. "Hello, Abba."

"Hello, my sweet Bettie," he said, ignoring his wife, the piles of food he had to dodge, and the jar he tripped over as he made his way toward his daughter. He leaned over her shoulder and inhaled the smells from the pot. "What are you making?"

"Saffron rice, Abba."

"It smells delicious, Bettie. You're a good girl." He turned and looked at his wife, who locked eyes with him. Neither one spoke. He turned and saw his other two children standing in the doorway, wide-eyed, waiting to see how Abba would react to the destruction of their storage-room-turned-sleeping-quarters. He turned back to Bilqees. "Your mother has changed something, but what? Wait. Let me guess. Is that a new dress?"

Tayab and Sayeeda started to giggle, and Bilqees grinned.

Jamila could keep silent no longer. "We need new living quarters."

"We do? What happened to the living quarters we had?"

"Those weren't living quarters! They were storage rooms."

"So what happened to our storage rooms?"

"Two men tore them down, Abba!" Tayab shouted.

"Hush!" Bilqees said.

Tayab ignored his sister. "You should have seen them, Abba! They had big hammers, bigger than I ever saw!"

He lifted the little boy into the air and hung him upside down, "Well then, we'd better call the police to arrest those men."

The boy giggled, breathless, as Sayeeda said, "Amma Ji asked them to do it. It was a surprise!"

"I see. Well, I am surprised!" He sat on the floor with his children, who gathered around a dinner cloth spread with simmering dishes as they did every night, and winked at Sayeeda. "Perhaps I'll call the police to arrest Amma Ji."

"No you won't, Abba!" Sayeeda squealed, and all the children laughed. They knew their father was joking because of his smile.

Jamila slapped him gently on the shoulder with an open hand and joined in the laughter.

"So," he said, "It seems we have no choice but to build new living quarters."

"Don't worry, Abba." Jamila turned to a nearby shelf, pulled down a large jar, and sat across from him. "If you had let me finish yesterday, I would have showed you how much money I've saved. We can afford to expand our house without borrowing."

"Okay, so we'll expand our house, but may I eat this delicious dinner first?"

IT WOULD BE DIFFERENT
FOR HER DAUGHTER

As with everything, Jamila knew exactly what she wanted her new living quarters to look like. She made a small sketch and made sure that her husband showed it to the contractors. The new quarters would effectively turn their 50 percent house into a small but respectable 100 percent house, no longer linked to the home of their former co-owners. The new home's design would change their opponents across the *angun* from co-owners to neighbors. When construction was finished, family and friends came over to see for themselves what they had heard: Jamila and Hanif finally had a home that could hold up among the nicer homes of the village. Everyone agreed that Jamila's layout was a good one that made optimum use of the sun and air according to the season.

"Why, this is a perfect place to relax in the sun in the afternoon!" her older sister-in-law said, "and you say you designed this?"

"My sister is a woman of many hidden talents," said her half-brother, Taqi.

Hanif turned a proud gaze on his wife, who smiled graciously but said nothing, silently savoring this small victory of respect from her former adversaries. Jamila and Hanif had come a long way since their first penniless days of marriage. Thanks to her clever and assertive planning, and his hard work and network of friends, they had built a secure and comfortable home. Their children wanted for nothing and, in fact, had more than most.

Jamila and Hanif did not worry as much over the birth of their next three children as they had over their first three. In 1929 and 1935, two more sons were born, Tahir and Mutahir, and in 1937, another girl, Zubaida. Each one born into the 100 percent house, a home filled with hope and promise.

However, the couple was still too poor and too far from modern doctors to protect their children from health threats, common in large rural families, that slipped into this house or that, scattering devastation regardless of age, sex, abundance of love, or hopeful prospects. Illness came and went without name or diagnosis so often that people rarely spoke of it.

One morning, not long after little Zubaida was born, Jamila woke with a start. The sun was high in the sky, and she realized she had slept through the night. She felt rested, but this only made her anxiety worse. She never slept the whole night through without being wakened by the tiny cries or stirrings of her baby girl, a sweet child so swaddled in sibling love that Jamila wondered if she would ever learn to walk because her brothers and sisters insisted on carrying her everywhere, passing her from arms to arms.

Jamila's heart pounded as she scurried to the next room, trying not to run—to run was to give in to the kind of fear that could tempt Allah. She reached the side of Zubaida's cradle and stared at the still child. She touched her. Jamila let out a wail, waking the entire house. Her predictions had proven too true.

After the funeral, sometimes the remembered cooing and gurgling of her lost daughter would float to her on a breeze. If her heart was broken, she did not speak of it. The death of babies was so common in her village that talking of such tragedy seemed a waste of breath. If all mothers gave in to their tears, they could not bear to go on for fear that another child would be stolen from them. Jamila kept the sorrow within the spaces of her heart and spread her love and hope on the children who remained.

She resisted the temptation to marry off her eldest daughter at thirteen. Jamila turned twenty-eight that year, and the passage of time had revealed to her just how much of her childhood and youth she had given up to become a wife and mother. Not that she was unhappy with her life, but in the time since her marriage, she had glimpsed a wider world, and she wanted her daughters, and her sons, to find a greater place in that world than her own fate had allowed.

Pur Qazi only had a grammar school and only boys could go. Jamila insisted that they find a home tutor for Bilqees and Sayeeda so that they could learn more than just the Quran. Unlike their parents' generation, Jamila and Hanif understood the benefits of teaching girls reading, writing, and math. If either of them had had more education, their early years together would have been much easier.

Jamila did not know if it was her daughter's ability to read, the good parenting she had received, or a natural personality trait, but Bilqees seemed to carry herself with a self-confidence not shared by other girls her age, even those who had already taken their adult place as married women. The young girl's eyes focused both inward and outward, as if she were equally curious about the world within her and the one around her.

One day, when eighteen-year-old Bilqees was playing with a cousin's baby, lifting the child in the air to rub noses, it struck Jamila that her eldest daughter was the same age she had been when she used to lift her in that way.

"It's time we look for a suitable match for Bilqees," she said to Hanif that night.

"Do you have anyone in mind?"

"I was hoping you would have some ideas, Abba."

The rules of purdah allowed Bilqees to only talk to men who were part of her family. She had no opportunity to know much about the young men of her village except what she heard through gossip.

"I'll find out if my cousins have some ideas," Hanif said.

The subtle community planning of a wedding began. It started with a dropped hint here and there among family members, neighboring families hearing about an eligible bride, questions and recommendations slipped subtly into conversations during visits, and then offers that filtered down the grapevine.

Jamila and Hanif discussed a few offers from respectable local families whose sons were educated, well-mannered, and presentable. Jamila felt a surge of pride, knowing that she had allowed her daughter to complete her childhood and that the girl was now much more ready for marriage at eighteen than she had been at thirteen. She was also pleased with herself and her husband for taking greater care in selecting their daughter's mate than her own Amma had taken in choosing hers, though Jamila had learned to love him.

In the end, Bilqees had no say in the matter, and her parents informed her of their choice. Her broad smile told Jamila how truly grateful she was. They had picked a groom who was close to Bilqees' age, educated, with good prospects, and from a respected family of reasonable means. Many of her friends had settled for much less.

When Bilqees finally met Rauf Ahmed in the company of her parents, her eyes lit up behind the little square opening in her burqa, and Jamila's eyes smiled back. Bilqees would not have a chance to get to know the young man before their wedding, but she knew that her parents would not pick someone rude or arrogant, or someone who was not intelligent or well-bred. She saw that he had thoughtful eyes and nice skin. Marriage was a mystery, and the two would have their whole lives to discover the rest.

Jamila was taken aback when her husband began to describe the wedding he planned. For a man not known for his imagination or ambition, he had dreamed up quite an affair that included thousands of flowers, the best musicians, and fine food for hundreds of guests. "It will be a wedding more beautiful than Pur Qazi has ever seen," said Hanif. "Everyone will talk about it for years to come."

Jamila stared at her husband in surprise. Luckily, most of her face was discreetly covered in front of her daughter's future father-in-law, or they would have seen her mouth hanging open as if it had come unhinged.

She certainly supported the idea of a big wedding, as she understood that this was not only about their daughter; it was an opportunity for the Kazmi family to show how far they had come. Their beautiful, intelligent, first-born daughter was the flowery centerpiece of their success, and their new son-in-law certified their return to the higher class that had once been Jamila's birthright. During the first twenty-one years of her marriage, everything Jamila and Hanif had done had been part of her plan to increase their financial standing. Here was their chance to showcase the fruits of that labor.

In 1939 India, it was not uncommon among Muslims and Hindus alike for families to break the bank for a daughter's wedding. Large weddings were not just indicators of family status; they could raise a family's social status overnight. Peer pressure played a role in the size of weddings, as families of similar status tried to outdo each other. As messengers ran far and wide to deliver the traditional verbal wedding invitations, they not only announced the wedding of Bilqees and Rauf but the graduation of the Kazmis from penniless peasants to an elite family of genuine standing. The fact that they had come so far on their own added to their respectability.

Jamila stepped back in awe, almost a little afraid, as her husband grinned with childlike pleasure while doling out large sums of cash for food, decorations, and expensive silk wedding clothes for his daughter. Their roles had reversed. This time, Jamila begged Hanif to be reasonable and not spend so much money.

"I think you should be careful," she said. "We haven't worked so hard all these years just so you can put us into the poorhouse with a few days of celebrating."

"Don't worry, my dear, this time I'm the one who has been saving for this day. Relax. This will be the happiest day of our lives together, except for our own wedding day, of course."

She gave him a reluctant smile. "Oh, be honest, we were so nervous that day. Neither of us knew what we were doing. You were right the first time; *this* will be the happiest day of our lives."

It was the kind of thing one says whether one believes it or not. Jamila could not have known her oldest child's wedding would be a pivotal moment of joy before a terrifying season of change.

Bilqees, my sister at her wedding

- 10 -

MORE THAN A WEDDING

Whether Muslim or Hindu, a traditional Indian wedding is not a one-day affair but a series of ceremonies and celebrations that stretch over many days, weaving the families of the bride and groom together with multiple strands of memories. The *mangni* was the formal engagement ceremony, at which the families of both Bilqees and Rauf gathered to bestow prayers and blessings on the young couple and to decide the wedding date. A gap of a few months followed before the wedding itself.

After exhausting planning and preparation, Jamila guided her now nineteen-year-old daughter through the final series of rituals that would slowly draw a veil between Bilqees' life as a daughter and her new life as a wife. Fifteen days before the wedding, Bilqees began her *mayun*, a period of seclusion. For the next two weeks, she would not leave the house or see anyone but her immediate family and the female members of her fiancé's household. During that period, according to tradition, Jamila turned Bilqees' chores over to Sayeeda. This would give Bilqees two weeks to rest and prepare for the wedding, to contemplate the serious new role she was about to undertake, and to beautify herself for her new husband.

She was not alone in that last endeavor. Each day, the groom's mother and sisters walked across the village in a small procession, their matriarch carrying in her hands a jar of homemade *uptan*: a paste of turmeric, sandalwood powder, herbs, and aromatic oils. On the first day, Jamila formally greeted them at the door. "Welcome, welcome! Come in, come in! May I offer you some chai?"

"Thank you, and we'd like to share the gift we've brought for your daughter, who'll soon be my daughter."

"Of course. Let's go out to the angun, and I'll send Bilqees to you, and the chai, too."

With a smile, Bilqees' future mother-in-law invoked blessings over the bowed head of her future daughter-in-law. The women and girls broke into an hour of giggling and chattering, as Rauf's mother and sisters each dipped their fingers into the jar of soft, golden paste and gently massaged it into Bilqees' hands and face. (Many years later, Bilqees' daughters and nieces would like this ritual to a beauty shop facial.) The hands that gave her this facial were those of her new family, and their touch imparted love as well as beauty. Though Jamila giggled with them, she felt moved when she saw how eager Bilqees' new family was to make the girl feel welcome and accepted. Whenever Jamila felt tears threatening, she jumped up to refill everyone's cups of chai to the brim.

As the mother of the bride, Jamila took her younger daughter, Sayeeda, to visit the groom with their own jar of *uptan*. Because Rauf would soon be Jamila's son, she could break through the veil that usually separated her from men and apply the paste to the young man's face and hands. Even her own sons no longer let her touch them this much.

The day before the wedding ceremony, all the women of Bilqees' family and family-to-be gathered again to treat the bride to a final day of love, music, and beauty for females only. This was called the *mehndi* party. Several women and girls focused themselves to her hands, while the rest assigned themselves to her feet, as they took turns applying swirling, flowering, and snaking patterns of dark amber henna from fingertip to forearm, from ankle to toe. Those who weren't painting lifted their voices in song, each woman trying to outdo the last. Bilqees leaned against her Amma, and they both drifted on the harmonies rising and falling around them like a joyful wind in a mango grove. Jamila stroked her daughter's hair and felt the joy she'd missed at her own wedding.

When Bilqees' hands were done, she waved them around her face in answer to the wavering sound of her sister-in-law's voice. With such a frame, Jamila saw how much her daughter truly was a lovely sight to behold. I can imagine that Jamila thought, "Her eyes are her finest feature. The secret is in the intelligence. I can see it in her eyes."

As some women continued to sing, others performed *sadka* on the bride to ward off evil. They circled her three times, holding money over her head and then spilling it in her lap until she was buried in notes and coins and laughing under the pile. Her Amma Ji likely tried to keep a running tally in her head, balancing it against the money her husband was spending on this wedding. Bilqees would get to keep the money to add to her dowry, but it was nice to know that their investment would at least bring a return for their child. It was a daughter's security against future uncertainty. Jamila would never forget how quickly her own mother's fortunes changed when her father died. Education, money, and the freedom to approve her own husband were the *sadka* with which Jamila encircled her daughter. It was hard to imagine any bad luck at that moment while gazing at a daughter softened, perfumed, painted, and sung into a portrait of family love.

The multiplied adoration of two families was a powerful thing; it bound the young couple together more powerfully than they could accomplish on their own. Jamila found this idea comforting rather than oppressive. She knew that power was only as good or bad as those who wield it, and she had taught her daughter all she knew, while also giving her the gift of knowledge that she herself did not possess. She believed that Bilqees' future was as secure as she could make it.

After all the guests left and her younger daughters slipped off to bed, Jamila pulled Bilqees into her room to talk to her about the duties of a wife. The conversation was brief, but afterward Jamila said, "I have a special gift for you."

"But Amma, you've already given me too much."

"You must humor your Abba and me, and let us give to you while we still can, because after tomorrow you'll join your husband's family, and you'll no longer be ours to spoil."

She opened a drawer and pulled out a small book.

"Abba and I have already given you a holy Quran, but we wanted you to have another book," Jamila said.

She gave Bilqees the *Behshti Zevar*, which was a common practice in northern India upon the marriage of a daughter. The literal meaning of *behshti zevar* is "jewelry of heaven." It was written by a conservative Muslim man, and it teaches women how to be good, subservient wives and mothers. If a woman follows the ways outlined in *Behshti Zevar*, it is said that she'll ensure a happy family life on earth and earn a place for herself in heaven after death.

Bilqees thanked her Amma for this mysterious book, as Jamila had thanked her mother before her and as Aisha had thanked her mother before her. Other than the holy Quran, it was the only book Jamila had ever owned.

Bilqees' wedding day was a flurry of silks and flowers, foods and sweets, music and laughter, and a shifting tapestry of faces. Jamila had seen many of these faces off and on throughout her life in Pur Qazi, but half of the respective names escaped her. This wasn't surprising, as women spent so much time at home among their own kin. It was disarming, however, to realize how much more a part of the world her husband was; Hanif greeted almost every man by name.

The day started with people she knew, as the *baraat* made its glorious procession to their home. Two young boys led a horse wreathed in flowers, and Rauf sat atop it, wearing a silk turban and a shining tunic with a high-braided collar. He was followed by grinning family and friends, and a small band brought up the rear. The musicians had not mastered the art of playing in unison while walking, making them sound like a collection of mewling calves, but they made up for it with their exuberance.

The aroma of roses, the oiled groom, and the perfumed wedding guests was intoxicating as they arrived outside the house of Jamila and Hanif. The odor of a sweaty horse faded as the bride's family rained rose petals around the heads of the groom's family and placed garlands of flowers around the necks of Rauf and his parents.

The men and women split into two groups. The men sat outside under a large, open tent strewn with cushions, and the women gathered inside where they could not be seen.

Finally, when both tent and house were so full that Hanif might worry that his wife would suggest they needed yet another addition to the house, the official wedding ceremony began. During the *nikah*, the bride and groom sat apart from each other for the main part of the ritual, which took place outside under the tent full of men. The fathers of both the groom and the bride announced the terms of the marriage contract. It included the bride's right to divorce her husband, though nobody present knew of any woman in Pur Qazi who had ever availed herself of that right. It also included the *meher*, the small amount of money that the groom would give the bride. This was considered a "safety net" that protected the bride in case her husband fell into financial trouble, though it was a trifling amount and mostly symbolic. After reading the marriage contract, the *Maulana*, or imam, read selected verses from the holy Quran.

If everyone under the tent listened silently, the women in the house practically held their collective breath as they strained to hear the ceremony that was about to change the life of the bride. Jamila's mind drifted back to her own wedding day, which was a quiet and secreted affair. She was lucky, as Hanif had turned out to be a devoted and hardworking husband. He still exasperated her at times, but now she could chuckle at his stubborn resistance to her headstrong ambitions—each one pulled in opposite ways like mules resisting a master.

The imam was waiting for the father of the groom to propose to the father of the bride. Jamila heard Hanif accept on behalf of his daughter. The imam, the fathers, and two male witnesses took the contract to the bride. The imam read the dry details of the contract to Bilqees.

"I accept," she said and signed the paper with a flourish.

"Your daughter has beautiful handwriting," someone whispered to Jamila, who beamed silently.

The small entourage took the contract to the groom, and the imam read it aloud to him.

"I accept," he said.

The imam recited the *Sureh-e-Fatihah*, the first verse of the first chapter of the Quran, a simple prayer to Allah to guide his people on the path of righteousness and forgive them for any shortcomings. Finally, he formally announced the marriage of Bilqees to Rauf.

The bride's family served a dish of dates and unrefined sugar to Rauf to welcome him to their family. With that, the bride's father and three brothers escorted the groom to his new wife. It was the first time that the couple sat side by side. They were nervous, not sure what to make of this anticlimactic finish to so many weeks of buildup. Bilqees remained mostly hidden, reflecting light from an array of sequins, beads, and cut glass, her hair and the lower half of her face still a mystery under her sparkling veil.

Though excited as a young girl, Jamila refrained from leaping from the floor when her part finally came. She slowly unfolded herself and floated to join her husband. Together, they guided the young couple to a mirror where Bilqees removed the veil from her face, unconsciously looking down perhaps for fear of catching a look of disappointment on the face of her husband. When she gazed up at the mirror, he was grinning at her, all his teeth showing. She smiled back but kept her lips closed over her own teeth. She would not have wanted to appear unladylike in front of her Amma and Abba. Jamila held out a plate of sweets to the bride and groom, and they fed pieces to each other, giggling as their fingers brushed each other's mouth. Rauf reached out to catch the juice that was about to drip from Bilqees chin, and they both laughed. The parents of the bride shared a chuckle. Yes, these youngsters were going to be fine.

According to the custom of the time, even neighbors not invited to the reception would show up to congratulate the families, but uninvited guests were not expected to stay for dinner. One after another, as guests arrived outside and shook Hanif's hand, he looked as if he'd suddenly been struck by an amazing idea and say, "But you must stay and join us for dinner!"

"We don't want to impose," they said.

"It's not an imposition at all," he replied. "There's plenty for everyone, and it would make our day more complete if you shared this happy occasion with us!"

When his wife caught wind of this from inside the house, she could not hide her panic. Her eyes wide and jaw clenched, she muttered to her closest female friends that she was afraid her husband's generosity would outpace the food. The women whispered among them, and passed word to their husbands, who finally got word to Hanif.

"Your wife is on the verge of a nervous collapse for fear you'll run out of food," one man said.

Hanif moved toward the doorway of the packed house and politely asked a husband to ask a wife to ask the women inside to clear a path to his wife so that he could talk to her.

They worked their way to another room and shut the door where Jamila burst out, "Abba, what are you doing?! You must stop! We're going to run out of food!" When she saw his mouth working as if he were about to laugh, she put her hands on her hips. "It's not funny. What if we run out of food?"

"I planned to ask all these extra people all along. I've made arrangements for additional guests. We won't run out of food."

"You couldn't tell me this?" She was not sure whether she was irritated that he had almost caused a nervous collapse or tickled to find that her husband had planned such an elaborate gesture. "Who would have thought you could ever surprise me?" she laughed.

"All those years that I didn't surprise you? It was all part of my long-term plot just so I could make you laugh today," Hanif said.

After a few more hours of eating and celebrating, the groom paid an exorbitant ransom to Sayeeda and several of Bilqees' female cousins for the return of his missing shoes. He and his bride bid then farewell to her family. This was the most emotional and drawn-out part of the wedding, the moment when Bilqees' home ceased to be hers. From then on, she would become a member of her husband's family and household and would only return to her parents' house as a guest. There was not a dry eye in the Kazmi family. Jamila took her daughter's hands and pulled her close, inhaling her first-born's unique scent amid the perfumes and oils. She then reluctantly let her go.

In such a conservative community, Jamila and Hanif would never think to make physical contact in public, but they stood so close that they almost touched as they waved goodbye to their daughter, watching until they could no longer pick her wedding veil out among the bobbing heads of colorfully dressed wedding guests heading to the Groom's house.

On that day, Jamila was only thirty-four and Hanif thirty-six. They had predicted correctly that the day would be the happiest of their lives in Pur Qazi. Happiness comes and goes in life. They knew this from experience, but it still came as a shock to find out how fleeting happiness could be.

That year, my parents' youngest daughter was born. My sister Sajida became another constant in my life when we were growing up and, later, when we became adults. Looking back now, with all my other siblings, Salim and Kalim included, it seems that my sister Sajida and I became the closest.

-11-

TWISTS AND TURNS

Jamila and Hanif had high hopes for all their children, but Tahir seemed destined to become a scholar. He was curious and lively, always asking questions, often coming up with his own excited conjecture before anyone had a chance to respond. The talent that made his parents most proud was his phenomenal memory. From the time he was a small boy, he was learning to recite the Quran by heart. Hanif beamed as the boy recited verse after verse, and when he finished, Jamila placed an approving hand atop his head. At night, Jamila whispered her greatest praise out of her son's hearing, to prevent him becoming arrogant, "He has the voice of an angel. When we're too old for work, Tahir will sit with us, and his sweet voice will remind us of the hope of Allah and the words of the prophet Mohammad, peace be upon him. When we pass away, Tahir will visit our graves and read to us while we listen from heaven."

When Tahir was a teenager, the talk of India's independence from Britain caught his imagination. India would become a great country, he told his mother, and its people would have a part to play on the world stage. He would go out to see that world. Jamila did not doubt that her second son was meant for great things.

One day, Tahir complained that he was too tired to help his father in the mango groves. "It's because you study too hard, work too hard, and play too hard," Jamila said. "You must get more rest."

Tahir got more rest, but he remained quiet, not lively and talkative as he used to be.

"It's just growing pains," Hanif said. "He's going through puberty."

About a month later, he lost his appetite. "What's wrong? Where does it hurt?" Jamila asked.

"I don't know. All over, I guess," Tahir said.

In those days in rural India, consulting a modern medical doctor wasn't a preventive measure but a terrifying last-minute resort. There were no such doctors in Pur Qazi, only the *hakeems* or professional herbalists. Jamila gave her son the time-honored herbal remedies prescribed by their hakeem: soothing teas, healing plant extracts, and pain-killing poultices.

Tahir thanked his mother. "I feel much better, Amma. I'm sure I'll be well soon."

He wasn't. He barely ate or drank for two weeks and lost so much weight that his limbs looked like sticks. "Maybe we should take him to a doctor in the city," Jamila said.

"Maybe you're right," Hanif said.

Tahir died before they had a chance to go to a doctor. They never knew what killed him.

Jamila and Hanif were stunned. They felt all the guilt of survivors who discover there is nothing fair about life and death. "What did we do to deserve this? Parents should not outlive their children," Jamila lamented to Hanif. "All the hakeem's remedies, what good are they? They could not save my father, and they could not save my son. Maybe if we had gone to the doctor sooner . . . it's my fault, I know." The children were not around, so she took Hanif's hand in hers. "He was so smart that I thought our Tahir might *become* a doctor. Now he will never know what it is to have a wife or children of his own," Jamila said.

Even when the children were around, they did not hide their tears. Though their home was always full, it was now very quiet. Tahir had been a bright presence, and without him, the house felt dark.

After the funeral and several days of mourning, Hanif returned to the mango groves, taking solace in his work. Jamila did not know how she would ever overcome such grief, but she understood that life had to go on; her other children were still depending on her. She redoubled her efforts to care for those children, determining that they would all find successful futures to make up for the loss of Tahir.

The chaos of fate never rests. It was not long before death struck again, this time with no warning at all. Bilqees and her husband, Rauf, were married less than four years, and he was in his early twenties when he died of a massive heart attack. Rauf left his widow with two young sons. Salim was two and a half, and Kalim was only six months old. A stunned Bilqees moved back in with her parents.

Bilqees had loved Rauf very much, but the needs of young children do not wait for sorrow, and a young mother without a husband would never stay that way for long in a village like Pur Qazi. Just as nature abhors a vacuum, rural Indian society abhorred the idea of a fatherless family. Bilqees was still young, pretty, and healthy, so she did not have to wait long for an offer of marriage. A widower related to a local family decided that he and Bilqees could help solve each other's problems. She needed a husband, and he needed a wife to help him care for the five children his late wife had left behind.

Bilqees' new husband, Yahya Rizvi, was almost old enough to be her father, but this was not unusual in Pur Qazi. Jamila and Hanif knew they could not be picky when it came to a second husband for their daughter, and Bilqees, no longer a childless virgin, was in no position to decline.

This new marriage would break her heart into yet more pieces. She had lost her beloved first husband and was now about to lose her parents and siblings. She was to move to southern India where her husband worked for the state of Hyderabad. Not only that, but at her parents' suggestion, she would lose one of her two children.

"When you move in with your new husband, you must leave Salim with us," Jamila told her daughter. "Kalim is too young to be separated from his mother, so he must stay with you, of course."

"I've already lost my husband, and now I must give up one of my children?"

"If you think about it, you'll see the wisdom in it. Your new husband has five children, and you're still new to motherhood. You'll kill yourself trying to take care of seven children. Six is more than enough to handle, and you know I have some experience with stepbrothers. It is not always easy between children from different parents. Kalim is only a baby, so your stepchildren may learn to think of him as their own brother, but with Salim, there may be conflict. I think this is a good way to protect him."

"You're not giving Salim up," her father reassured her. "You're entrusting him to the care of his grandparents. We have only three children still at home, and another will be a blessing. It is better this way for all of us. Salim will always know you are his mother. "

"I know you're right, Abba," Bilqees said, though her heart ached, "and I know that Salim loves his grandma and grandpa, so he will be happy here. Anyway, a new man might scare him. The idea scares me."

That statement turned out to be wiser than she knew. Bilqees had loved Rauf, and she knew that finding love with two husbands in one lifetime might be too much to hope for. In most ways, Salim's new stepfather was an honest, fair, straightforward man, but at home, he was a strict disciplinarian.

In Indian culture, Hindu or Muslim, the man is the undisputed head of the household, and although a woman with a strong personality might hold sway in domestic matters, a man will always have the last word.

In the midst of death, life sprang again, renewing the Kazmi family's sense of hope. About a year after the deaths of Tahir and Rauf, I was born. Though Amma and Abba knew they could never replace my absent brother, they saw my arrival as a kind of balancing of fate... Tahir had died, but I would fill the hole in their hopes. Amma was in her forties when she gave birth to me, the last of eight children, six of whom survived the vagaries of rural life.

I was only a year old when my parents celebrated the marriage of their second daughter, Sayeeda. She married sometime in 1946. It was a simple ceremony, no match for the elaborate wedding of Bilqees. The times were changing both for my family and for all of India. My oldest brother, Tayab, did not attend Sayeeda's wedding. Tayab had left home to attend high school and then engineering school, but he completed only two years before dropping out.

He later said that he was worried that our parents' finances were wearing thin.

"No, no, son, don't give us that excuse," Amma said. "We never told you to quit school."

"I know you wouldn't, Amma, because you're too generous."

She gave him a suspicious frown. She would never say aloud that she suspected he was more bored with school than concerned with her security.

Still, Tayab had enough credits to earn a diploma of surveyorship, and he became a surveyor in the army engineering corps. He held the rank of Havaldar Major. In addition to his regular salary based on rank, he also earned a trade allowance. The gross total was 110 rupees a month, which was a good salary at that time, but he became a soldier at what may have been the worst possible time.

I was a baby and would not understand until years later that I was born into what were both the best and the worst moments in Indian history. India's freedom movement was in full swing.

The question was not whether the Indian subcontinent would be able to throw off the yoke of British colonial rule; everyone knew it was only a matter of time. The question was what the India left behind would look like, how it would govern itself, and whether it would remain one country or become two. Would India remain united by cultural ties or become divided along religious lines?

Until that time, my father's family never had any major players in politics, but in the 1940s, people who had never thought much about their part in the grand scheme of things were stirred to get involved. The son of one of my father's cousins, Syed Murtaza, ran for mayor of Pur Qazi. During his campaign, he asked my mother to take charge of a group of women to drum up the female vote. On the Election Day, my mother was also in charge of monitoring the women's polling place and counting the votes. Murtaza won that election and a few more until he ultimately won a seat on the National Assembly. My mother remained in charge of the women's groups that had helped to elect him.

My mother and father had opinions on India's independence, as did most people in those days, even the uninformed and illiterate. Amma and Abba were very vocal in their support of the freedom movement, and they supported the two-nation proposition.

There had always been a certain level of mistrust between Hindus and Muslims in India. That's why the All-India Muslim League, led by Mohammed Ali Jinnah, saw India as two distinct nations within a nation, one Muslim and the other Hindu. The League believed that it would be impossible for the people of two fundamentally different religions to live together in peace under one flag. They wanted a separate country for Muslims, comprised of those provinces that already had a Muslim majority.

The second most influential political leader of the Muslim League, Liaquat Ali Khan, lived in the same district as our family. That district included Pur Qazi and several surrounding cities and villages. When Liaquat Ali Khan ran for National Assembly, my amma and abba were active in his election campaign. They helped achieve a majority of votes for him in Pur Qazi, and he won the seat. Our family was divided on the Pakistan issue: one group favored the creation of Pakistan while the second group disagreed with dividing India on religious grounds. Mohammad Ahmad Kazmi, who ran against Liaquat Ali Khan, was from the part of our family who opposed the creation of Pakistan.

Another group, led by Maulana Abul Kalam Azad, believed in Hindu-Muslim unity. His followers opposed the partitioning of India on religious grounds. They believed that language, culture, and customs, not religion, formed the foundation of a shared national identity. They also believed that dividing India on the basis of religion was not in the interest of the Muslims of India.

The irony was that most Muslim religious leaders favored Hindu-Muslim unity, while most liberal, secular Muslims taught in an educational system designed by the British advocated the division of India based on the Two-Nation Theory. The only religious leader who had a following throughout India, and who favored creating a separate country for Muslims, was Maulana Shabbir Ahmed Usmani. He happened to be the uncle of my brother-in-law.

The War of Independence of 1857 (or Mutiny, as the British called it) shook the British into realizing how close they came to losing control. As part of the study and causes of the War of Independence, the British realized that in order to rule India freely, Hindus and Muslim must not form an alliance as they did in the 1857 uprising. The British saw their rescue in Hindus and Muslims considering each other the enemy instead of their common enemy, "the occupier of their homeland."

To achieve their goal, the British use a policy of "divide and rule," also known as "divide and conquer." By political, economic and military means, a party is able to gain and maintain control by breaking up a larger group into smaller, less powerful groups.

Almost 40 percent of India was administered by independent rajas, nawabs, feudal lords, and maharahjas. These states were commonly known as Princely States, and these states acknowledged the supremacy of the British, but the leaders were in charge of administering and maintaining the order. The race relations were better in the Princely States than in the remaining 60 percent of India that was administered by the British, because the Princely States did not follow the communal policies of the British.

After the World War II, it became almost impossible for the colonial powers to keep their colonies under control. They started giving those countries political freedom, but that did not mean they were willing to give up all control and possibly suffer a backlash or lose economic and political sway in their former colonies. They divided their colonies in such a way as to create new countries and put them at odds with each other. It was in Britain's interest to divide India into two sets of enemies, thus creating two weak countries where there used to be one.

Ultimately, a British-led Border Commission undertook the identification of Muslim-majority areas and carved out a new country. Pakistan would contain two noncontiguous enclaves, East Pakistan and West Pakistan separated by more than one thousand miles. Britain gave several Muslim-dominated districts to India. Among them was Gurdaspur, where 51 percent of the population was Muslim.

Gurdaspur contained important road and water connections to Kashmir, the source of four major rivers. The ability to control access to such a plentiful source of water was of strategic importance to every bordering country. Giving Gurdaspur to India was one of several concessions that led Kashmir to become a disputed territory in a tug of war between India and Pakistan, a dispute that continues to this day.

In spite of the bitter arguments over the new border, my mother and father never imagined that they might have to pay a personal price for freedom from British rule. They expected to simply continue their lives in the homeland where their forefathers had lived for centuries. Though they believed in the Two-Nation Theory, they thought Muslims should have a right to live in their own country if they wished and that no Muslims or Hindus should be forcibly relocated. They thought that these countries would be based on democratic principles, and they assumed that people would not have to go anywhere they did not want to go.

Like most of their neighbors, my mother and father had no desire to leave Pur Qazi. They did not wish to severe their ties to family, friends, and neighbors or to abandon the sights, sounds, and smells they had known their whole lives. The smell of sugarcane and mangos, the coolness of the home Amma fought to own, and the laughing women who had once gathered at that home to buy kitchenware—these formed the backdrop for the secure family life she and Hanif had worked so hard to create. Amma had ambition, but not ambition that required uprooting them from their land. She hoped to increase their hold on that land and their position in the community. Amma and Abba were planted, like the trees in the groves. Their presence was perennial, like the hot season and the monsoon.

Jamila had learned to trust her own judgment. She did not believe she had it in her to be naïve, but who could have expected the horror to come?

On August 14, 1947, Pakistan was born as a new homeland for the Muslims of India. It would be a bloody birth.

Among Hindus and Muslims, elated with freedom from Britain but angry over splitting the spoils, a rabid nationalism took hold of millions, especially the young. That nationalism took on different meanings to different people, and those differences became deadly. Many Hindus blamed Muslims for breaking up India. Many Muslims blamed Hindus for shortchanging them in Pakistan. The argument over whether Kashmir rightfully belonged to Pakistan, because of the territory's 77 percent Muslim population, or to India, because of its connections to Indian waterways and roadways, fanned the flames of hatred among people who had peacefully coexisted for centuries.

Millions of Hindus, Sikhs, and Muslims became foreigners in their homelands. Throughout the summer of 1947, riots broke out in northern and eastern India. The most violent riots arose in Punjab and Bengal, the two provinces in the center of the newly divided India. The fear of religious violence and persecution instigated the largest human migration in modern history. Roughly fifteen million people migrated, more than eight million Muslims fled India for Pakistan, and nearly seven million Hindus and Sikhs fled homes in Pakistan where they had lived for centuries. Angry mobs from all three religions looted businesses, burned down houses, and massacred men, women, and children of all ages.

Many people fled the violence by walking across the country. Others fled by train. Those who could afford the train tickets were not the lucky ones, as mobs of religious fanatics from both sides attacked train after train. Thousands of women and girls were raped, mutilated, and murdered in front of their loved ones. The attackers amputated the breasts of the women, sometimes while they still held babies in their arms. Several trains arrived at their destinations without a living soul on board.

Robert Trumbull, a veteran correspondent of *The New York Times*, wrote in the September 12, 1947 issue:

"Death by shooting is more merciful than to be beaten to death with clubs and stones and left to die, their death agony intensified by heat and flies."

"Horror had no race, and the terrible anguish of those August days in the Punjab was meted out with almost biblical balance . . . an eye for an eye, massacre for massacre, rape for rape, blind cruelty for blind cruelty."

Lal Khan, an Indian writer, lamented the devastation in this way:

"The partition of the Indian subcontinent was a wound inflicted upon the living body of one of the oldest civilizations on earth. A civilization that was rich in art, architecture, music, literature and other forms of human culture. Its cultural diversity was its greatest beauty. The pain will remain and has left an indelible scar upon millions of people."

It is estimated that more than one million people paid with their lives for India's partition. A majority of the Hindus, Muslims, and Sikhs who died were innocent, naïve, and illiterate. Most of them were peasants and day workers on farms, people who understood little about the politics of partition. They only understood one simple fact: flee or die.

Pur Qazi was in the state of Uttar Pradesh, a Hindu-dominated state, and my parents were Muslim. My amma was middle-aged, a time when her life had become comfortable and, to some extent, predictable, but now all comforts and predictions were off. She had no clear picture of what was next.

Though Pur Qazi was far from the worst of the massacres, it was not immune to the plague of discrimination, violence, and death. At night, Amma and her friends met on their rooftops under cover of darkness to whisper of the news, the rumors, and their fears.

"My friend's cousin was walking home when a group of boys started taunting him and throwing stones. His wife had to take him to the hospital."

"They burned my sister's house at night, when everyone was asleep. They were lucky to escape with their lives, but they lost everything."

"I heard a Muslim, a shopkeeper in Muzafarnagar, was beaten up just for daring to open his doors. They forced him out of business."

"I heard there are some Muslims also attacking the Hindus."

"Maybe in places where their numbers are larger, but we're the minority here, aren't we? What power do we have to attack someone, much less protect ourselves from attack?"

In bed with Hanif at night, Jamila said, "Do you think anyone will attack us here?"

"Don't worry. Pur Qazi is a small community, and we're far from the migration routes. The violence won't come this far. That's not what I'm worried about. Our problem is that I can no longer safely make the trip to visit many of my customers."

"Will we lose more business?"

"I don't know."

Abba's agricultural trade had already slowed to a trickle. He could no longer safely transport livestock or mangoes on the road, and some of the Hindu customers who had been friendly to him all their lives suddenly treated him with surly suspicion. A few denied that they owed him money; some refused to speak to him at all. Fearing for his life, he stopped going out at all. Luckily, Amma had a habit of saving, so they had money set aside.

"It won't last forever," she said.

"This conflict can't last forever, either."

They waited to see which would end first: the climate of fear or their savings.

There was still reason to hope. They still had many Muslim customers, and even some of their Hindu customers remained loyal.

A few of Abba's Hindu employees quit working for him, but most of them did so in embarrassment. "You understand, of course," one said, "You have been a good boss, but some of our neighbors don't understand."

"Of course, of course," my father replied. "You'll come back when this craziness dies down." He couldn't blame them, and it saved him the trouble of trying to decide who to let go when the business declined.

One faithful Hindu friend refused to quit. Pancha had become my father's right-hand man and a close friend of the family. He often brought treats or toys for the children. He had even shared meals with our family on occasion. Though she had to stay behind her veil and take part in the conversations from another room, my mother had also come to regard Pancha as a member of the family.

When times grew tough, Pancha told my parents, "I will not quit just because men decide to twist God's laws to their own purposes. This is not about religion but about fear. People are so afraid that someone will hurt them or take from them that they pull away or strike out before anyone has a chance to do anything to them. In the end, this is how they lose everything. With all this fear and suspicion, they're just creating their own destruction. Well, I won't let fear turn my friends into my enemies. Everything I have I owe to you, and you can count on me to stand by you to the end, whatever it may be."

"Hindu or Muslim, you are family, Pancha," my father said. "You always do what God asks of all of us, in any religion: to be honest and faithful to family. No matter what happens on the streets, you're always welcome in this house."

Ultimately, the only two men left at the business were my father and Pancha. My father had no desire to leave the only home he had ever known. It was my mother who wanted to go.

-12-

MIGRATION

Like most of the young people of his time, my oldest brother had long supported the idea of a separate country for Muslims. Right after independence, Tayab resigned from the army and moved to Pakistan. If he had kept his position, he would simply have been assigned to the Pakistan Army, but the start of a new country seemed to call for the start of a new life.

Tayab wanted to go into business for himself, but Amma's brother Zaheer had already moved to Lahore, Pakistan where he had a job in government administration. Tayab went to live with Zaheer, got an office job, and saved enough money so he could afford to get married.

In 1949, Tayab returned to India where our parents helped him find a bride. Amma hoped that he and his wife would settle down with us, the way it had always been done in the Muslim community of Pur Qazi. The tradition was for the bride and groom to live with the groom's family.

Tayab had other plans, and he explained them to Amma as they sat in the kitchen late one night, shortly before the wedding. I was too young to be in on the conversation, but I learned enough later to have some idea of how it went.

"Amma, Pakistan is my country now. Muslims have a limited future in the old India, but in the new Pakistan, things are just beginning. There I'll have more opportunities and can give my family a better life. Isn't that what you've always wanted for your children?"

"Yes, of course, but Tayab, family should stay together. In a family, we all support each other. If you're so far away, how will you set an example for your younger brothers? How will you help look out for your baby sister? Who will you turn to if you need help with your family?"

"My younger siblings can't have much interest in a brother who's almost old enough to be their father, and you all have each other. My wife and I are young and strong, and we can take care of our own family. If we need help, Uncle Zaheer and Uncle Jamil aren't far away, and we can always come back to visit."

"Yes, of course. I'm sure you know best."

In her heart, Amma was not so sure, and she knew it would be difficult for Tayab to come back and visit. It had been a long and difficult process for him to obtain a visa for this trip to come home and get married. It was unlikely that he'd go to that much trouble just for a simple visit. She didn't want to argue with her son and drive him away emotionally as well as physically, so she tried to accept.

My second-oldest brother, Mutahir, didn't understand why Amma was upset when he decided to go with Tayab and his bride to Pakistan. Mutahir was about fourteen and eager for adventure. In a country where Muslims were the majority, he imagined a land of increased opportunity, and far from home, he imagined independence from his parents.

This was not the future Amma had envisioned when she was a young mother. She had expected to lose her daughters when they moved in with their husbands' families, but she had imagined that her sons would stay by her side until her death. The death of Tahir had taken away one boy, and Tayab's move to Pakistan would deprive her of another. Was she also going to lose Mutahir?

I was only five, but she looked at me, sighed, and said something like, "I suppose when you get big, you will leave me, too?"

"No, Amma, I will never leave you," I replied.

She smiled, leaned over, and held my cheek in her hand, "No, my precious baby boy. I don't think you will."

I suspect that she struggled not to cry as Mutahir, Tayab, and his bride Sajida—who had the same name as my third sister—all said farewell and left for the train station.

The three of them did not return to Lahore, where Uncle Zaheer lived, but instead moved to Sialkot, where Uncle Jamil lived. The city of Sialkot is situated right under the peaks of Kashmir, northeast of the Punjab province in Pakistan. Its recorded history goes as far back as five thousand years. One of the founders of Sialkot was from Sia Caste, and it is believed that the word *Sialkot* means "Fort of Sia." Sialkot is famous for leather garments, musical instruments, sporting goods, and surgical instruments. In the modern era, Sialkot also is birthplace of two famous scholars, Muhammad Allama Iqbal and Faiz Ahmed Faiz.

The poetry of Muhammad Allama Iqbal in Urdu and Persian is considered to be among one of the best in modern era. His vision of an independent state for the Muslims of British India became the inspiration to create Pakistan. Though involved in politics he is best known for his poetic work which also earned him a British Knighthood.

Faiz Ahmed Faiz is also renowned for his poetic work and probably one of the most famous poets of the Urdu language in modern era. His progressive writing earned him the Lenin Peace Prize by the Soviet Union.

At the time of independence, Sialkot was a much smaller city, as compared to Lahore, which promised to grow, and I suppose that Tayab wanted to get in on the ground floor, so It was there that he started a grocery store with his humble savings.

Sometimes he sent short letters home, which Abba read aloud to us because Amma did not know how to read. The letters were few and far between. "And so short," Amma said. "Why doesn't he tell us more? Maybe things aren't going well, and he's afraid to tell us."

"You worry too much," Abba said. "I'm sure the letters are short because he's so busy."

Amma folded her arms and was not convinced.

Bilqees and her family soon moved to Pakistan, too. They traveled to Dadu, a city in the province of Sind. Amma accepted this with a show of calm. Bilqees had lived hundreds of miles away for several years now, and whether she was in southern India or Pakistan seemed to make little difference. To Amma, it seemed that her whole family was quickly slipping away.

With two sons gone, Amma began to convince herself that Pur Qazi was not the same anymore. By now, my abba had become familiar with a certain faraway look in his wife's eyes and impatience in her stride as she scurried from one part of the house to the next, starting one task and dropping it for another. It was as if she did not know what to do with herself.

He then learned of the new scheme she had in mind. She said that she wanted to move to Pakistan.

"No, no, no. This is our home. This is where I was born and where I plan to die. I don't know anyone in Pakistan."

"What do you mean, you don't know anyone? What about our two sons? And my brothers, Jamil and Zaheer, who we raised as our own sons? In Pakistan, we can start a new business without worrying whether Hindus will dare to buy from a Muslim. We'll be surrounded by people like us."

"We're already surrounded by people like us. We're happy here. Things are just getting back to normal. Have patience, my dear."

"That's just like you. You're afraid of change, always expecting things to stay the same. The world is moving on without us. Our sons are moving on without us, and I, for one, don't want to be left behind."

Abba did not point out the irony that Amma was arguing to move precisely because she feared she would see the home she knew changing around her. He knew that, as always, he had already lost the argument, but he insisted on one point: he would not leave until he had wound up his business affairs in India in an orderly fashion.

"Many of my customers still owe me a lot of money. If we go to Pakistan now, I'll never get paid. I'll just stay long enough so that I can collect these debts."

"But that could take a long time, and I want to see my sons. I want to be there when Tayab's first child is born. I want to make sure Mutahir is all right."

"Then you will have to go ahead without me."

"Do you think that's wise?"

"I don't think it's wise to leave in the first place, but yes, I think it's the wisest choice. You don't want to start our new lives with no money, do you?"

"No, no. I know you're right. We'll need that money if we want to start a new business."

"Stay home, my dear. We can always go next year."

Amma was afraid that if she gave in to him, she would lose her nerve. One year would turn into two, two would turn into three, and she would never see her sons again. She also believed that if they wanted to go into business in Pakistan, now was the time. The country was new, and one could get in on the ground floor of whatever the opportunities would bring.

A few years after independence, in the summer of 1950, Amma packed what she could fit into a trunk and two suitcases. She took my hand, and my sister Sajida took little Salim's hand, and we boarded a train bound for Pakistan. My father stood alone at the station, lost in a sea of people and waving at us as our train pulled away. Amma waved until she could no longer see him and then reached a hand up under her burqa and wiped her hidden face.

I did not know when I would see my father again, but I was not worried. My Amma and I had left the house together before, and we always saw Abba again that night. Surely it would not be long. Besides, I had never been on a train before, and there were so many people, foods, noises, and colors to grab my attention that I soon forgot about my father standing alone on that platform.

Though my Amma seemed a bit nervous, I was too young to understand why. For the most part, law and order had been restored in India. The violence that had erupted right after independence had subsided, and it was more or less safe to travel by train, at least physically. That did not mean this journey was a safe move financially, emotionally, or socially. My mother was about to take her family from a place where it no longer felt like home and transplant all of us to a new home.

My real memories began when our train reached the refugee camp at the border. My life before that had been a series of images, flashes, glimpses, but that day was the start of my life story. Even though everywhere I turned the world seemed strange and incomprehensible, I was eager to discover what it all was and who I was in the midst of it.

I have only two clear memories about that refugee camp. The first is the small makeshift restaurant with the tin roof that sat next to the camp. It was not a restaurant in the usual sense but rather a bread-baking shop—more of a shack, really. I stood for endless minutes, or hours, staring at the baker in amazement as he transformed a plump lump of dough into a thin, round sheet, tossing it high into the air, catching it, and then throwing it against the inside wall of a hot clay oven. This was the first time I had seen someone baking *naan*. "How does it stick to the side of the oven?" I wondered. That was the only exciting sight at the camp; the rest was a nervous, roiling energy where I alternated between boredom and the fear of getting lost and never seeing Amma again.

There was not much to do except wait for the train that would take us to our final destination. The refugee camp was on the side of Pakistan next to the Indian border, far removed from the nearest town. There was no sign of population nearby, and no sign of vegetation or trees. It was nothing but an open field in the desert where families set up tents to protect themselves from the sweltering heat.

My second vivid memory was of sand. To protect us from the relentless sand, the ground was covered with *daris*—a *dari* is a sort of throwaway carpet made out of cotton—but they did not help. There was no escape. Soon the *daris* were covered with sand, and our skin, hair, and clothes felt gritty. Everyone was coated in the same gray dust. All of our food was crunchy, and I wondered if I would break a tooth. If we sat still long enough, the entire refugee camp would have been covered with sand.

Most of the refugees had just enough space for their families, elbow to elbow, knee to knee. There was no running water or electricity. Water was brought in tanks from nearby towns. Everyone's eyes kept gravitating to the far end of the camp, where the small train station stood. Trains from various parts of India dropped migrants off on the Indian side of the border, and people walked to the Pakistani side of the border, blinking with the realization that they had crossed into a new country.

If a train was not available immediately, people waited in the camp for the next one. The trains had started running less frequently, maybe every two to three days. When we arrived, the train had left a day earlier, so we had no choice but to stay at the camp and wait.

Our train finally came to take the four of us to our new life. Sajida, Salim, and I were still very excited about traveling by rail. I remember that it was nighttime when we left and began our rocking and clacking, chugging journey in the pitch dark.

A middle-aged man, perhaps in his fifties, sat next to us, though he seemed very old to me. I remember him as vividly as if he were sitting before me now. His hair was completely white, and his beard nicely trimmed. Out of politeness, kind concern, or just the desire to kill time, he started chatting with us. Later, he treated us to the small sweets he was carrying.

"*Bibi* (sister), are you traveling by yourself with the kids?" I remember the man asking my mother.

"Yes, *bahi sahib* (brother)."

The man gave her a look of astonishment. There was no judgment in his voice, only concern. "How come, bibi? Where is their father?"

"Bahi sahib, their father is still back in India. He'll be coming later. He has a business, and all of our funds are tied up in that business. We decided that he'll come at a later date, after he collects the money that his customers owe him."

He shook his head, his eyes sad. "Bibi, you and your husband made a big mistake. You should not have come by yourself with such young kids."

My mother was not offended. For her, this was not nosiness but the true sense of community and caring she had learned to expect from her people. She did not wish to appear weak or needy before a stranger, especially because she knew herself to be strong and a survivor. She was proud of how well she had faced and overcome every challenge and obstacle in her life. She believed that the future was bright because she had already made a bright future of her past and she believed that things would turn out all right. The alternative was too frightening to consider.

"Thank you for your concern, bahi sahib, but I'm not worried. My two older boys are in Sialkot, and we're going there."

"Bibi, I hope you're right, but I still wish the kids' father had come with you. I hope and pray that Allah will keep all of you safe."

"Thank you, bahi sahib," she said.

I was too young to understand the look on my mother's face, but it seems that a crease of worry appeared there. As the stranger had placed sweets into our hands, he had pressed a kernel of doubt into her mind.

It is the first adult conversation I remember listening intently to because the man seemed so worried about us. It left me wondering if we should be afraid. I quickly shook off his prophecy of doom. I was only certain that I once lived in one house with my family and would now live in another. The distance between them seemed unreal, rolling along the tracks in the dark, but as long as my mother was near me, the idea of a "new place" seemed exciting. I peered out the window into the dark and tried to see our new life approaching. I never forgot the old man in the train. I often wished I would see him again to thank him for his concern and for the sweet treats. Since that time, the feeling of concern has been connected with a grayish bearded middle age person. I've rarely boarded a train without peering into the elderly faces before me, as if trying to find him again.

The train stopped at several stations before we arrived at our destination. At each stop, we met with a number of vendors who sold items such as samosas, sweets, fruits, and tea. This was all new to me.

We got off the train in Dadu, Sind. This was where Bilqees lived, my *baji* (older sister). I had always thought of Salim as my brother, but I learned that he was Baji's son. I could not wrap my brain around the idea that this grown woman was my sister or that this boy, who was older than me, was my nephew. Bilqees still seemed like a stranger to me, and I decided to continue thinking of Salim as my brother. When we left her house a few days later, her other son from her first marriage came with us. It was not long before Kalim, too, became my brother. He was Salim's brother, so he must be mine.

Our next stop was in Rawalpindi to see my Uncle Zaheer. Zaheer seemed like a stern and important man. I still felt out of place among all these strangers who were supposed to be my family. My brothers, my sister, Sajida, and I bonded more tightly together, playing among ourselves, creating our own private world in this wide new one.

Finally, we were on our way to our destination in Sialkot. I knew we were to live with Tayab, my *bahia* (elder brother), his wife, and my other brother, Mutahir. I did not remember either of my brothers, as they had both lived away from home since I was a baby, but my mother was so eager to see them. Because I felt so safe with her, I felt no fear at the prospect of living with them, though to me they were more strangers on this strange journey.

When we arrived, it finally hit me that our old home was gone, but that did not bother me. When we left Pur Qazi, one of my father's brothers had recently died in one of the rooms of our home. As he was dying, the home had been kept dark in deference to his need for rest. The house had been dark, as far back as I could remember, so home in Pur Qazi had always seemed gloomy to me. By comparison, this new home appeared filled with light.

While the light was welcoming, my grumpy little-boy eyes squinted at the unwelcome intrusion into my sleep. By the time we arrived at our new home in Sialkot, it was late evening. Our arrival woke me, and I was feeling very hungry. Amma had some sweet bread in one of her bags, and I asked her for a piece. My teenage brother, Mutahir, did not like my insistent tone and admonished me not to talk to Amma in that way. I might have forgotten his comment if he had not also teased me about my accent, which had also been his accent until recently.

"You sound like a country boy," he said, mimicking my speech.

I had never known I had an accent until that moment. "What's wrong with how I talk?"

Mutahir laughed. "You'll learn. It's not important, but it *is* important to respect your elders and speak politely to your amma. Don't tell her, 'I want sweet bread'—ask her, 'Amma, may I please have some bread?'"

"You are not my father."

"No, but he is your elder brother," Tayab said, "and you must respect him."

I looked at my mother, but she said nothing. Amma seemed content to let my big brothers boss me around. This was how it was with big brothers, and I was not sure that I liked it. Though I was skeptical, I stared at Mutahir and listened carefully each time he spoke, trying to catch the music and rhythm of the local city accent that he had adopted. I muttered under my breath, trying to imitate him. He caught me and grinned, and I was not sure how to take it. I did not understand that he was simply taking the liberties that many older brothers take with little brothers. If he had not left our house a year before, I might have been used to his teasing, but for the moment, it felt like an intrusion into my peaceful relationship with my amma.

I thought of the man on the train, so soft-spoken, concerned, and polite, and wished that Mutahir would talk more like him. That old man was not my brother and this young man was, though I did not remember him. Moving toward this unknown destination had been less confusing than the actual arrival.

I don't think I understood that we were in a new country, but I was certain that I had entered a new life.

-13-

NEW COUNTRY, NEW PEOPLE, NEW CHALLENGES

Although the first life experience I clearly recall is the train journey to Pakistan, my first distinct memories of home are those of Sialkot, and my first distinct memories of Sialkot feature the face of my mother. She was beautiful to me, small and delicate, with smooth, creamy skin and dark, intelligent eyes. Years later I would realize that her imposing nose often kept others from recognizing her beauty. "God gave me plenty of nose," she used to joke. Her sense of humor only made her more beautiful to me. I remember walking to the shops holding her hand, looking up at the burqa she still wore and recalling the familiar features that lay under that cloth, hidden from our new neighbors but known to me.

The first thing I remember her saying to me came in response to something I gave her. Our new kitchen had the same kind of wood-burning stove that we had in India, but it was missing something. I sat in a corner and watched as my mother poked, prodded, and fussed over that fire. Smoke filled the kitchen, and she started to cough.

She sputtered and swore at the stove. *"Ye kumbakhat gili lakrian too julnae ka nam hi nahe lateen."* (These damned wet woods won't catch fire at all.) We'll all choke to death before we even get to eat dinner. I need one of those, those, things . . . I need a *phooknee.*" Amma Ji was not talking to me, but I knew what she was talking about. I had seen a *phooknee* before. It was a small handheld pipe that would blow air onto the fire. There was a sweatshop across the street where they made knives and little tools, and I knew that the object she wanted was something the craftsmen there might make. I had lurked in their doorway many times, and they often called out, *"Salam o alaykum"* and had sometimes gone so far as to make small talk with me. As my mother waved her hand back and forth waiting for the fire to catch, I ran across the street and into the shop. I rushed between the men sitting at small benches or squatting on the floor and made my way to the man who had always been friendliest to me, never tiring of my many questions. I directed my breathless request to him.

"My amma needs a *phooknee* to make a fire in our stove. Do you have one?"

He smiled and said, "It so happens I have an extra one. Wait a minute."

He walked into the back room and returned with an object that looked like a large whistle. "Tell your amma this is my gift to her, to welcome her to the neighborhood."

Moments later, I walked up to my mother, still bent over the stove, and held out the small pipe. "Here, Amma. Is this what you need?"

"Why, yes, exactly. Thank you." That night she told everyone in the family, "I didn't think to buy one, but Zahir, he thought of it. What a helpful boy." It was just a simple expression of gratitude, yet all these years later I remember it as the moment on which our future relationship was founded.

I was a hero. I wanted to do everything for her and take care of her so that she would be proud. She needed someone to help her in that new city, in that new home, but there was no one. We lived with Tayab, my big brother, but this was not enough. Amma Ji relied only on herself.

Tayab's house was comfortable. The ground floor consisted of three commercial shops, two entrances, and a small living area. The sleeping quarters were on the floor above it. Tayab operated one of the shops as a convenience store that sold mostly groceries. The house had previously belonged to a Hindu family that migrated to India right after independence. When Amma's brother Zaheer moved there from India, he had taken possession of the house. These kinds of switches came along with the partition of the nation. A Hindu family suddenly might find themselves on the Pakistani side of the new border and decide to abandon their home and head to India, while a Muslim family could find themselves on the Indian side of the new border and walk away from their home and head to Pakistan. Each would move into a house vacated by someone heading the other way; it was not necessarily the same two families and rarely an even exchange. It would take years for the governments to wade through the paperwork required to reimburse people for their losses and to get those who had moved into bigger, better homes to make up the difference to those who had lost them. Of course, few people were happy about the lost property or the lost cash.

I did not know such things back then. All I knew was that Zaheer had moved with his family to Rawalpindi, leaving Tayab in control of this large house where we now lived. This was Tayab's property, and though we were his family, we did not have a sense of ownership. I was excited to leave behind the dark house of mourning in Pur Qazi, but that did not mean I immediately felt at home there.

I was surrounded by a language and culture that my mother did not understand, and because I was still young enough to interpret the world through her eyes, I inherited some of her sense of not quite belonging, not quite comprehending, not quite relaxing in this new world. I spent most of my time in the slow-moving streets of our neighborhood, my feet always ready to take off here or there, never quite landing at home.

We left behind the religious and cultural tensions of the old country for the cultural and language issues of a new one. The dialect spoken in Sialkot was Punjabi. We spoke Urdu, and though the locals understood Urdu and a few people spoke it, our dialect raised eyebrows and sometimes brought laughter or disdain. Punjabi-speaking people thought our accent was funny and strange, a mark of country simpletons. In turn, the newcomers who spoke Urdu like we did believed that they were more sophisticated and educated than Punjabis. Everyone made fun of each other's accents and assumed their superiority, but since Urdus were in the minority, it was harder for a boy like me to remain convinced of my culture's superiority for long. There were too many voices and sounds that disagreed with that notion. I often felt embarrassed among Punjabi speakers, and as I picked up some of their habits, I grew to feel embarrassed among Urdu speakers—I never landed solidly in one world or the other but floated between them. After the massive upheaval of national partition, this was what it boiled down to for a seven-year-old boy. I was forever being an outsider no matter where I roamed.

"Hey, *ae bahia ki olad* (Urdu-speaking boy)," kids sometimes taunted me, "go back to where you came from!"

While I felt embarrassed, I was not afraid of them. "You want me to go back where I came from? My mother says we all come from the earth and go back there when we die. I am not afraid of earth, are you?"

It was not just the language that was different. The style of clothing common in Punjab was different, too. In northern India, it was common for Muslim women to wear *Chori-Dar-Pajamas*. These pajama pants were loose from hips to knees but skintight from knees to ankles. Due to the tight fit, they were not easy to put on. The women in Punjab mostly wore pants known as *shalwar*. They were loose-fitting, easy to put on, and more comfortable. Though my mother was middle-aged, there were some aspects of assimilation that she was more ready for than any of us. After spending nearly fifty years of her life confined in the heavy, disguising, confining clothes of her sex, her religion, and her culture, Amma was eager to adopt anything that might make her daily life more comfortable. She quickly exchanged her *Chori-Dar-Pajama* for *shalwar*.

Although my mother was a devout Muslim, she was open to anything that made more sense. Cultural habits for their own sake did not have a hold on her. "I can't believe I spent all those years wearing something so uncomfortable," she said of her old *Chori-Dar-Pajama*. "So silly, when I could have moved around this easily all along. Everyone should wear these." Once she started wearing the loose-fitting pants, she never struggled into tight clothes again.

Amma's adaptability had always been her strength. Back in India, when she used to visit Jamil in Delhi, she noticed people wearing sweaters during the winter. Back home in Pur Qazi, people wore tight, quilted jackets with heavy cotton padding to keep warm in winter.

She thought the sweaters allowed for more comfortable movement and they were prettier, so she learned how to make them. Her children were the first to wear sweaters in Pur Qazi, and because the neighbors respected Amma's sensibility, they followed suit.

When we moved to Sialkot, however, she did not try to learn to speak Punjabi. She always spoke in Urdu to her children, her neighbors, and the shopkeepers. Because Punjabi was not so much a different language as it was a dialect, and because Urdu was the formal language of Punjab, most people understood her so long as she spoke slowly and clearly. "I'm too old to learn a new language," she said. "Why should I when I can get everything I need by using the language I know?" She was uncomfortable in pajamas, so she switched to shalwar; she was comfortable speaking Urdu, so she stuck with Urdu. We children spoke Punjabi outside and in school, but the language used in our house remained Urdu.

It was not as if she went out of her way to fit in with our few Urdu neighbors when it was not convenient. Many Urdu people like to chew *paan*, a combination of betel leaf, areca nut, and lime paste. They consider it a palate cleanser, a breath freshener, and a digestive aid. Many consider it polite to offer *paan* to guests who come to your home, especially right before or after a meal. Almost every Urdu-speaking household in our neighborhood had a *pandan*, a container filled with the ingredients for *paan*, and a special urn, like a spittoon, for spitting out the remnants. Most houses were Punjabi, and when my mother noticed that those houses did not have those items, she said, "Good. Chewing *paan* is a messy habit. I say we don't need it." Because we alternately clung to old traditions or assimilated new ones, people from both cultures found us strange.

"You don't have a *pandan*?" an impertinent Urdu-speaking guest once asked my mother.

"It's too messy," she said.

"You've given up on the old traditions under pressure from the Punjabis?"

"No one pressures me. I keep the traditions that make sense to me and those that honor the holy word of the Quran."

A new language, new clothes, and the subtle differences between two intersecting cultures in transition were not our biggest problems in negotiating our way through a new life in Pakistan. The main issue we faced as a family was family. My mother had uprooted her life because she could not stand the thought of being so far from my two older brothers, yet Tayab and his wife, Sajida, made it clear that they believed their lives would have been easier if Amma had stayed in India.

The bad blood began to flow even before we arrived. My Uncle Zaheer owned a small retail business in Sialkot, and Tayab had engaged in a few transactions with him. Both men ended up believing the other had given him the short end of the deal. Tayab accused Uncle Zaheer of not dealing in good faith and vice versa. When Amma arrived, her son tried to lay down the law. "If we're going to live together, we must be united as a family. Zaheer is not an honorable man, and I no longer consider him family. Amma, you shouldn't trust him either. He cheated your son, and you should have no part of him."

"I'm sure you believe that's true. And I'm sure he has his own side of the story, which he believes is true. I'm not going to choose between my brother and my son. You're all my family, and until I have some proof of wrongdoing by either one of you, so you will both continue. The bonds of family are what make us strong in the face of a difficult world," Amma said. "I wouldn't break those bonds so easily if I were you. You don't know when you'll need that strength later."

"Yes, Amma, the bonds of family are strong, but I'm not the one who has broken them. Zaheer is the one. You're too trusting. You don't know what he's capable of. Just remember, by keeping your bond with him, you may be weakening the bonds of the rest of the family. If family is so important to you, you should know that sometimes you can't have it both ways."

"When it comes to family, I do not think there are two ways, only one," Amma said. "You're young yet. Someday you'll see what I mean."

With that, Amma dropped the subject. Although it did not come up again, an invisible line had been drawn: Tayab and Sajida on one side and Amma on the other.

My mother did her best to prevent most of the other tensions that came with a blended household by drawing another line. Just after we arrived, Amma said that her daughter-in-law deserved her own kitchen and suggested that our family have a separate kitchen.

"With so many people in the house, it's natural that we'll run into each other," she told Sajida, "but in some parts of the house this could cause problems, even if we all do our best to avoid them. The kitchen is an important place for a family to relax and have a space for themselves. You are newlyweds, and you should be able to enjoy each other without the noise and chaos of five small children who aren't your responsibility, and without the meddling of a mother-in-law who has her own ideas about running a kitchen. I was a daughter-in-law, too, you know, and I know how difficult it can be. We also have different incomes, and it could make it awkward when I'm feeding my family on my budget while you're feeding your family on a different budget. If we each have our own kitchens, you don't have to worry about any extra financial burden, and I don't have to reassure you that we have what we need. Do you see?"

"But we don't see you as a burden, Amma," Tayab said. "Right, Sajida?"

"No, of course not. We are happy to have you," Sajida said.

Amma stood her ground again. She had been an eleven-year-old girl when she was introduced to the ways that money issues could pull a family to pieces, and our finances were far from certain. At first, our only source of income was from our father in India. He had been having trouble collecting money from his mostly Hindu clients ever since the revolution. Now that many of his debtors knew he was planning to leave the country, even fewer clients seemed inclined to pay. Some Hindus still felt bitter toward Muslims for splitting the country, but it seemed that both Hindus and Muslims were simply trying to wait him out, hoping that he would give up on collecting and leave. Our father sent very little money and only intermittently.

"You two shouldn't be burdened by our financial problems," Amma said to Tayab.

"But if you need help, it's our duty to help you," Tayab replied.

"Let me put it this way. If you find that you're able to later, you're welcome to help us, but you're just getting started, so for now let's not worry about it."

Amma hoped to lessen the chances of friction between our two families, and more importantly, between daughter-in-law and mother-in-law. In traditional Muslim Indian culture, this particular relationship was doomed to foster resentment and frustration. These two people had no choice but to share a home where an older woman felt she was being pushed out of her domain and a younger woman believed she was being stifled and controlled. Amma hoped to avert that seemingly unavoidable conflict, but she soon found out that such a gesture was no help when the recipient had no room in her heart or mind.

Though she never said so, Tayab's wife made it clear that she wanted no part of us, especially Amma. She made baseless, silly accusations against our family at every opportunity. The easiest target was my sister, Sajida. She was a young girl and therefore expected to be more compliant. She also was at an age where she was expected to take some responsibilities in the household yet still young enough to make mistakes. My sister-in-law may have resented having to not only share her house but also her name. The elder Sajida often accused the younger Sajida of not doing what she was told, doing chores incorrectly, or using household items that were not hers. It was clear that the elder Sajida made up most of the accusations to vent her unspoken frustrations. I knew my sister, and only around Tayab's wife did she suddenly turn into this irresponsible, untrustworthy, clumsy person I did not recognize.

Looking back, I wonder if the elder Sajida might have envied the younger Sajida because of one thing my mother gave little Sajida, something my brother did not want her to have. When we moved to the city, once my mother changed her pants and threw out the *paan*, her openness to change did not stop. She began questioning which traditions truly seemed in keeping with the holy Quran and service to God and which ones only seemed to serve the misguided, silly, or selfish interests of certain people. One of her questions was this: why should her daughters be kept from going to school just because they were girls? Her answer was to send Sajida to middle school.

"Absolutely not! No girl in my house is going to school. I won't allow it!" Tayab said.

"You're not her father. You have nothing to say in the matter," Amma said.

"When my father isn't here, *I* am the head of this household, and I say it's improper for a girl to go to school. A proper girl needs only to learn to read the Quran so that she can learn what she must know to be a good wife and mother."

My mother was not one to raise her voice, but when she felt strongly about something, her insistence was like a wet fire in a woodstove, her smoke choking off all argument, her flying sparks threatening to ignite. She looked fierce as she laid down the law. "Wrong, Tayab! When your father is not here, *I* am in charge of my children and the matters of my household. If you learned your Quran, you would know that. You would also know that the first verse was revealed to the prophet Mohammad, peace be upon him, was about the importance of education, period. There is nothing in our faith that says learning is only for boys. I do not see how knowledge will make my daughter a bad wife. If anything, a smart wife can be a better support to her husband. If both your father and I had an education, we would not have had to struggle so hard. *All* my children must have an education. My daughter is just as smart as my sons. Why should she be denied to learn just because she happens to be female? It makes no sense."

"Amma, what will people say?"

"You're worried about what people will say? Is that what you've learned from the Quran? Shame on you, Tayab."

"Well, you don't have a lot of money, you know. How will you afford yet more books and supplies?"

"If you're worrying that we'll ask you for money, Tayab, there's no need. I won't ask you for a penny."

Its likely Sajida butted in at some point to say something like, "I think Tayab is also concerned that if you spend money on sending Sajida to school, you won't have any money to invest in her bridal clothes and jewels or in finding her a good husband."

"Is that what you're saying, Tayab?" Amma asked.

"No, but the cost could be another problem."

"If so, then that's my problem and not your concern."

The money did become an obstacle. Amma thought she was sending Sajida to the equivalent of an American public school, but a few months later, Sajida brought home a piece of paper requesting tuition. Amma went to the school to ask why she was being charged a fee when she never had to pay anything before.

"No?" the administrator said. "According to our records you paid for her first semester."

"No, I didn't pay anything."

The administrator discovered that one of Sajad's teachers had paid the fee. The next day, my mother and Sajida walked to the school before classes began to find the teacher. While Sajida sat outside, my mother talked to her teacher alone.

"I heard that you paid the tuition for my daughter, Sajida."

"Oh, I knew that you had probably just moved to the area. Moving is expensive, so not everyone has the tuition handy right away. I knew you would pay as soon as you settled in."

"Yes, yes. Well, we're settled in now, so I insist on paying you what we owe you."

"Sajida is an excellent student and, as a teacher, it's a great honor to help her achieve her potential. Keeping her in school from now on is all the payment I ask."

"No, no, it's not right. I must pay you back."

"And I'm telling you, it's a gift to welcome you to the neighborhood. I've told you how to pay me back, and I'm afraid that's the most I'll accept."

Amma smiled. She knew it was poor manners to reject a gift. "Thank you. You're very kind. I promise I'll honor your gift by making sure Sajida has all the education I can give her."

Amma had not planned on the expense of Sajida's tuition, which she would have to pay from then on. Our budget had little room for new expenses, so she simply bargained harder for our food at the market.

During our first year in Sialkot, Tayab bought two more stores, one of them located in the wholesale market. He started making good money. One day, just when the future looked bright for him and his wife, Tayab announced that he had sold all his stores, including the inventory, and would be moving to Lahore in a few days.

It was too late for my mother to suggest to Tayab that he leave the store for her and Abba to run once he joined us from India. Too late for her to argue her oldest son out of giving up an investment that was doing well and taking the risk of starting all over again. Too late to appeal to him that it was not a good plan to leave her alone with five small children and no man in the house. Amma would never have begged—it was not her style—but given a chance, she might have tried to make him see the error of his decision. I doubt it would have made a difference.

"You sold the store to complete strangers, Tayab? Why? Your father is coming soon. He could have run the stores. What will we do to make a living when he leaves the business in India?"

"Amma, I have to think of my own family now."

"I don't see how your family can benefit from this decision. You're leaving a working investment, and for what? You have no plan, no other business. You'll have to start all over. Just who does this benefit?"

I doubt he had stopped to consider the peril he was putting us in, leaving an uneducated, middle-aged mother of five children, ages seven to sixteen, alone with no business, no job prospects, and no husband. Even if he did not realize this, he had to know the risk he was taking with his own fortunes. The only possible explanation was that his wife, Sajida, had convinced him that she could not take another minute of living with us.

My mother brought us to Sialkot in hopes of reuniting with her two eldest sons, and now half of that reason was leaving. I have no idea how frightened my mother must have been, as she never let it show. In our early days in Pakistan, I thought I had the power to rescue her with such heroic weapons as the small pipe that blew wind onto the stove fire, but she was the one who single-handedly would now have to rescue us all.

Shortly before Tayab left, the power department cut off our electricity.

-14-

LEARNING TO READ
AND WRITE

Amma woke up one morning, a few days after Tayab and his wife left for Lahore, and grabbed the handle of the kitchen water pump, working it up and down with her muscular arm. At the beginning of each day, she used a little of this water to splash her face hen set a pot full boiling for our morning tea and porridge. This morning, the water slowed down to a rusty trickle and then stopped altogether.

Like our electricity, our water supply also had been cut off due to unpaid bills. Tayab had left all our utility bills unpaid for some time and had given us no warning. During those days, water in Sialkot was in short supply. Corruption was rampant in the power and the water departments, among others, so it could be a very lengthy, difficult process to restore both our electricity and our water connections, if we could manage it at all.

We could live without electricity but not water, so solving the water dilemma became my mother's first priority. While my brothers and sister were at school, Amma gently pulled me by the hand down street after street, hurrying me to keep up with her, until we reached the offices of Sialkot's water department. After waiting a very long time, I listened as Amma patiently explained our situation to a man in a suit. He bobbed his head back and forth in a response that meant neither yes or no but only indicated his inability to answer and his denial of any responsibility for an answer. I was too young to understand, but

I realize now that if only Amma had a little extra money, above and beyond the cost of our overdue bill, she might have had the power to restore our water service. She asked to speak to another man, but he also shook his head in that same sorry-but-not-sorry way.

We had the same experience at the power department. My mother walked out of both buildings with her head held high but her lips pressed together into a thin, quivering line, as if she were holding something back. The walk home seemed very slow compared to our scurrying earlier.

Although we had no water hookup with the regular city lines, we still had access to a hand pump on the ground floor. The store's new owner owned only the shop itself, not the other rooms on that floor or the associated water pump. Every day, my brothers, my sister, and I took buckets down to the ground floor, filled them up at the pump, and carried them back upstairs. I remember the first time I lugged a water bucket up the steps, holding it in front of me with two hands, the bucket bumping from side to side against my knobby little knees. A lot of the water sloshed over the sides and dribbled down the stairs, and when I reached the top, the bucket was only about half full. When I stood before my mother, the bucket in my hand, she smiled and said, "You are such a big help to me, Zahir. Thank you."

I grinned from ear to ear, not worrying about the spilled water, and then went off to school where I had just started my first year of study.

That night, Kalim, Salim, Sajida and I gathered in a tight circle around the light of an oil lamp to study, as we had done for several nights. I strained to see my paper as I traced the letters of the Urdu alphabet in pale strokes of pencil. Amma sat in a corner and slowly fanned herself with one of our old notebooks, staring up at the ceiling fan, which hung as unmoving as a dead spider. Luckily it was not the height of summer, or the room would have been suffocating instead of merely stifling. None of us complained about the heat or the dim light. We knew how hard Amma had tried to restore our electricity.

One night, as we studied by lamplight in the quiet hours after dinner, listening to children with less education-obsessed mothers playing games in the street, a soft rap came at the door. My mother gave us a nervous glance and said, "Its okay. Keep working. I'll get it."

Amma opened the door to see the face of a man who lived across the street.

"Hello. I couldn't help but notice the beautiful light from your oil lamp, and I can see that your children are trying to study. I know the electric department can sometimes be a problem, turning off electricity for no good reason," he said.

"Unfortunately, my grownup son had to move away, and he forgot to pay the bill before he left. I tried to give them money to turn the power back on, but . . ."

My mother bobbed her head in the way of the men at the utilities offices, but this time the gesture merely communicated a polite uncertainty.

"Oh, yes. I know these city officials can move as slow as honey on a cold day. I didn't mean to be nosy, only to offer a neighborly hand. You see, we have access to power and a couple of good extension cords, and I thought maybe in the evenings we could run a cord to your house to give your children a good light to study. I'm sure you'll agree it will be better for their eyes."

"It's so kind of you to offer, but we don't want you to risk getting your electricity shut off, too, if the authorities find out what we're doing."

"Who will tell them? We have good neighbors here. If the electric department is too busy to turn on your service, it is certainly too busy to come out here and investigate why a few extra watts are leaving our house."

"I see what you mean. We would insist on paying you for the extra electricity, of course."

"Sure, sure. So you see it would be no real sacrifice for us and a big help to you."

"Thank you so much. What's your name?"

"Abdul Ghanee."

"It's good to know we have such generous neighbors. My name is Jamila."

"Welcome to the neighborhood, Jamila."

We ran an extension across the street high enough not to be hazardous for incoming traffic. No one ever tripped, and no one ever took a notice of the long extension cord running from one house to the other. After that, Amma became fast friends with our new electrical suppliers and often carried extra samosas and other small treats to their home whenever we had a little food to spare. That wasn't very often, but it was just often enough to give Amma a chance to show her generous nature.

Our neighbors were mostly middle-class and working-class people. We were poor by comparison, but my mother always held her head high when she walked down the street, even when entirely covered in her burqa. She taught us to hold ourselves the same way. We learned from her that it's not the level of money one has that determines a person's character or respectability of a person and that there is no shame in hard work.

"When you're educated, you're rich in here," Amma said, tapping the side of her head. This statement came from a woman who could not read, though I was only beginning to notice that detail. She asked my brothers and sister to read our father's letters to her and then dictated her replies to Sajida, who would write them in her shaky, round, oversized script.

Our parents must have left many private expressions of love and concern unwritten because they did not want to worry us or were afraid to show feelings that propriety dictated they share in private, away from the eyes and ears of their children. For a time, all we knew from Abba's letters was that he was still doing his best to collect on client payments and that he missed us, and all we learned from Amma's dictated replies was that she was proud that we were all doing well in school, disappointed that Tayab had moved away, and we still had a roof over our heads and food to eat. Praise Allah.

Each time she listened to one of us read Abba's letters, each time she watched us laboring over our homework, it seemed like a school bell went off in her head, waking her to the importance of literacy. She was in her late forties, in charge of a household, and poor. Attending school seemed out of the question, but Amma had a gift for recognizing unique moments when opportunity accompanied desire. She had small children who were learning to read and write and who brought home the tools to do so.

One night, she asked me, "Zahir, what is that letter?"

Urdu has a different alphabet than English, but if it had been English, my answer would have been something like "A."

"And what sound does it make?"

"Aaah."

"And this one?"

"B—buh."

She asked me a few more questions and then went on with her cooking or whatever she was doing, but little by little, day by day, she learned the entire alphabet and all its sounds.

She continued to ask questions, first of me, and then of all of us. She glanced over our shoulders or held up one of our books and asked, "Sajida, what is this word?" or "Kalim, am I pronouncing this correctly?'

At first, it was strange for the woman who was my teacher to ask me to become her teacher. Each day she guided my steps, admonished me to study, and taught me right from wrong; now our roles seemed reversed. "Will you look at this sentence, Zahir, and tell me if it's right or wrong?"

She had no time to sit down with us while we did our homework. When I look back, I realize that she was always working, first at housework and soon at more difficult labor. However, Sajida, Kalim, Salim, or I often shared a word or a sentence with her and, the next day, I saw a piece of paper with that word or sentence written in careful, firm handwriting, over and over. She showed us those papers and asked if she had done it right.

I saw that she was never embarrassed to ask—her desire to learn was greater than her pride, and this later helped me. When subjects at school did not come easily to me, I knew that things did not always come easily to Amma. I did not grow up afraid of failure or afraid to try, though sometimes I felt a touch of shame that I was not nearly as motivated to study as Amma.

At the time, it didn't occur to me that Amma must have given up some of her sleep so that she could practice her reading and writing, but later I thought, "Of course! When else would she have done it?" When I went to bed, I sometimes saw her with paper and pencil in hand, practicing short sentences. I suspect that she may have sometimes drifted off to sleep with one of our schoolbooks in her hands.

I remember once seeing her sitting tall and straight in a chair, writing a full page with a look of deep concentration on her face. She must have been writing a letter to Abba, proud that she could finally do it on her own without anyone's help. I do not remember exactly when she stopped asking us to read our father's letters to her, but I do remember that it was not long before our roles reversed yet again and we all gathered around Amma as she told us, "Abba has sent us another letter. Would you like to know what he has to say?" I like to think that once she started writing letters to him, my father knew they had some privacy and perhaps said loving things to her. She finally had the privilege of keeping them secret from our ears.

Long before that, she had another secret to keep from us. We were dangerously close to ending up starving on the street. If our mother had not been such a resilient woman, we might have. The money our father sent was not enough to keep body and soul together, and with my brother gone, we had no other source of income. There was no such thing as welfare in the new Pakistan, nor do I think my mother would have used it except as a last resort, and perhaps not even then, considering our experience with the power and the water authorities. It came down to my mother, and she had been raised in a society that discouraged women from working outside the home.

Though she must have worried, Amma Ji never let us see it as her eyes calmly ranged over the five faces gathered around her on the floor at dinner each night. Seventeen-year-old Mutahir, twelve-year-old Sajida, eleven-year-old Salim, nine-year-old Kalim, and I looked up at her and saw eyes always full of intelligent life. Although I did not know what she was thinking, it was clear that she was always thinking about something.

As our money dwindled, two thoughts must have circled around in her head: How will I feed my children? How will I keep them out of the factories? It was common for families in our situation to send children of Sajida's age, and sometimes even those Salim's age, to work in sweatshops. Down the block from our house stood a row of cottage industries that manufactured a variety of items such as surgical instruments, shoes, sporting goods, and clothes. Sometimes while playing in the streets with my friends, walking to school, or walking with my mother to the market, I would peek through the open doorways of those buildings. Inside, I saw up to several dozen heads bent over objects, their hands moving through repetitive tasks. They all worked on different items, but nearly half of them had one thing in common: they were eight to fifteen years old.

My mother knew that once we started down that path, our educations would be lost, and our children, too, might be doomed to end up in those dim, hot, packed rooms, working at repetitive tasks, bringing home just enough money to keep starvation away. She had spent some thirty years helping her husband build a business so that they could give their children the kind of comfort she could recall only in faint childhood memories of bright colors and herbal jars, memories awash in the scents of mango and sugarcane. She must have thought of Bilqees' wedding, the golden threads of her gown, the garland of flowers around her neck, and the henna patterns on her hands. She recalled the women she had urged to go to the polls and to vote for the men who would split India in two halves. Now here she was in that other half, in Pakistan, wondering where the time had gone, wondering if she had the energy left to win back the safe, comfortable life she had once again lost.

Amma did not for a moment consider sending us to those factories. The question was not whether she would send us to work but what she would do to avoid it. She could not go to the factories herself. No factory employer would take a woman in her late forties, with no experience, when they knew they could easily train a younger worker with more energy. She could not leave her children alone for the long work days that such jobs required—often twelve hours or more.

If Tayab had left us the shop, we all might have pitched in to work the counter a few hours each and made enough money to survive, but that option was gone. Amma could go to her brother, Jamil, and ask for help, but whatever help he could give could only be temporary. She needed a long-term solution that would keep us fed, clothed, and housed, one that would pay our tuitions until every one of us had graduated from high school and preferably college.

She needed to find a way to keep us going for the next few months until Abba joined us. Allah forbid, she might need to keep us going for years if Abba could not get the money from his clients and was forced to arrive in Pakistan empty-handed.

Each night when we went to bed and Amma turned out the lights, I suspect she lay awake in her room, staring into the dark, wondering when she would see Abba again, wondering what kind of work a middle-aged mother with no education and no training could do. She might have cried, but I doubt it. Her children needed her, and I do not think that she would have wasted the tears, not even when she was alone. Amma was a problem-solver, and for that, she needed a clear head.

She was not educated, but that did not mean her brain was weak. If she thought long enough and hard enough, she was to think of an answer. Her options were few, but surely she would have considered the pros and cons of each one, even those that seemed farfetched or ridiculous. That was her way, the way of a true leader. She knew how to cook, but not well enough to work in a restaurant. She had sewn sweaters for her children, but she was no skilled seamstress. If only she had gone to school!

Even if she had not gone to school, she had started to read, proving she still had it in her to learn, and once again she would teach herself to do something new. She had plenty of motivation to add a new skill to her growing repertoire, because whatever she did, it had to keep the family together. She was not sure what that might be, but she could feel an idea rising within her. Sooner or later, one always did.

-15-

THE SEAMSTRESS

I was accustomed to my mother pulling me by the hand through the streets of Sialkot. Whenever we left the house together, I knew we might go to the shops to buy school paper or clothes or kitchen utensils, but most likely we would go to the market to buy food, spices, and tea. Amma had to stretch every rupee, and sometimes our meat portions were hard to find in the midst of vegetables, rice, potatoes, and sauce. She always made sure to buy enough so that each of her five children got a bite, and each night, she carefully picked over each bone to make sure that the servings came out even. We were poor, but if Amma worried that we might descend into homelessness and starvation, she never showed it.

On this day, we did not head in the direction of the market or any of the usual shops.

"Where are we going, Amma?" I asked.

"Today, we will buy a sewing machine, Zahir."

"Are you going to sew me some clothes for school?"

"Sometime, yes, of course, but first I'm going to make clothes for other people."

"Who?"

"I'm not sure yet, but I'll make beautiful clothes for people, and then they'll pay us, so we can buy more meat for our dinners. Won't that be nice?"

"More meat would be good, Amma."

She walked into a shop filled with small, black tabletop machines. Amma passed her hands over several newer-looking models, but she did not linger. She headed to the back of the store and toward a group of old-fashioned hand-crank sewing machines. These made more sense for Amma: they were cheaper, and because electricity was expensive and unreliable, we were still piggybacking on the electricity of our neighbors. She walked to the cheapest, rustiest one, the black rubbed away in places by the sweaty hands of previous owners. Amma haggled with the shopkeeper to lower the price.

It was always fun to watch Amma bargain as she and the seller volleyed numbers back and forth. The look in her eyes could change from serious to surprise, then to mildly outraged and even amused, all in the matter of a few minutes. Sometimes she grabbed my hand and pretended to walk away, but she always kept her cool, never shouting or losing her temper. "Always know how much you can afford to spend before you go into the store, Zahir, and never let them convince you to go higher, no matter how tempting it is. Maybe you will have to leave the store. If he can afford your price, he will call you back. If he can't afford your price, maybe the next store can." I did not completely understand her tactics, but I thought Amma must be very smart.

Amma grabbed my hand to leave the shop twice. I was certain that the machine must have been expensive if she was willing to walk out two times, but she finally haggled the price down to an amount she could live with. She offered to have Mutahir pick it up later, but the man said he would have a delivery boy drop it at her house, free of charge. Amma gave him a grateful smile. The cost of the machine had taken most of her meager savings, and she could not afford to pay extra for delivery.

That evening, after she set up the sewing machine in our main living area, we all stood around admiring it.

"Do you know how to use it, Amma?" Sajida asked.

"The man at the store showed me. It's simple." Amma sat down to demonstrate. "You put the thread here. This is called the bobbin. Then you push the cloth through here while you turn the wheel, which makes the needle move up and down to push the thread through the clothes." She smiled at us with quiet confidence, though she had never sewn anything on a machine. In the past, she made sweaters for us and mended our clothes to make them last, but she had always done the work by hand.

Mutahir looked skeptical. "How will you get customers?"

"I'll tell our neighbors that I'm a seamstress now, and I'm sure some of them will give me orders. I'll charge less than the fancy stores, so I'm sure word will get around, and we'll get plenty of customers."

I gave Mutahir a triumphant grin, confident that our mother could do whatever she said she could do.

"Anyway, this is a perfect way for us to make extra money. I'll be my own boss, so I won't have to worry about getting hired or fired, I'll be able to stay home to take care of all of you and the house, and I can make my own hours. Soon things will be looking up again for the Kazmis. This is just a start. You'll see."

Amma did not put up a sign or take out an advertisement in the papers but simply dropped a subtle word to our neighbors: our first Punjabi-speaking friends, the ones who shared their electricity with us, Ghani and his wife, Mahmooda. The day after the sewing machine arrived, Mahmooda came to the door to say hello. Knowing my polite but shrewd Amma, the exchange probably was quite calculated.

"Come in and share some chai," Amma said.

"Thank you, just for a few minutes," Mahmooda said. Surely she had seen the delivery boy bring our package yesterday and must have been curious to know what it was. Her eyes scanned the room. "Ahhh, I see you have a new sewing machine."

"Oh, yes," Amma said, as if it was something she'd been casually considering for a long time. "I'm sewing for customers now, so I needed a good machine."

"You sew?" Mahmooda asked.

"Yes," Amma said. "Haven't you ever seen my red shirt? I sewed that myself."

Mahmooda might or might not have seen the shirt, but either way, she would have said something polite. "Yes, of course. It's lovely. You must be very talented."

"Enough I suppose. The great thing is I work at home and don't go through a store. This means that I can sew clothes cheaply. If you'd ever like some nice clothes at a discount, I'd be happy to make something for you."

"As a matter of fact, I could use a new dress," Mahmooda said. "Do you have time soon?"

"Yes, I could fit that in tomorrow. Why don't you come by in the morning with the fabric that you'd like? Oh, and remember to bring one of your dresses. I'll need it to get your proper measurements."

Amma shrewdly gave the impression that she was the experienced seamstress of a growing business and was generously fitting Mahmooda into her schedule instead of a homemaker who had no idea what she was doing. She asked Mahmooda to bring her dress not to get her measurements, which she could easily do with a tape measure, but to see how the dress was put together so that she could reverse-engineer something similar. Mahmooda probably suspected as much but wanted to support her friend's new endeavor.

The next afternoon, I watched as Amma turned Mahmooda's old dress inside out. She took a deep breath and cut some of the threads with scissors to see how the seams had been put together. I held my breath and observed my mother put the dress back together on the sewing machine, hoping it would work. She restitched it slowly, pushing the cloth under the needle with one hand while turning the handle on the wheel with the other. Faster, slower. Faster, slower. It was hard for her to crank the wheel with one hand while holding the cloth in a straight line with the other. The seam veered off track a couple of times, but when she had closed the gap, she held up the dress. There were a couple of false starts where the seam was off its target. "There! If I can do that once, I can do it again." This was on-the-job training without a trainer.

Amma probably spent ten hours making the dress when it should have taken five. She still had to charge less than the stores, as she had promised, especially if she wanted Mahmooda to spread the word. It was clear that Amma's work was that of an amateur, but if Mahmooda noticed, she did not complain. She only thanked my mother for the lovely work.

"And such a good price! I'll tell my friends," Mahmooda said.

"Thank you so much. You're a good friend," said Amma.

"Not at all. You're a good seamstress."

That was a polite fib, but with practice and determination, Amma did get better. Word spread and more work came her way, and Amma improved until finally she was truly a good seamstress. During the holiday seasons of Ramadan, Eid, and Eid-ul-Adha, many women ordered dresses for parties and to give as gifts.

Amma did set her own hours, sewing during the hours when she was not cooking, cleaning, or shopping for us. During those years, I can only think of her in constant motion, moving from the stove, to the market, around the house, to the sewing machine, back to the stove, back to the sewing machine. Each night when I went to bed, she would still be hunched over the sewing machine, her upper back curved like the top of a cane, her eyes staring at the seam leading from the end of the needle.

Each morning when I awoke, porridge was already bubbling on the stove. "You'll study better if you eat a good breakfast," she said.

I do not think I ever saw her sleep, though she must have. I knew she was always tired. One could tell by the dark circles under her eyes and the way she rubbed, clutched, and pressed her shoulders. Every morning, I still saw pieces of paper with new practice words spelled out in Amma's careful hand, and through it all, she never stopped learning to read and write.

Even after she got better at sewing, turning the hand crank for hours remained difficult. A muscular man would have found it tiring, and Amma was a 120 pounds at most. Keeping the seams straight with one hand remained a challenge. Sometimes, while stitching a long piece of fabric, I spun the wheel for her so that she could hold the fabric with two hands. "A little faster, Zahir. Oh-oh-oh, a little slower. Perfect. Now keep it steady. Good, keep going." I was proud to help Amma and help keep her shoulders from hurting. Before I left the room to go to bed, I sometimes caught her rubbing those shoulders and thought, Maybe things will be better when Abba comes. He can do more of the work and give Amma a rest.

Amma became a pretty good seamstress. She was certainly skilled at making *kameez* (tunics) and *shalwar* (loose pants), mostly for women and children, although sometimes she made the loose pants for men that we called pajamas. Only once did she try to sew Western-style men's clothes. When I was in sixth grade, I begged her for a pair of Western-style slacks.

"Amma, none of the boys wear *kameez* and *pajama* to school anymore. They wear dress shirts with buttons tucked inside modern Western pants. I know we don't have a lot of money, but please can we just buy one pair? Everyone stares at my clothes."

"Why would I buy such expensive pants when I can sew them myself?"

"But you don't know how."

"I didn't know how to make *kameez* and *shalwar*, but I learned. It's not that I can't make pants, it just always seemed too complicated, and I already have plenty of customers without having to take on something new, but for my son, the one who always helps me, I think I can make an exception." She smiled at me.

I tried not to frown in return. "Amma, this style is different." I didn't want to insult my mother, but I had seen her first try at Mahmooda's dress, and I wasn't sure I could live with the humiliation of showing up at school with one pant leg higher than the other.

"It's that or no pants at all," she said.

I had asked for gray, so she bought some gray cotton twill fabric. When I first tried them on, I was relieved. Both legs were the same length. They didn't look as good as slacks I had seen in stores, but there were no puckered seams, and they fit well. Finally, I had real pants to wear to school!

The next day, as I walked to school and the material swished back and forth between my legs, the feel and sound was all too familiar. I looked around me at the other boys walking to school and realized my mother's mistake. She had made the pants in the right style, but the soft fabric material was too similar to the type used to make pajamas. This was worse than going to school wearing pajamas! I was wearing something that no one had ever worn to my school—a strange cross between Western slacks and Eastern pajamas with a shirt tucked into it. I looked ridiculous, and soon everyone at school would know it.

My pace slowed. Were those boys walking across the street laughing at me? I stopped walking and let them drift ahead. I quickly untucked the shirt from the pant waist and let it hang loose. As long as I did not draw too much attention to myself, people would think I was simply wearing pajamas. As far as I could tell it worked; none of my friends seemed to notice. When I returned home, I put those pants in the bottom of a drawer and never wore them again.

I did not say anything to Amma about the pants, and she said nothing to me, but she never made pants for anyone again. A few months later, the weird pant-pajama hybrid disappeared from my drawer. She took me to a shop where used clothes from countries like America and Britain were sold. We selected two pairs of slightly oversized pants, and Amma took them in for me on her sewing machine.

When I put them on, she gave me a crooked smile and said, "They don't look as comfortable as pajamas, but you do look very handsome."

For a long time, I had no idea that we were poor. Amma saw to that. She was careful with money, but she never was shamed of our financial challenges. Amma always held her head high wherever she walked, and I learned to do the same. I didn't like the pants she made for me, but I still walked to school with my head held high. Amma bought a sewing machine so her children did not have to work in sweatshops, and when the customers came in to our home, she handed them their clothes with her head held high. The money those clothes brought did not buy us much extra meat, but it kept the meat coming, and it kept a roof over our heads. Most importantly to our mother, it paid our school tuition.

"Sajida, do you know you'll be the first girl in our family to graduate from high school?" she told my sister.

"Yes, Amma."

"If you study hard, maybe you'll even go to college, and you'll never have to sew clothes for other people."

The Reverend Jesse Jackson, the civil rights leader, once said, "I may be poor, but I am somebody. I may be on welfare, but I am somebody. I may be uneducated, but I am somebody." He suggested that real poverty is ingrained poverty, the kind that grinds generations down because they see no way out. Poverty was never ingrained in us. Amma was always working toward a better future for us. She made it clear we had the potential to improve our lives, to be more than what we might be in the moment. Whenever we faced hardship, Amma always treated it as a temporary phase on the way to something better.

Though we were among the poorest people in a mostly middle-class neighborhood, Amma treated all her neighbors with the dignified friendliness of equals, never acting obsequious, subservient, or embarrassed. Whether they were customers, friends, or acquaintances, she smiled at all with the same equanimity and offered chai and brought homemade samosas or other treats to those she visited.

My mother's hospitality allowed me to think nothing of befriending a neighbor kid who was about my age. For a few months, we visited each other's houses, sometimes careening in and out as our mothers smiled indulgently or called out, "Stop running in the house!" We spent most of our time running in the street playing games. Our favorite was *gulidanda*. The idea was to place a cone-shaped piece of wood on the ground and hit it with a stick to make it pop up so we could hit it with the stick again, almost like a baseball. Whoever hit it farthest would win that round. I often hit the ball much farther than my new friend, but he was a good sport about it. "Wow! I'll bet you're great at cricket!" he would say. We appeared to be on our way to becoming lifelong friends.

One day when we went inside my house to take a break, Amma offered him some sweets she had made. "No, thank you," he said.

"There's no need to be polite. I know you boys are playing hard. Go ahead."

"No, I really don't want any, thank you."

"But you must."

"I'm sorry, I can't."

"Why can't you?"

"I'm sorry, but my amma told me not to eat anything when I came over here."

I had rarely seen such a furious look on Amma's face, but she did not raise her voice. "And why shouldn't you eat our food?"

"I don't know," he said.

"Surely your mother gave you a good reason."

"I think it's because you're a *durzun*. You sew her clothes sometimes. Maybe she thinks you can't afford it."

"If I couldn't afford it, I wouldn't offer," Amma said.

"I'm sorry, but I have to do what my amma says, or she'll get very angry."

"Of course, you must obey your amma."

I watched this exchange in embarrassed silence. I knew better than to eat the treat that had been offered to me. My friend and I both took a drink of water from the hand pump and ran back outside to keep playing, but our hearts were no longer in it. He went home a few minutes later.

"Zahir, I want you to understand something," Amma said when I returned. "It's not because his mother is worried about what we can afford that she doesn't want him to eat here. It's because she thinks she is better than we are. This is not true, and we will have nothing to do with people who are so prejudiced. I'm sorry, Zahir, but you cannot play with that boy anymore."

"But Amma, it's not his fault."

"No, you're right Zahir. It is his parents' fault, but they are the ones who are teaching him what kind of a man he would become. Now, no arguing, you must do as I say. I'm sorry. I know you'll miss your friend, but you'll make other friends. You'll see."

"Yes, Amma." I was sad, but in another way I was relieved. The boy had humiliated my amma, and I did not want to ever see him or anyone else like that again.

Amma never visited their house again. The next time the woman came in to order clothes, Amma said she was too busy to take on any new orders, and the woman never came again.

The incident made an impact on me, but it barely caused a ripple in our lives. Some people thought that our neighbors were better than us, but they were few and far between. Amma had many friends, and after just a few months, many of them came to her for advice and friendship—poor, middle class, even a few of our somewhat wealthy neighbors.

I was aware that some people thought of us as poor, or believed my mother to be ignorant, but I did not buy into that reality. I learned to define myself on Amma's terms and then on my own terms. Amma showed me how. She knew where she came from, she knew where she was going, and she knew in which direction she was pushing us, and it was far beyond where she could go.

There was one thing my temporary friend pointed out to Amma that did hit her where it hurt. It was true that she had no husband at home to help her. She was not ashamed of it, but every difficult day was another day to regret the decision she made to leave India without him. She knew that he had stayed behind to collect the money his clients owed, but it was becoming clear that most of them would never pay. The money he sent had slowed to a trickle. It seemed there was no reason for him to stay in Pur Qazi anymore, so why did not Abba come back to us?

Though she had learned to read his letters, Amma had yet to learn to read "between the lines." At first, she did not realize Abba was hiding something, but with a family as big as ours, you cannot hide things for long. A visiting cousin finally brought the news to one of my uncles, who passed the word to my older sister, who brought the word to us. Abba was ill.

"What's wrong with him?" Amma asked, as they sat cross-legged on the floor, drinking chai.

"No one knows. Abba wouldn't even admit to being sick. They could just tell. He's very thin, he has dark circles under his eyes, and he walks as if he's in pain. I think he tells people he is only feeling a little poorly, but it's been going on for a long time."

There was only one way to find out the truth and one hope to bring our family together again. Amma would have to return to Pur Qazi. As difficult and frightening as it had been to come to Pakistan, attempting to cross the border back into India would present my mother with the greatest obstacles she would ever have to face.

-16-

TRYING TO GO HOME

After we turned out the lights on the night we received the news about Abba's health, I suspect that Amma remained awake in her room, staring into the dark, wondering how sick Abba was and whether she would ever see him again. I imagine her whispering to her absent husband, "Maybe the old man on the train was right. Maybe we made a big mistake. Maybe I shouldn't have come here alone with our children and you shouldn't have stayed behind in India."

In the morning, she announced her decision. "Abba is too sick to work, and there's no chance for him to collect any more money in Pur Qazi. For some reason, he's not coming here. Perhaps he's too sick to travel. We don't know, but I must return to India, and someone must go with me." I sat up expectantly. I was Amma's constant companion whenever she left the house.

She said, "Mutahir, you must go." My disappointment must have been obvious, as she put a hand out and stroked my hair. "I'm sorry, Zahir, my little man. I wish you could come, but for this kind of trip I need a big man to come with me, and you're not quite tall enough yet."

"When will we go, Amma?" Mutahir asked.

"As soon as possible."

They would have to obtain visas and apply to the High Commission of India. That would mean taking a bus to Lahore, 100 kilometers away.

When they returned, Amma looked even more stricken than when she left. She removed her traveling burqa and gathered us in the living room, where we sat in a circle on the floor. She took a deep breath.

"Mutahir will be going to India alone. The High Commission wouldn't give me a visa."

"Why won't they let you go home, Amma?" Sajida asked.

"I don't know. They wouldn't tell me."

Home? Oh, she meant India. To me, Sialkot was home, not Pur Qazi. I did not hear the heaviness when the word *home* fell from her mouth, like a stone dropped in a pond, but I felt the ripples. At the time, Abba's illness and Amma's desire to see him seemed reason enough for her to be devastated by the rejection of the request.

A couple of days later, we all saw Mutahir off at the train station. I will admit that I had a sense of excitement. I was surrounded again by the pulsing energy of the station full of surging bodies, pumping train wheels, stacked boxes and suitcases, all going to hundreds of destinations. I thought back to our long train ride and how it had changed our lives. I wondered where all these people were going and envied the many changes they were about to experience.

Mutahir's train pulled away, and we all stood waving amid the jostling crowds. It must have seemed to Amma that everything was moving in the wrong direction. She had come here to keep our family united, but now Tayab had moved to Lahore, and she was sending Mutahir back to Pur Qazi. I was not exactly sorry to see Mutahir go. He was so much older than me, rarely home, and not a part of my daily life. I was glad that he was going to get our father. I knew I was not big enough yet to protect my mother the way I wanted to, and I knew that she needed Abba's help. I hid the real truth. I was sorry that Abba was sick, but I did not miss him all that much. It had been more than two year since I had seen him. I was fond of him, but I could barely remember his face, his voice, or his touch.

As we ate dinner in our usual circle on the living room floor, everyone was strangely silent. I was puzzled at what had made the room so quiet. Mutahir was gone, but he had rarely been at home anyway.

Several weeks passed with no news. As I turned the wheel on Amma's sewing machine while she ran a seam under the needle, she sometimes muttered, "Why doesn't Mutahir send word? I hope nothing has happened." Sometimes I saw her on her prayer rug, facing

Makkah, asking Allah to take care of Mutahir and keep him safe. She asked him to restore the health of her husband, the father of her children, and bring him home to us. She asked him to bring her family together again, safe and well.

Sometimes she gave a sadqa, a sacrificial offering of alms to the poor. Even though we were barely scraping by, she would give a few of our precious coins to an imam collecting for charity or give directly to a beggar in the street.

"Giving money to that old man will help Mutahir and Abba?" I asked.

"When we give money to the poor, it tells Allah that we're willing to help others. When we open our hearts to others, we open ourselves to receive the help Allah wants to give us, but we can't always understand what Allah wants for us. We must wait on his will."

"So maybe Allah will help us?"

"Allah always helps us, but I also hope he'll show us soon that Mutahir is safe and that Abba is well."

I was not sure I understood her answer. I sometimes pulled out Mutahir's prayer rug and tried to pray, just in case it might help. I knew this would please Amma.

There were times that Amma took more direct action, bypassing God and heading to the telegraph office. She took me with her, and I listened as she dictated telegrams to the clerks.

After sending several telegrams, we finally received a brief letter from Mutahir. It confirmed both his safe arrival and Abba's sickness. Mutahir wrote how Abba was taking medicine and hoping to be better soon, but there were no details.

"That's it?!" Amma cried. "That's all he has to say? Oh, I could strangle that boy!"

After couple of months when Mutahir came back, Amma questioned him closely, and we all sat listening.

"Why didn't you write to me?"

"Didn't you get my letter, Amma?"

"Yes, yes, but only after I sent several telegrams!"

"Well, since everything was fine, I didn't see any reason to write."

"It never occurred to you that I might worry?"

"I thought you knew I would write if there was bad news."

"Stop, stop!" Amma said in frustration. "Just tell me. How is he?"

"Abba's health was not very good."

"You just said he was fine."

"Well, I meant he was as well as could be expected, and he's not dying or anything. He has diabetes, and he's taking medicine for it."

"So he has seen a doctor?"

"I think so. I'm not sure. I think Abba said that from his symptoms it was obvious what he had. Anyway, I'm sure he saw a hakeem to give him the herbs he's taking."

"Abba is treating himself?" Amma shook her head. I could tell she wasn't happy about this. "I hope he's right."

Now that Amma knew about Abba's illness, she asked about his health in every letter she wrote to aba. His answers were brief, and after another six months, he was still not well enough to join us in Pakistan. Once again, we had to hear the full story through the family grapevine. Abba appeared to be getting worse and was suffering from so much pain and exhaustion that he was often unable to get out of bed.

Amma and Mutahir went again to Lahore to apply for visas, and again, Mutahir received a visa while Amma's application was denied. Again, Mutahir went to India and came back with no good news. Abba could not come to us, and Amma could not go to him. She sometimes paced the floor, asking Allah what she should do. I do not know if God answered her, but one day when we came home from school, she had an announcement for us.

"I'm going to India to see your father. This time I'm going to apply for a visa by myself. I'm going to go to India by myself, and no one but Allah himself is going to stop me! Zahir, how would you like to come with me to Lahore?"

I nodded enthusiastically—I went with Amma everywhere else. The only times I had not gone out with her were the last two times she went to apply for a visa. If I was with her, maybe I could help. "Maybe you'll be my little good luck charm," she said.

We stayed the night with Tayab and Sajida at their home. In the morning, we went to the High Commission, and for the third time, a visa officer turned down her application. I thought he was mean, pounding that stamp down on her paper like he hated her, like he did not care about what happened to her husband. If I had been bigger, like Mutahir, I would have asked him why he told Amma no, and I would have tried to change his mind, but I was a boy, and he was a man. I frowned at him over my shoulder as Amma took my hand and we walked away.

We returned the next day, and Amma demanded to speak to someone about her visa application. We sat on a stiff bench against a wall and waited a very long time for a man to call us to his window.

"*Bahi sahib* (brother sir), you have to tell me why your officers keep denying my visa application," Amma said.

"*Mata ji* (mother), I'm not the visa officer, and I'm not allowed to share the reason for the denial with you."

"Bahia sahib, please, you must tell me. My husband is very sick. I must go to India."

"I don't know the reason. Unless I know the reason, I cannot fix it."

"I won't leave unless you give me the reason. I beg you, please!"

He sighed heavily. "Mata ji, I'm telling you at the risk of being reprimanded for violation of policy. It was the policy of the Indian government not to give a visitor a visa to visit a spouse. However, the Indian government would give you a permanent visa if you want to move back to India."

"Bahia sahib, that's not possible, I can't go to India permanently. I have five kids at home. I want to go to India so I can bring home their father, my husband, who's very sick.

"I'm sorry, mata ji, I can't help you in this. I don't think even a visa officer can help you."

"There must be a way. Please tell me, is there anybody who can help me?

"The only person who can help is the High Commissioner. He's the only one who has the power to overrule this regulation in extreme situations."

"Then I need to see the High Commissioner."

"I don't think it's possible. He doesn't have office hours. To see him you have to make an appointment, and to make an appointment you have to go through his assistants, and I don't think they'll give you an appointment. You'll be wasting your time."

"Then I'll go to see him at his residence. Can you please tell me where he lives?"

"I don't have that kind of private information. All I know is that he lives in the Cantonment area of Lahore, but I don't know the address. Mata ji, please don't tell anyone that I told you even this much, otherwise I'll be in big trouble. I could lose my job."

Amma gave him a reassuring smile. "Bahia sahib, don't worry, I won't tell anyone. I'm grateful to you for your help. I pray God will reward you for your kindness."

"Mata ji, I hope you're successful, but I'll warn you, the security guards may not let you inside the residence. I wish you luck."

The Cantonment area of Lahore was a wealthy neighborhood, full of towering walls, high edges, and security guards. If she was found wandering there, Amma would surely to be viewed with suspicion, but that did not cause her one moment's hesitation.

Because Tayab was busy in his work, Amma decided that she and I would go by ourselves to see the High Commissioner. The Cantonment neighborhood was far from Tayab's house, and Amma could not afford a taxi or tanga, so we used public transportation.

Armed only with the general location of the High Commissioner's residence and no specific address, we got up early in the morning to start looking for him. Amma asked several bystanders at bus stops for directions, and learned that public transportation was not available all the way to the Cantonment area. The people who could afford to live there had little need for it, and their servants had to make their own arrangements. This problem did not deter Amma. We took buses as far as we could and then walked, stopping a few times to rest and to ask the locals for more directions.

It took us more than two hours to arrive at Lahore Cantonment, and we were still far from our destination. We still did not know the exact address of the High Commissioner, so Amma asked a police officer. He said he did not know but guided her to the area where most foreign high officials lived. When we reached the neighborhood, Amma questioned more bystanders until she found the exact address.

After some three or four hours of riding buses and walking, we found ourselves standing in front of a mansion in a secluded area surrounded by other large houses. We approached the tallest gate I had ever seen. Armed guards stopped us.

"May we help you?" one of them asked. He didn't smile. I didn't think he wanted to help us. I looked from his gun to his stern face and back, wondering if he might shoot us. Amma explained why we were there. His face relaxed. "I'm sorry, mata ji, the High Commissioner is gone for the day. Even if he were here, you wouldn't be allowed to see him here. You must go to his office."

"I already tried that," Amma said, "and they told me I would never get an appointment. My husband is very ill, and I must go to him. I'm sure if I can only explain to the Commissioner, he'll understand and make an exception. Meeting him here is my only real chance."

"Even on the small chance that he would talk to you, it's not going to happen now, because he's not here."

"Then I'll return tomorrow. Will you please tell me what time he usually leaves?"

"Mata ji, can't you see we're security guards? What kind of security guard would I be if I gave away that sort of information?"

"Can't you see that I'm a harmless old mother? All I want to do is see my husband. Obviously I'm not here to harm the Commissioner. I just need his help."

The second guard, who had been silent all this time, suddenly spoke. "If you come back before eight o'clock, you'll have a better chance."

The weather conditions were not hospitable, to say the least. It was early July. If Amma traveled to India during this season, her children would be out of school on summer break and could safely take care of each other.

The temperature ranged between 110 and 115 degrees in Lahore. By the time we headed back to Tayab's home, the sun beat down on us relentlessly. I was panting and listless with the heat. Covered in a burqa from head to toe, Amma must have been even hotter.

A few times Amma stopped to clutch a tree or wall, swaying as if she might faint. I was stumbling over my own feet. I was too big for her to pick me up and carry me, and that made me sad. We stopped once to buy *naan* and water, but it seemed as if the piece of flat bread only made me hungrier. Within the next half-hour, I was thirsty again. I wanted to cry, but I held back tears. I knew Amma was worried about Abba, and the last thing I wanted to do was upset her.

When we finally arrived home, we went directly to the hand pump to splash our faces and drink copious amounts of water. We ate dinner early. I'm not sure what Amma did next, but I crawled into bed and fell asleep.

In the darkness of the early morning, we headed back to the High Commissioner's house, taking bus after bus and then walking. At least this time we knew where we were going. Once again, the security guards stopped us at the gate. Though I was no longer afraid they might shoot us, I remained quiet. "Mata ji, I can't tell you whether he's home or not."

"I can see as well as you that he's home. That big car wasn't here yesterday, and now it is."

"Either way, we can't let you in."

"Then my son and I will wait for him to come out."

"Suit yourself. I doubt that he'll talk to you."

"Come on, Zahir." Amma tugged me over to a tree near the gate. From there, we could easily see when the gate opened and could quickly run back toward it. We sat for a long time, mostly staring into space. Amma sometimes played a clapping game with me or asked me to spell words for her to pass the time. In the middle of one of the games, we saw a car coming out.

"There he is!" Amma jumped up and ran toward the car, but it sped away. She watched as the car moved out of sight.

"Do we have to try again tomorrow?" I asked. I did not want to complain, but I wondered how much more of this walking I could take.

"No, Zahir. This time we'll wait for him to come home. Maybe he'll talk to us when he comes back from work." We returned to the trees and sat in the shade. This time, Amma had bought *naan* in the morning and brought it with her. We sat through the heat of the day and into the evening.

I slept off and on. It seemed like the longest day I'd ever known. It grew darker and darker, and still there was no sign of the High Commissioner.

Amma walked back to the gate and begged the guards to give us some idea of the Commissioner's whereabouts.

The guard gave her a sad look. "Mata ji, I'm sorry, I really don't know where he is. I don't suggest that you wait, because sometimes he comes very late, and sometimes he goes out of town without us knowing about it."

"I understand. I realize you're just doing your job and you probably don't know his personal schedule."

"I really wish we could help you," the man said.

"You're very kind. Thank you. Come on, Zahir." She took my hand in hers, and we began to walk through the darkened neighborhood. It was not as hot as it had been the day before, but I was still exhausted.

Though Amma was tired and frustrated, giving up was not an option. She was not one to leave a mission unaccomplished.

The next day, we again rose early and headed back to the Commissioner's house. Later, Amma admitted that she had made a promise to herself: "No matter what, I won't let the guards stop me from seeing him this time."

This time, the gates were open, and she saw the Commissioner's car parked inside. The guards stood there with their guns. She walked up to them. "I'm sorry, I know you are doing your jobs, but you cannot stop me from seeing the High Commissioner. My son and I are going in. Please don't shoot us." My eyes grew wide as she gripped my hand firmly and scurried past the guards toward the front door.

"No, no, no! You can't go in there," one of the guards shouted.

"Stop! Please stop! I'm begging you to stop! We don't want to hurt you," the second guard shouted.

Both guards rushed up to her, trying to block her way. She ducked around them and kept walking, never turning to look at them and continuing toward the door.

I saw an expanse of grass and a little girl singing as she skipped across the grass. Everyone stopped. The guards stopped shouting, and Amma stopped in her tracks. My mouth dropped open. The girl was not much older than me and unexpected in the midst of armed men, gates, big cars, and towering homes full of officials.

She stopped, her mouth snapped shut, and she blinked at Amma. Apparently we were not what she expected to see either.

"Hello, Beti (sweet young girl), is your father home?" Amma asked. The girl nodded.

"Will you please tell him that an old lady is out here who would like to see him?"

"Okay." She smiled and ran up to the door and went inside.

The guards looked at each other and shrugged. Amma's exchange with the girl had broken the spell. My mother no longer appeared to be a threat; she was more clearly a harmless old mother who just wanted help.

The guards conferred for a moment. One of them followed the girl inside the house while the other walked back to his post at the gate.

Amma and I stood between them, waiting.

After a few minutes, a door opened and a man, most likely a servant, invited us to come inside. He offered us a seat in the hall and said, "Wait here, please." I looked around me at the rich furniture, paintings, and vases. I rose to look at some little curio, but Amma grabbed me by the waist and pulled me back to the bench, saying, "No, Zahir. Stay with me."

After a while, a woman brought a tray with cold drinks. We sipped them slowly and wiped the condensation from the glasses onto our clothes, careful not to drip anything on the fancy tile floor.

A few minutes later, the High Commissioner entered. He smiled at Amma and then at me. "Well, hello! What brings you all the way to my home?"

Amma explained her predicament. When she explained that she had camped outside the High Commissioner's home off and on for the last three days, there was a moment of silence before he smiled. "You're certainly a determined woman. I hope if I ever got sick and my wife was separated from me, she would go to that much trouble to reunite us. Your husband is lucky that you're so concerned for his well-being. I'll tell you what, you go back to the visa office tomorrow, but this time you make sure everything you've told me is written down on a piece of paper and include that paper with your visa application."

"Excuse me sir, you're very kind, but I've told them my story every time, and I've always been denied. How do I know it won't happen again?"

He smiled again, broader this time. "Don't worry. Just go back to the office."

It was common in Pakistan that at any official building frequented by the public, one or two people were posted outside the building at a table with a typewriter to provide secretarial services.

Early the next morning, we went to see the typist in front of the visa office. We were his first customers of the day. Amma asked him to help her fill out her application, and she told him that the High Commissioner himself had also asked her to tell her story. The typist listened and typed out her story on a separate sheet. Armed with these two documents, we headed toward the window where the visa clerk was seated.

By now, the staff knew Amma and had become fond of her. One of the young men saw her approaching the window and shouted, "Mata ji! Mata ji! You got the visa!"

The word "visa" was a gift from heaven! I looked up at Amma, and her smile confirmed it. She closed her eyes and moved her lips silently. I knew she was thanking Allah for answering her prayers.

As soon as we returned to Tayab's house, Amma began to pack her bag.

"Are we going home, Amma?"

"Not yet, Zahir. You know that your Abba needs me, so I don't want to make him wait anymore. I'm going to leave straight from here for Pur Qazi in a couple of days. While I'm gone, you're going to stay here with Tayab."

"Why can't I go home and stay with Kalim and Salim and Sajida?"

"Because I can't put you on a train by yourself, and I know how you and your brothers fight when I'm not around to stop you."

"We don't fight that much, Amma."

"Anyway, it will be good for you to get to know Tayab. He's your brother, too, you know."

"Yes, Amma." What else was there to say? She was my mother. Arguing was not an option. Even if it had been, I did not want to give her more to worry about.

I was a little frightened to be left with Tayab, who had such a stern face and never spoke to me, and even more frightened to be left with his wife. Sajida did not seem to like Amma and who only spoke to me to scold. I wondered how she would talk to me when Amma was not there.

Two days later, Tayab and I took Amma to the train station, and he and I walked home together. "Are you hungry?" he asked.

"Not really."

"I wonder what Sajida has made us for lunch," he said, as if I hadn't spoken.

He said nothing else the rest of the way home, and I was glad of it. He was a grownup and I was supposed to mind him, but he was not my father or my mother, and I did not feel comfortable with him. He had never said much to me before. I never knew what to say to him. The silence was awkward, and I soon began trying to calculate the smallest possible number of days before my mother returned. She might be gone for a week or three months, but in my young mind, the uncertainty held the potential of years.

-17-

GOING BACK TO INDIA

Now at my older brother's house, I began to understand what it might feel like to be an orphan. I was eight, and Tayab was twenty-eight. Maybe he just did not know how to relate to me. He was neither kind nor unkind. Most of the time, he did not even look at me. I might as well have been a stick of unnecessary furniture in the house, something to be tripped over or walked around until someone finally came to take it away.

Sajida, my *bhabi* (sister-in-law), was another story. After Amma left for India, I became the focal point for her nervous discontent, and unlike Tayab, she did have a use for me. Too many uses! Never before or since have I known anyone as disorganized as Bhabi. I became the victim of her inability to plan ahead. All day, every day, I was busy running errands for her. This was bad enough, but in the summer heat, it bordered on abuse.

Bhabi rarely bought enough groceries to last for more than one day, sometimes not even enough for the next few hours. I was constantly picking up vegetables, fruits, meats, grains, and the many different spices she needed to prepare our daily meals. She never made a list of what she needed. Instead, she waited for the moment she needed an item, looked for it, and then screamed for me.

"Zahir! I need you to go to the market and get some salt. Here are two rupees. Hurry now."

I rushed to the market and back, and when I handed her the salt, she said, "What took you so long?" She often added, "In any case, you'll have to go back. I need turmeric."

This is the way it would go. She would send me to buy one item at a time. Go get yogurt, go get peppers, go get curry powder, go get cumin.

"Do you need anything else?" I would ask, hoping to save the extra trip that I knew was coming.

"No, Zahir. That's all. We don't have so much money that I can buy extra things I don't need. Just do as I tell you."

I'd go and come back again, and she would remember that she needed yet something else.

The spices came wrapped in small twists of paper. Whatever she did not use, she left scattered on a counter in the kitchen and forgot about. Because the packets were not sealed, and she made no effort or plan to store them, she knocked most of the contents to the floor as she scurried around the kitchen, never able to find what she needed, often tossing unwanted items aside in her search.

"Where is the bay leaf? Bay leaf, bay leaf . . ." She opened and closed packets, spilling more on the floor, before shouting, "Zahir!"

I often walked through the house barefoot, experiencing the gritty, sticky kitchen floor. Bhabi, who always looked busy, never seemed to get around to sweeping. I thought of home, where Amma swept the floors daily. I thought of Amma's shelves where spices were stored in small jars. I thought of the market in our neighborhood where Amma did not send me back and forth on errands but did her own shopping and brought me with her. Back in Sialkot, I walked up and down the rows of vendors with Amma's hand clinging to mine, but now, I ran back and forth from Bhabi's kitchen to the market and back again, my sweaty shirt the only thing clinging to me.

I did not play with the other children in the neighborhood. There was no time to make friends. Bhabi kept me too busy.

Tayab worked long hours, and when he returned in the evening, he always groaned to Sajida about how tired he was. Amma told me she wanted me to get to know my big brother, but he did not speak to me at all, only stared at his plate while he ate dinner. I sometimes wondered if he remembered that I was sitting there. Though he was too tired to talk to me, he had plenty of energy for loud arguments with Bhabi. Often, he and Bhabi would scream at each other, oblivious of my presence.

I wondered when Amma would come get me and take me away from this messy house where my brother treated me like a stranger, my sister-in-law treated me like a servant, and where I ran through the streets as unkempt as a beggar.

When Amma first brought me to Lahore, she believed we would only be staying for a day or two. She brought only a single change of clothes, but when she finally received her visa and decided she could no longer delay going to see Abba, she did not want to waste time returning to Sialkot just to get me more clothes. I am sure Amma assumed that either Tayab would get me new clothes or that Bhabi would simply wash one set of clothes while I wore the other. That is not what happened.

If Tayab did not notice me, he certainly was not going to notice the state of my clothes. As for Bhabi, washing was one of the other things she did not have time to do. When clothes piled up so high that the wash could no longer wait, she would send it to a laundry service. Sometimes it took a few days to get the laundry back, and for those few days I ran back and forth in heat of more than 100 degrees in the same grimy, sweat-stained garments.

The highlight of my stay with Tayab was a visit by Bhabi's relatives from Karachi. Sajida was cooking a special dinner, and she kept me busy all day long running back and forth to the store, right up until it was almost time for the guests to arrive. Bhabi was behind as usual when she finally turned to look at me.

"How did you get so filthy? Go wash up! I don't want my cousins to see you looking like that."

"I don't have any clean clothes."

"I don't have time to argue with you. Just go wash up."

There was no separate room for bathing at their house, just a water tap in the corner of the courtyard and a bar of soap sitting on the nearby bricks. Whenever I needed to shower, I had to take a cot and put it in front of the tap to create some privacy.

I went into the courtyard and as usual placed a cot in front of the water tap. I took off the clothes I was wearing and washed them as best I could, scrubbing them against the bar of soap. Even wet, the stains were still visible, but it was the best I could do. I threw my shirt and pants over the top of the cot to dry. On those hot, dry summer days, it usually only took a couple of hours for clothes to dry. I did not think I had that long, but I could wear them when they were just a little damp.

I stood under the tap, running the soap over my thin frame. The water felt soothing and cool after another day of toiling in the burning sun. When I finished, I turned off the tap and reached up to feel the clothes hanging over the cot. They were still soaked. I sat on the bricks and waited. Maybe the guests would be late.

The sun started to set, the air cooled, and goose bumps rose on my skin. I was old enough to know that I needed the sun's heat to help dry the clothes, so when the sun went down, I wondered how much longer this would take. While I sat naked and shivering behind the cot, the guests began to arrive. It was dark, and there were no lights near the tap. I sat quietly behind the cot and hoped that no one would notice me.

Tayab and Bhabi brought their guests out into the courtyard to entertain. This was common during the warm, pleasant summer evenings. It was a way to escape the stuffy heat of Pakistani or Indian houses, which had no air conditioning, only fans. The guests of honor sat on a cot brought out from the house, while Tayab and Bhabi sat in patio chairs. For once, I was glad that my brother and sister-in-law never noticed me except when they needed something. They did not seem intent on presenting me to Bhabi's aunt and uncle or making sure that I joined them at dinner. At first, no one even mentioned me. They shared casual conversation, discussing a recent journey from Karachi, the events of the day, and laughing at jokes—the murmuring of adults that I did not yet understand.

When I reached up to check my clothes for the fifth or sixth time, I stumbled into the cot, and it squeaked. The female guest who had been speaking, whose face I had not yet seen, stopped talking. Everyone became silent.

"Is something wrong?" Bhabi asked.

"Is there someone behind that cot over there?"

"Oh, that must be Zahir," Bhabi said. "That's where he takes his shower."

"Who is Zahir?" the man asked.

"My husband's younger brother," Bhabi said. "He's staying with us while their mother is in India. I think we mentioned her to you."

"Oh, yes. You told us she went to see your father. How is he?"

"He's been quite sick, but in his letters he says he's getting better. He has diabetes."

"Why doesn't Zahir come out?" the man asked.

"I think those are his clothes," the woman whispered.

"His mother didn't bring enough clothes," Bhabi said.

"Poor thing. Don't you have any clothes for him?" the woman asked.

"None that will fit," Bhabi said.

"Well, let's not embarrass the boy," the woman said. "Let's just continue our conversation, and let him come out when he's ready."

I was grateful that they were polite enough to move on with their conversation, saving me further embarrassment.

As soon as my clothes were dry, I put them on and slunk out from behind the cot. I could not avoid the guests sitting on the other side. I stepped forward, grateful that the only light drifted out from the house. They could not see my face in the shadows.

"Zahir," Tayab said, "Say hello to Bhabi's uncle and aunt, Azhar and Rani Usmani."

I looked at the ground. "As-Salamu Alaykum," I said.

"Wa Alaykum As-Salam," they replied.

"It's nice to meet you," Rani said. Her voice was soft and kind.

"Excuse me," I said. "I'm not feeling well."

I walked into the house and did not come back to join them for dinner. I was too humiliated.

Eighteen years later, when we were living in Karachi, Amma went to visit some relatives, and Rani Usmani happened to be there. Rani did not know her connection with me until I came to pick up my mother.

"You're the brother of Tayab Kazmi?" she said.

"Yes."

"Is your name Zahir?"

"Yes."

"What a strange surprise!" Rani said. "I guess you never know when the past will come back to visit you. Do you remember meeting me at your brother's house?"

It took a moment, but it slowly came back to me.

"You know Zahir?" Amma asked.

"I could not forget meeting him." She told Amma that she'd met me when I was a little boy, hiding naked behind a cot at Tayab's house, waiting for my clothes to dry. She chuckled.

I ignored the story but said, "It's nice to see you again."

Amma said nothing until we got in the car.

"Why didn't you ever tell me about that, Zahir?"

"I was only a little boy, Amma. I didn't realize it was something I should tell you, and later I tried to forget about it. It was a long time ago."

"I can't believe Tayab let that happen to you, his own brother. You poor boy!"

"He didn't do it on purpose, Amma. He just wasn't thinking."

"Clearly," she said.

"Amma, it was a long time ago. I think he has changed. Let's forget about it."

"I'll try," Amma said, but she shook her head and remained silent for the rest of the ride home. I knew she would never forget how she had left to take care of her husband, and no one had really been taking care of her youngest son. The only thing that would have helped if she could have created multiple copies of herself that followed each of her children at all times. That might have prevented her sons from making mistakes or from ever being left naked or neglected.

I stayed with Tayab and Sajida for nearly two months. They never did buy me an extra set of clothes.

One evening, there was a knock at the entranceway. "Get the door, Zahir!" Sajida shouted.

When I opened the door, Amma was standing on the doorstep.

"Amma! Amma!"

I threw myself against her with uncontained joy, though I knew I was growing too big to hug my mother. I think that until that moment, I worried I might never see her again, that government officials might make it even harder for her to come back to Pakistan than they had made it for her to go to India. She patted my head, smiled, and then backed away and ran her hand over my hair and face, frowning.

"Did you bring Abba?" I asked.

"No, not this time. He still has to get his passport and visa. It will take some time."

"Those visa people are mean sometimes, aren't they, Amma?" I decided that the people who gave out visas liked nothing better than to keep families apart. I hoped I never needed a visa.

"Sometimes they're not very understanding, Zahir," she said, smiling.

"Amma!" Tayab joined us at the door. "Why didn't you tell us when you were coming?"

"I guessed you would know when you saw me. Tayab, would you please get my luggage from the tanga, and here, give him this. I haven't paid him yet." Amma handed him money. "I'm so tired."

"Come in, Amma," Sajida called out from the kitchen. "You must be exhausted."

Amma walked in and sat down, rubbing her neck and sighing.

A few minutes later, Tayab returned to join us.

"Tayab, where did you put my luggage?" Amma asked.

"It's over here, Amma," he said, pointing to a small suitcase in the corner.

"But where's the big suitcase?"

"What big suitcase? There was no other suitcase. This small one was the only one in the tanga."

"No, I had another one inside the space under the passenger seat."

"I didn't look there. I thought this was everything."

"Oh no! No!" Amma cried out. "Don't just sit there, Tayab! Please hurry and go back out to see if you can find the tanga. Maybe the driver is still around."

Tayab ran outside but returned empty-handed. "I'm sorry, Amma. The tanga is gone. I couldn't find it again."

"Nooo, noooo," Amma moaned. For a moment I thought she would cry, something I had never seen her do. She put both her hands up to her head as if trying to hold it atop her neck. "Everything I bought was in there. So many things we need. So much money I spent. All gone. I don't know how long it will be before I can afford it again." She recited a long list. I do not remember exactly what was on it, but I imagine it included clothes for me and for my brothers and sister at home, material to sew her new outfit, things for the kitchen, foods and sweets, maybe some special tea.

"I'm so sorry, Amma," Tayab said.

Sajida said nothing but reached out and touched Amma's hand.

"It's okay. There's no sense crying about it. It's gone. I'm so tired. I think I should just go to bed." Amma looked almost as stricken as she had when she'd heard that Abba was sick.

For the next couple of days, Amma walked around in a daze, occasionally muttering about the suitcase and all she'd lost as if she had lost a chest full of gold, jewels, and fine treasures. Even then, I understood the loss seemed so great because we had so little. Today, I understand that the loss seemed even greater because it was a reminder of everything else she had lost, including her home in Pur Qazi and including her husband. It had been Amma's first trip back to India since we migrated to Pakistan. Perhaps seeing Pur Qazi again, she had yearned to stay. Leaving her husband behind again, this time suffering from diabetes, was surely almost more than she could bear. That suitcase had been her only evidence that the trip had not been for nothing, and now it was gone.

Did she have any idea at all when Abba might get his visa and come to Pakistan? Tayab and Sajida asked her the next day. Amma did not know. She would only talk about the suitcase and what a loss it was.

Even with all her losses, she did not forget me. "Don't worry, Zahir. You don't ever have to stay here again."

I put my hand in hers, and she smiled at me. I was not as big as the lost suitcase, but she was no longer empty-handed, and I was no longer invisible.

-18-

WRONG DIAGNOSIS

A mma left Abba behind in India twice, but this second time, she refused to leave until he agreed to follow her the moment he got a passport and visa. She would have waited in Pur Qazi with him if her five youngest children were not waiting for her in Pakistan. It took Abba months to get his visa, partly due to his ill health, partly due to the newness of the Pakistan government, and probably partly due to continuing suspicion and animosity between the two countries. Immigration officials often treated those trying to cross the border like suspected criminals.

Once Abba had his passport, Amma returned to India to accompany him on the journey to Pakistan. If anything, he was sicker than the last time she had visited, barely able to stand up or walk, and she was worried that he could not make it by himself.

On this trip, Amma left all of her children in Sialkot. Even though she did not know about the shower incident, she had immediately surmised from my dirty and disheveled state that my big brother had been less than attentive to my needs. She thought that I would be safer with the brothers and sister who were closer to me in age. Even though we were all young and we fought sometimes, she knew we would all watch out for each other, and we did.

About a week after Amma left for India, we heard the front door open, and we all ran to greet Amma and Abba. Though Abba looked gaunt, this was not the first thing that caught my eye. He wore a large turban on his head, which was unusual. We followed him into the living room, all of us calling out "Abba" and "Salam" and "Welcome

Home!" He nodded and reached out to pat our heads while hunching forward toward the living room. The weight of the turban seemed to bend him over even more, but it wasn't the turban he was holding, it was his lower back. It was obvious that he was in pain.

He sat down, unwrapped the turban, and removed it, and I realized that it was a large bed sheet. There had been no space for it in his suitcase, and there were strict restrictions against carrying too many goods between India and Pakistan. Amma and Abba had already lost so much, and they did not want to give up any more of their belongings than they had to. The sheet had been placed on his head, and to all appearances, it was just part of his wardrobe and a common sight in that part of the world.

The next day, Amma took Abba to see a local family doctor we had been seeing him since we had moved to Sialkot. Dr. Bashir Khan was the trusted physician of several of our neighbors, and we relied on him because we relied on them. Children did not go into the exam room with their parents, but afterward Amma told us everything that happened.

The doctor took one look at Abba and immediately knew what was wrong. "Shah Sahib (a title to show respect), I've seen many patients with this kind of pain. Diabetes does not send this kind of localized pain to the back and the abdomen. I'm sure you have a kidney stone."

"Dr. Khan, I'm sure you're an excellent physician, but you haven't even examined me yet, while my hakeem has, and he says I have diabetes. I'm afraid your diagnosis is wrong"

"Herbal medicine is very useful in many ways, but in this case, I'm sorry, it's your herbal practitioner who is wrong. We have to do an x-ray."

The x-ray confirmed what the doctor already knew. Abba had a large stone lodged in his kidney, and he needed an operation to remove it as soon as possible. Because we were poor, we had to rely on the public hospital, and it had a long list of people waiting for surgery. Abba would have to wait two months for a surgery that had already been delayed for months.

When my father came to live with us, Amma had someone to take care of her—at least that's what I thought. Instead, Amma added "nursing Abba" to her already busy schedule of sewing, cooking, cleaning, and caring for the rest of us. My father was weak and bedridden. I knew my Amma was strong, but it was profound to see how much stronger she was than Abba at this point. Our father tried to hide his pain from us, but living with so many people in such a small space and suffering as much as he was, it was impossible. Whenever I watched him hobble to the bathroom, I knew that he would be there for a long time, and I tensed my shoulders, waiting to hear the moans of pain he couldn't hold back through the closed washroom door.

Torrential rains had poured down for days. Most of the local rivers had overflowed their embankments. Sialkot was cut off from most of the world.

Tayab could not come on the day of Abba's surgery, but our next-door neighbors, Abdul Ghani and Abdul Rauf, braved streets knee-deep in water to come to the hospital and hold vigil with our family. Their wives stayed home; it would be unseemly for them to travel openly without necessity. The women sent pots and platters of food with their husbands. We had something to eat while we waited to see if our father would live or die.

Throughout the day, more neighbors came and went, as well as people who attended the mosque across the street from our home. They did not know Abba, these men, though they knew from word of mouth that the Kazmi family was an old and respected one. They knew firsthand that Amma was a mother who took good care of her children, who politely helped their wives by running errands or giving sound advice or watching over their children now and then, and who often sent over plates of food when their families were sick.

After the surgery, Dr. Khan came out to see us. He told us the surgery had gone well, but our father's problems were not over. The kidney stone he had removed from Abba was the size of an egg. It was unbelievable that he had been walking around with that monstrous growth lodged inside him. He had a long and difficult recovery ahead. Years of living with this pain had sapped his strength, and his immune system was not as strong as it should have been. If the surgery would have been done sooner, it might have gone easier, but this was not worth belaboring now. All we could do was pray, which Amma did faithfully, night after night.

When Amma was not at the hospital by Abba's bedside, she was at home listening for the call to prayer from the mosque. She was able to share in the strength of her female neighbors, as they all gathered on the connected roofs of their homes and kneeled to pray. After evening prayers, they gathered under the cover of darkness, finally able to stand outdoors free of their burqas and headscarves and to let their hair down in front of each other, both literally and figuratively.

A little boy would not be privy to such women's talk, but I knew our Punjabi neighbors, and I imagine that their conversation that first night was filled with kindness.

"I was thinking of you sitting in the hospital all day, Amma Ji, and I'm sure you didn't have a chance to cook. I always make too much food for dinner, so I brought you some of the leftovers," said Abdul Ghani's wife, Mahmuda.

"Oh, I hope you have room for more," said Sakina, Abdul Rauf's wife, who had also brought a container of food.

"You're both too kind. Your husbands already brought us food at the hospital today," Amma said.

"Don't say any more about it," said Mahmuda. "We know you'd do the same for us."

"I pray you would never need me to return the favor. I can't thank you enough."

Mahmuda brushed off the thanks and said, "So did you get to talk to your Abba Ji after the surgery?"

"No, he was still sleeping when visiting hours ended, but the doctor said it went well. It will be good when the waiting is over. It seems I've been waiting for my husband for so long, for years, and now, more waiting."

"It's good for him to rest. I'm sure you'll get to talk to him tomorrow."

"Yes. I'm just glad he had the surgery. In the end, he'll be better off, Allah willing."

"I have the feeling that Allah will be willing. You and your family have been through enough."

They fell silent for a time, enjoying the soft relief of the evening breeze that caressed their exposed necks and stirred their loose hair.

A few days later, Abba came home, thin and pale but happy as a child to be surrounded by his family. We took pleasure in fussing over the father we had been deprived of for so long, while he amused himself by showing us the container that held the kidney stone that had almost killed him.

"If you threw it at someone, it would make quite a weapon, don't you think, Zahir?" he said. I laughed, but it seemed to me that it had been weapon enough without being thrown. It had shrunk my Abba to almost the size of a boy, and I wondered if he would ever return to his normal size again.

As Abba struggled to return to his feet physically, our family fought its way back financially. My parents had long ago abandoned any hope of salvaging much money from their dead business in Pur Qazi, so it was no surprise that Abba arrived in Sialkot with little but pocket change. Our neighbors had already begun helping us before Abba arrived, and that help had come in the form of information.

Shortly before Abba came home, our neighbor Mahmuda Ghani came to visit Amma. She told Amma that her husband, Abdul Ghani, had just found out that the person to whom Tayab had sold the shop under our house was now planning to move and sell the shop.

"We know your husband has been ill and that when he gets better he'll need a job that doesn't require hard labor," Mahmuda said. "My husband and I were talking about it, and we think it would be wonderful if you bought the shop."

"Yes, I always thought that would have been a good idea," Amma said. "I wish Tayab hadn't sold it in the first place. Because Abba doesn't have a college education, there are so few options to make money without hard physical work. I think this is our only chance. My husband isn't here yet; do you think your husband would negotiate a price on our behalf?"

"Yes, I was just going to offer. You leave it up to us. We'll bargain as if it were our own money we were spending. We'll get you a good price."

They agreed on a price of Rs.300, but Amma still had no way to pay for it. She did not say anything about this to her friend. It was her problem to solve.

Although Amma had no savings whatsoever, she had a few gold bangles that she had brought from India. The next day, she took the bangles and told me that we were going to see my Uncle Jamil. Once again, I put my hand in Amma's as we left the house on another mission to save our family.

After the partition of the country, Amma's brother, Jamil Usmani, knew that he would have trouble remaining successful as a Muslim businessman in the primarily Hindu city of Delhi. He had exchanged his furniture business in Delhi for a ginning factory in Sialkot, where the Hindu owner faced a similar problem. The ginning factory did well, and Jamil soon began buying a number of other businesses and became one of the wealthiest men in the city.

Uncle Jamil lived simply, so at first I had no idea how rich he was—perhaps Amma did not know either. Amma's cousin Usman Usmani visited us from Karachi and took me with him to visit Uncle Jamil's factory. Jamil gave us a tour, and at one point, he opened the door to a massive storage room full of empty jute bags.

"What are those bags for?" Uncle Usman asked.

"Rice, wheat, sugar, things like that."

I wondered why Uncle Usman's eyes were so wide, "Bahi sahib, how much do those bags hold?"

"Maybe 150 pounds each, something like that."

"How many bags are there?"

"I'm not sure exactly, but there must be at least one hundred thousand," Uncle Jamil said.

"And the value of each bag?"

"About half a rupee."

Uncle Usman let out a long, low whistle. The conversion rate of rupees to dollars was about one to one at the time. Uncle Jamil had about $50,000 worth of empty bags lying around, but from the offhand way he responded, it did not seem as if they were of much importance to him. It was only a fraction of all he owned.

As little as Uncle Jamil seemed to care about the details of his business, he was so busy that he rarely visited the sister who had raised him, even though I often saw him drive past our house on the way to his factory. On one of the rare occasions he stopped by to say *salam* to Amma, our neighbor Abdul, who was also a businessman, saw my uncle entering our house.

The next time Abdul's wife, Mahmuda, saw Amma on the rooftop after evening prayers, she asked, "How do you know Usmani?"

"He's my younger brother."

"No! Really?!"

The next evening, Mahmuda met Amma again, "My husband was wondering if maybe I misunderstood you. Maybe Mr. Usmani is not your brother but a cousin or some other relative?"

"No, he's my brother. Actually, in a way he's almost a son to me, because my husband and I raised him from when he was small."

"Then how come we never saw him visit you before?"

"Jamil is very busy."

"Too busy to visit his own sister, practically his mother?"

The next time she met Amma, she said, "My husband and I are very disappointed that your brother has so little respect for the big sister who took care of him. He will not help you at all. Here you are working yourself to death to keep all these children fed and housed, while he's sitting on a fortune. It's not right. My husband knows him, and I told him to give this man a good scolding the next time he sees him."

"No, no!" Amma said. "You must promise me you'll do no such thing. I know you mean well, but this is a family matter. My brother is a good man, he's just very busy, and we're not starving. I'm sure if we were desperate, he would help us. Until it comes to that, I will not push him."

"What, you must wait until you're starving to get a little compassion from your flesh and blood?"

"Please, promise me you'll ask your husband not to say anything to him."

"Of course Jamila, whatever you say, but I still think your brother's actions are very wrong."

This was the man we were about to turn to for help.

At Uncle Jamil's shop, Amma and I sat with him as Amma explained our situation and asked him to lend her Rs.300 to buy the shop. She pulled off her bangles and sat them on his desk. "I want you to keep my bangles as collateral. I promise to repay you from our sales every month, but if I don't pay off the loan within a year, you can sell the bangles."

Jamil shook his head and pushed the bangles back, "I can't take these from you, Appa (older sister)." It was odd to hear him call her "big sister." I couldn't think of her as anyone's sister or daughter—it seemed that she had been a mother forever. His next words lent truth to my thoughts. "You and Abba were like a mother and father to me. I'm lucky I can finally pay you back. I'd be honored to help you, and I don't need collateral."

"Your heart is in the right place, Jamil, and I appreciate that, but I've seen how issues of money can tear a family apart. I know you love our family, but this transaction must be treated like business. I won't take the money unless you take the bangles. They're little enough. Consider it an act of good faith."

"But what will people say?"

"What will people say if you force me to take these bangles and sell them to get the money? That's what I'll do if you don't take them. You're only holding them for me, little brother. Don't worry, we'll pay you back."

My uncle heaved a sigh. "Okay, but I won't sell them. I'll just keep them safe for you until you're ready to come back for them." He stood and turned to the safe behind him. I stared, fascinated with the secretive combination dial, which vibrated and clicked like the gears on a bicycle as he spun it back and forth. I peered around the corner of the desk and over his shoulder into the safe, where I caught a glimpse of multiple stacks of multicolored bills, more cash than I had ever seen at once. He peeled away what seemed like a very small stack, considering the weighty conversation that had produced it.

I wondered how it was that my uncle had so much money and we had so little. The answer came to me instantly. Hadn't Amma told me time and again? Education.

Once Abba began to feel better, he and Amma began to stock the shop with groceries. We bought the food partly with cash and partly on loan. Amma was well respected in town, and soon Abba was, too. All it took was a few friends and neighbors to vouch for Mohammad Hanif Kazmi and his wife, Jamila, and with that, several local suppliers were willing to give them the food products they needed and to wait for them to sell the inventory to pay the invoices.

Mutahir, Sajida, Salim, Kalim, and I helped open the boxes and stock the shelves. I loved looking at the little stacks of cans and the rows of cartons. As we loaded the shelves, Amma explained to us how our father was still not fully recovered and might remain weak for some time.

"Abba will need all of us to help him tend the shop, but what always comes first in this house?"

"School?" Sajida said.

"That's right. We're lucky that we have so many hands in this family. That means you'll all still have time to do your homework as well as help in the shop for a couple of hours each day. To do enough business, we must open the shop at least sixteen hours a day. We'll open at six o'clock in the morning and close at ten o'clock at night. Before school starts, from six to eight, one of you will watch the register. During the day, your father and I will share the duty—not that many people shop during the day anyway. When you get out of school, one of you will watch the store while the rest complete your homework, then someone else will watch the store, while the other one does homework. I don't want to hear any of you ever saying that you couldn't finish your homework or that your grades are falling because of this store. Do you understand?"

"Yes, Amma," we all said.

We were not just being obedient. We could see how sick Abba was. We had long seen how hard Amma worked day and night to keep the family going, and we wanted to help.

"And Amma," I said. "We'll get even more education from working at the cash registers, because we'll have to count money and make change." I thought about the stacks of money in my uncle's safe and wondered if our store would ever make as much.

I enjoyed selling groceries to our neighbors before and after school. I learned everybody's names, and they treated me as if I were a grownup as I put their items into bags, took their crumpled bills, and handed them change. We did have a safe, but I was not allowed to look inside, only to push small stacks of bills through the slot when the register got full. I was happy neatly pressing bills into the orderly little troughs in the register drawer. Each time a customer handed me money and I put it in the drawer, I felt as if I had a role in renewing our family fortunes, which surely must be on the increase.

The drawer always had the same amount of money in it every morning, but it seemed that our financial situation slowly improved.

My father got better and gained some weight, but he still seemed shrunken, delicate, and frail. Sometimes at night, he told us stories about life in Pur Qazi, which had taken on the feeling of a make-believe place for us younger children. He often grew tired and went to bed before the rest of us.

Amma continued to be the last to bed, sometimes sewing or practicing her reading late into the evening. Even Amma found time for homework. Education did not seem to be making our lives a whole lot easier, but I believed everything Amma told me. I stared at the little stacks of money in the register and waited.

A HOLY MAN

Abba in 1950

Our father's family name indicated that we were direct descendants of Imam Mussa Kazim, a revered saint, the seventh of the twelve imams, a spiritual successor to the prophet Muhammad, peace be upon him, and related to the Prophet by blood. Though we were one of the few Urdu-speaking families in a neighborhood of native Punjabis, our mother's perseverance, generosity, and pride brought her a reputation for respectability in the neighborhood. When my father arrived, the name Kazmi alone made him revered even before the neighbors discovered that he deserved it.

Abba maintained a strict prayer schedule, visited the mosque every day, and was otherwise a quiet and unassuming man. Like many men of few words, he created the impression of being exceptionally scholarly or holy, though he really was as simple and straightforward as he seemed. If he had wisdom, it was mostly the wisdom of keeping things simple and accepting things as they came. He took his time in making decisions, so much time that Amma continued to make most of the big family decisions without waiting for him. As she did so with Abba's support, he continued to maintain his position as head of the household.

Neighbors now came to both Amma and Abba for advice. During his long recovery from surgery, he was less active than Amma and more disposed to sit and listen, a favored trait in any wise counselor. People who came to him often went away to do exactly what they had intended to do in the first place, but his beatific smile made them feel that they had the blessing of a descendant of the seventh imam.

We lived in a middle-class neighborhood with a small minority of wealthy businesspeople and a larger minority of poor. Throughout Pakistan, some 80 percent of the population was illiterate to some extent. It was not only poor people who tended to be illiterate but also many of the working class and some of the middle class. Many of our neighbors held conservative, even fundamentalist, religious beliefs. The tendency of some to put faith in prayer as the sole solution to their problems seemed to increase in direct proportion to their level of illiteracy.

Uneducated believers with little to live on but hope were ripe for exploitation. Unable to read the teachings of the Quran for themselves or only able to read by rote without understanding, they looked to others to interpret the teachings of the Prophet. They respected the imams of the local mosques, religious scholars, and spiritual leaders. Sometimes they gave a charismatic religious leader the title of piir.

Some piirs were indeed knowledgeable, and they acted as honest spiritual guides to their followers. The followers of such piirs were often better-educated and not easy prey for false prophets. For them, a piir was someone to whom they looked for straightforward advice as they followed their own individual religious practices.

On the other hand, some power-hungry, greedy men bestowed the title of piir upon themselves. They were in the business of selling false hopes and dreams to followers in exchange for money. Such men convinced their followers that they had a special connection to God, and if they prayed on someone's behalf, God would be more likely to answer that person's prayers, solve problems, heal diseases, or grant dreams. They charged substantial fees, which they called donations, offerings, or reimbursement. Some of these men were as popular in their way as American televangelists.

Abba was not one of those who gave himself the title of piir, but thanks to his revered name and quiet wisdom, others began to treat him like a piir. Our educated and well-informed neighbors found his advice helpful and realistic, and if they asked him to pray for them, it was only in the way that friends and neighbors might ask any fellow Muslim to pray for them in an hour of need. However, our illiterate and blindly religious neighbors sometimes turned to him in ways that Abba did not encourage.

When someone in our community got sick, their family would often come to Abba and ask him to pray for them. Abba was embarrassed and even a little angered by these requests. Though not very educated himself, he knew how to read and write, he had been involved in politics, he knew people from many different walks of life, and he stay informed by reading the newspaper. He was irritated that some people were gullible enough to ascribe godlike power to fellow humans.

When people, mostly women asked him to pray on their behalf, Abba would say, "Ari Kum Bakhat Meera pass Quoon Ai Hi? Ja Allah say Mang." You ignorant fool, why have you come to me? Go make your request to God yourself. They would insist that, as a descendant of Imam Mussa Kazim, Allah had specially blessed him and would be more likely to listen to him. Abba explained that according to the Quran, all people are equal before God. "You have the same level of connection to God as I do. You're just as close to God as I am. If you talk to him, he'll listen to you just the same as he would to me. It makes more sense for it to come from you. Who knows what you need and want better than you do?"

Some thanked him for his wise words and left, but others insisted, *"Shah ji, Khuda De Watsa, Toosi saade wasta duwa kurdo." Shah Ji, please for Allah's sake, just pray for us.* They wouldn't leave unless Abba prayed for them.

I witnessed one such encounter on a day when I was working the register at our convenience store. Abba was sitting behind the counter when a woman rushed in, holding a crying girl in her arms. "Shah ji," she cried to my father, "a poisonous spider bit my daughter! Please pray for her."

"Why are you here?" Abba said, "you should hurry up and take her to a doctor."

"No, shah ji, I need you to pray for her. I know there's special power in your prayers."

"I have no such power. No one has such power. Don't waste your time. You're putting your daughter at risk. If you're concerned about her, you must take her to a doctor now."

"No, shah ji, I'm not leaving or taking her to the doctor. No doctor has the kind of power you have. You have to pray for her."

My father stood up, shook his head, strode to a drawer, and opened it. "I'm sure God would not approve of you putting your daughter at such risk," he said as he took out a knife and lit a match along its edge. I stared expectantly, thinking that the knife might glow, but it only turned sooty black. "Did it ever occur to you that maybe God gave us doctors?" He walked around to the front of the counter, held up the knife, and said, "Show me where the spider bit your daughter."

The woman lifted the girl onto the counter where she sat with her legs dangling. The girl screamed in great hiccupping sobs, her face red, her mouth wide. "Shhh, shhh, this man is going to make it better." The woman showed Abba a small red bump on the girl's arm.

He gently took hold of the girl's wrist and said, "This will hurt for a moment, but then it will help."

The girl stared at him and then the knife. Her sobs quieted, but her eyes were wide as she watched the knife close in on her flesh, shrinking from his grasp. I flinched, too, as I watched Abba cut open the spot where the spider had bitten her. He put the knife down and pressed his hands against the sides of the wound to force blood to ooze out. The girl silently stared at the blood. After that, Abba took her to a sink, washed off her arm, and put a small bandage on the wound.

"Thank you, shah ji," the mother said, "and will you pray, too, please?"

He nodded, his eyes neither scolding nor laughing. It could not hurt, and it was not that he did not believe in prayer, just that he did not believe it replaced medicine or common sense. He put a hand on the girl's head, closed his eyes, recited a couple of verses from the holy Quran, and then said, "Allah, please heal this girl if it is your will." He opened his eyes and gave the woman a stern look. "Now, you still must take the girl to the hospital. Prayer is only part of our duty to God. We must also look after those he has entrusted to our care, and that means taking your daughter to a doctor."

"Of course, shah ji. Thank you, shah ji. I know she'll be fine, now that you've prayed for her."

A few days later, the woman came back to the shop with her daughter. "Look, she's much better, and the bite is already healing. You see, shah ji, I know there is power in your prayer."

"I'm sure there's power in all our prayers, and taking her to the doctor probably helped."

"No, shah ji. My girl is okay, but I never took her to any doctor."

"She's lucky we removed enough of the poison, or maybe the spider wasn't poisonous to start with."

"Why won't you just accept that you have healing power in your prayer?"

"I hope you don't go spreading that around. It's not right. You'll give people the wrong idea."

"Anyway, thank you, shah ji."

I seem to recall that Amma teased Abba, saying something like, "If our store fails to make money, perhaps you can make your fortune as a piir."

"What utter nonsense," he said. "That girl could have died, and then what? That woman would have been as good as a murderer, but she probably would have blamed me."

He still prayed for others, at their insistence. Some tried to pay him, but he never charged a penny. We certainly could have used the money, but even I understood that it would have been wrong to pay someone for a prayer.

Like my father, my mother combined faith with practicality. They prayed for our family to thrive, but they also worked hard to make it so. Though our little store never made us rich, it made us enough money to put food on the table and to put all of us through school. We still had to be thrifty, and Amma was our resident expert.

Sometimes when Amma was busy, Abba offered to go to the market, but she said, "No, let Zahir do it." I knew why she didn't want Abba to go. He always bought meat with bones. Whenever Abba insisted on going, she admonished him. "Make sure you buy meat without any bones," she said. "If you buy meat with bones, I won't be able to divide it up to make sure everyone gets a *boti* (a piece)."

When Abba showed up with meat full of bones, Amma would throw up her hands in exasperation. "What am I supposed to do with this?"

"Why are you complaining?" Abba said. "Isn't it even more meat than you hoped for?"

"What does it matter, since half of it is bones?"

"But the marrow is good for the children, and it makes the food taste better."

"Hmmph." Amma pursed her lips and shook her head, as she accepted the package.

At dinnertime, we all sat around the table and unconsciously imitated our father, who, after finishing his meat, sat sucking loudly on each bone. He would crack them open to get his tongue at the marrow within, slurping, gnawing, and chewing some more. None of us would stop sucking on those bones until we had consumed every last bit of juice.

Amma leaned back in her chair, staring at us, and laughed. "You sound like a bunch of animals."

"Yes, we're carnivores, aren't we, kids?" my father said. He growled, first softly and then loudly, until he reached out, grabbed me, and pretended that he was going to take a bite out of me. "Look at the ribs on this one! I think we'll chew his bones next."

Chewing on those bones never made Abba any fatter. He still seemed all bones himself, as if someone had chewed off all his meat and sucked at his marrow. As I grew older, I began to understand that Abba's health problems had never gone away.

I knew that we were poor, but that did not mean we had to sit back like victims and accept the status quo. We could take action to change our lot. I learned this by watching my mother. I had helped Amma as she sewed clothes, and now I helped Abba sell canned foods and dry goods in the convenience store, and through all this I came to understand the idea of making and selling things to earn money. We all understood it, and we all chipped in to help.

We saw how hard our parents worked, so rather than ask them for money for school supplies, we decided to make the money ourselves. One summer, Kalim, Sajida, and I decided to make paper bags to sell to the shopkeepers in the nearby business district. We started buying old newspapers, folded them, and glued them to create stacks of simple shopping bags. Salim helped us at first, excited at the prospect of making money, but he quickly tired of the endeavor.

"Then you don't get any money for school supplies," Kalim said, as he bent over his stack on the path outside the house.

"You know that's not true," Salim said. "Amma won't let me go without."

"That's not fair," Sajida said, because she knew it was true. Amma would never let any of us go without, especially when it came to school.

It also wasn't fair that Sajida could not go to the market to sell her stack. She was going through puberty, and it was not proper for her to go into public unless it was necessary. Sajida waved goodbye to Kalim and me as we carried our stacks of shopping bags to the local shopkeepers. When we returned, she was always eager to see the coins we brought back.

"Here," I said. "You take the money to Amma Ji."

"Thank you, Zahir." Her eyes shone with pride, and she ran into the house. "Amma!"

At holidays like Eid and Ramadan, I made some extra money by going to the market to buy stacks of small toys at bargain rates, setting them up on a table outside our house, and selling them at a small markup. It was a good way to make money, because it was traditional for children from extended families to exchange presents on holidays. I was always very proud to hand my profits to Amma.

She put a hand under my chin. "Thank you, Zahir. You're a big help. I know I can always count on you. This will help pay for your education, and someday you will be a big businessman and make a lot of money, I know."

"Just like Uncle Jamil."

"Something like that."

"Only I'll share with you, Amma."

"I know you will, son."

I was eleven.

Uncle Jamil and his family never did warm up to us and vice versa—we rarely visited each other. Like my toy sales, our family visits happened only on special holidays when custom dictated that families visit each other. We traded off: they visited our house one year, and we visited theirs the next.

On Eid and Eid-ul-Adha, it is a tradition for adults to give *edi*, or small gifts of money to young children. Our family had five kids, and Uncle Jamil's family also had five. Amma always gave one rupee to each of her nieces and nephews, and in return our *mommani* (aunt), gave one rupee plus ten pennies to each of us. If our *mommani* gave first, Amma would add a few extra pennies to the rupee she portioned out for each of their kids. I don't know what their kids did with their *edi*, but if we got ours first, we always immediately ran to give it to Amma. We knew Amma would use the money they had just given to us as *edi* for their kids, and it would make it easier for her to afford the few extra pennies. Even if we received our gifts second, we still gave Amma the money. We knew that she needed every penny she could get to keep our family going.

I did not care much for Uncle Jamil, but because I had to pass his factory whenever I walked to the home of a nearby friend, sometimes I could not avoid saying hello. He was not normally very friendly, but I remember that one day he seemed to be in a good mood.

"Salam, Zahir!"

"As-Salamu Alaykum, Uncle," I said.

"Where are you off to?"

"I'm visiting a friend."

"If you're visiting a friend, you should be embarrassed to have his parents see you looking like that!"

I looked at my clothes. "What's wrong with how I look?"

"It's not your clothes, young man. It's your hair. Why don't you get it cut?"

All the boys were letting their hair grow longer in those days, nothing like the later Beatles craze but still longer than people of my uncle's generation were accustomed to. I knew that many elders did not like it, but my mother didn't seem to mind.

I tried to sidestep the issue. "When I go home, I'm getting a haircut."

"Why wait until then? I'm on my way to the barber. If you come with me, I'll treat you to a proper haircut."

At first, I thought that it was a nice change to see Uncle Jamil in a friendly mood, but then I was not so sure. "That's very kind of you, Uncle, but it's really not necessary, and I don't want to be late to my friend's house. He's expecting me."

"Nonsense. It will only take a few minutes, and it will give us a chance to talk."

Which *he* did—I did not. I was too worried about him telling the barber to cut my hair short. At the barbershop, my uncle invited me to go first. I sat uneasily in the chair. "Uncle, please don't tell him to shave all my hair off. I just want him to trim a little bit off the sides, just a very little bit."

"Don't worry, Zahir. He'll only cut your hair to your specifications."

I do not know what passed between them—a wink, or a whisper, or a signal he had used with his own sons—but to my astonishment, the barber took out his hair trimmer and, before I could speak, sheered my head from one side to the other without stopping, leaving a thin, almost bald strip down the middle.

I pushed the barber's arm away, jumped out of the chair, and shouted, "I told you not to do that!" I turned to my uncle, breathing hard, arms rigid at my sides. "Uncle, you promised he would do what I asked."

My uncle chuckled. "Zahir, it's not the end of the world. It'll grow back. Trust me, you will look better this way, and you'll feel much cooler in the summertime."

I held back tears of frustration. How dare this guy, who had never before taken much interest in my family, suddenly decide that he could take control over anything about me? I wanted to leave, but I realized I'd look ridiculous walking out with that bald strip across my head. Instead, I flung myself back into the chair, crossed my arms, and said, "I guess you better finish."

I sat, quietly seething, staring into the mirror at my bald head, thinking how ridiculous I looked, thinking that I would never speak to my uncle again, wondering how I would pay him back for this betrayal. The moment that the barber finished, brushing the hairs off my neck with a towel and saying, "There, that's much better," I stood up, picked up the stool next to me, and before anyone realized what I was doing, least of all me, I swung the stool against the mirror on the wall in front of me. My shaved reflection exploded into shards of glass.

The chiming, shattering sound was still ringing in my ears as I ran out of the store and straight home. "Amma!" I shouted as I ran upstairs. "Amma!"

"What is it, Zahir?" she said. Then I was standing before her, staring at her open mouth. "What happened to your hair?"

I told her what Uncle Jamil had done.

"He had no right to do that, no right at all," she said. "I'm so sorry, Zahir. If that ever happens again, you tell him that your mother told you that you're not allowed to get a haircut, you understand?"

"Yes, Amma. Thank you." I looked down, self-conscious of my appearance.

She smiled. "Don't worry. It'll grow back before you know it, and you still look as handsome as ever."

I couldn't help but grin back.

I never told Amma about the broken mirror. I suppose my uncle paid to repair it, but I never asked, and I never had problems with him after that. My hair grew long again, and he never said a word about the incident. I wonder if Amma said something to him. Probably not.

Amma stood up for herself and her children, but she had sacrificed a lot to keep her family together. She was unlikely to allow a simple haircut to start a crack running through her family, dividing her from those she loved. Not if she could help it.

-20-

EMPTY NEST

Ather and my sister Sajida at their wedding

One by one, Amma and Abba's children grew up, finished school, and moved on. Little by little, running our family store was left to Abba and me, and business was not good. Abba was often unwell. He suffered from a constant sore throat, and stocking, maintaining, and updating the store and its goods was difficult for a man with an ailing body. Amma still insisted that school came first, so I could only help part-time. Business had never been brisk, and as new stores opened all around us, our clientele slowed to a trickle. The once soldierly lineup of colorful packages on our shelves dwindled in dusty disarray.

At a first glance, our family finances were waning, but when Amma looked at her children, she continued to see the success story she had dreamed about. My second-oldest brother, Mutahir, earned an associate's degree and moved to Lahore in the mid-1950s to work as a claims settlement officer. India and Pakistan were still buried in property claims from people who had to leave their homes and businesses behind when they moved across the new border, and that meant plenty of jobs for those interested in sorting out the mess.

Sajida, Salim, and Kalim were all in the same grade in school. After graduation in 1957, Kalim moved to Dadu to live with his mother, my sister Bilqees, and found a job in the settlement commissioner's office.

Sajida and Salim lived at home while attending college and earned their associate's degrees in 1959. Salim wanted a four-year degree, but Amma and Abba couldn't afford to pay for him to finish. Together, they and Salim decided he should move to Lahore and live with Mutahir, find a day job, and attend school in the evenings. Salim was excited to live the young bachelor life with his older brother. The two of them got along well, and Mutahir helped Salim find a job at the settlement commissioner's office.

Although the family sometimes hit financial obstacles, all of the children had already received education well beyond that of their parents. Mutahir finished his bachelor's degree and, later, earned a master's degree. Saleem finished his bachelor's degree, and Kalim completed a law degree.

One evening after I closed the shop, I walked into the kitchen to find my mother and father sitting and talking while Sajida prepared dinner.

"What are you smiling about, Abba?" Amma said.

"I was just looking at Zahir and Sajida. I was thinking that as soon as Sajida gets married, Zahir will be the last child at home. All the work you did planning for our children's future, the money we saved, the businesses we started, the struggles we've had, and how you were right—it all paid off. Our children will have a better life."

"Oh, is that all?" Amma said. "Sajida isn't married yet, so let's not be in too much of a hurry to congratulate ourselves."

I was fourteen years old, too young to understand why Amma still worried even though we now had fewer mouths to feed and most of her children were off to a good start on their own. If her sons continued with their education, their futures would be as close to secure as she could hope. Education was not enough to assure the future of her youngest daughter. Among Muslim families in the 1950s, marriage was still the best path to security for daughters, but it would not be easy to find Sajida an appropriate partner in Sialkot.

Even though Pakistan had been created in an effort to unify Muslims of India based on their religious beliefs, Muslims do not have one monolithic culture. Our family still belonged to an ethnic minority in our new land. We were Muhajir, which was the name given to Urdu-speaking migrants from India. Five other ethnic groups were spread throughout Pakistan: Punjabi, Pathan, Ballochi, Sindhi, and Bengalis (from the province of Bengal, which later broke off to become the country of Bangladesh). These six groups shared one country but lived as if they were six separate nations.

Sialkot was mostly made up of Punjabi people. Most of the Muhajirs, who spoke Urdu and shared our traditions, had settled in Karachi. After years of living among Punjabis, we had developed a Punjabi accent, but we were still considered different. Although many different Muslim people had left behind homes, families, businesses, and properties on the basis of religious unity, living side by side for years had led these different groups to focus not on what united them but on what divided them.

Though Sajida had spent most of her life among Punjabis, marrying a Punjabi was almost unthinkable. This was not because our family did not like our Punjabi neighbors or because they did not like us. It was because our lives were too different. Punjabis and Muhajirs just did not spring from the same cultural mold, and we did not fit into our shared world in the same way.

Finding a husband for Sajida could not be left to chance. Dating was out of the question—not just dating Punjabis but dating anyone. Sajida was a good Muslim girl. As such, she was expected to not seek the company of any man outside the family until the day she married, and that day would not come until her parents arranged it. Although my parents loved each other, this was a product of having never known any lovers but each other and a result of proximity, respect, and time. Falling in love was something that happened in books. Finding a mate was not up to Sajida; it was the responsibility of her parents.

This worry had been eating at my mother for some time. There were two problems. First, if Amma and Abba wanted to find Sajida a husband who could offer her a secure economic future, their best chance was marrying her to the son of a family of high economic and social standing. To attract such a mate, they had to provide a sizeable dowry. How would they do this when they had almost no money? Second, if they wanted to find someone with whom she would find a joyful and peaceful partnership, their best chance was marrying her to someone who shared her culture, education, and personal values. How would they do this when we were Muhajirs living in a city surrounded by Punjabis?

My sister was one of the prettiest girls in our community, and one of maybe a handful who had any college education. In spite of this, Amma knew from the moment we arrived that unless she planned ahead, her daughter might not get married. Amma had no intentions of letting her little girl grow up to become the town's prettiest, most educated "old maid." As usual, Amma had a plan and had thought and saved money for this plan for a long time.

Amma's own mother, Aisha (my *Nani*), had disappointed her by taking so little care in the choice of Amma's husband. Perhaps *Nani* (maternal grandmother) waited through the intervening years for the earth to turn on its axis enough times to return her and her daughter to a place where she could prove she was a much better matchmaker than Amma, her daughter, had given her credit for.

My *nani* Aisha lived in Karachi with her younger son, Zaheer, but she often came to Sialkot to visit her older son, Jamil Usmani, and her daughter Jamila—my Amma Ji. In her old age, *Nani* had made matchmaking her hobby. It was more or less a secret hobby that she pursued without anyone's knowledge or permission.

Nani (my maternal grandmother)

Nani now considered it her responsibility to find a suitable match for Sajida, but my amma did not. In fact, she still did not trust her mother's judgment at all.

Nani had spent the past few years prodding Amma, mentioning boys who she thought might be a good prospect for Sajida. She sipped her chai and talked about the weather, about family, about the aches of arthritis, and then casually mentioned a boy she had in mind.

"I met a cousin at that wedding who has a friend whose son would be perfect for Sajida. He's handsome, very polite and helpful, and he has a good job with the government," *Nani* said.

"You've met him?" Amma asked.

"No, but our cousin told me all about him," *Nani* said.

"Amma, please don't worry about it. When I'm ready for your help, I'll ask for it. Sajida is still too young to marry," my amma said.

"I'm only trying to help. Time will pass faster than you know. Just a few minutes ago, you were a little girl."

"Yes, and I was still that little girl when you married me off."

"Times were different. I understand that things have changed. You can trust me."

"No one said I didn't trust you, Amma."

"Hmph," Nani said. When I happened to catch Nani at such moments, I had to hide a smile. She looked so much like Amma Ji.

Nani didn't argue but did not take no for an answer either. She started approaching families on Amma's behalf without her knowledge or blessing. On Nani's encouragement, a few families approached Amma, proposing marriage of their son and Sajida.

In each case, Amma did not consider the son a suitable match and graciously declined.

She talked to one eager couple, saying, "I'm sorry. I know you've gone to a lot of trouble coming here, but my mother talked to you sooner than she should have. Sajida is not old enough to marry. When she is, we will be happy to talk to you again, although I am sure that by then such a fine young man will have already snatched up a perfect wife."

The couple looked surprised. "Your mother was very clear. We didn't go to her, she came to us, and she said that you had asked her to speak on your behalf."

"I'm sorry. My mother is getting on in years, and sometimes she's a little confused. Perhaps she misunderstood me."

The visitors seemed confused but politely took their leave. "Your daughter is a lovely girl. Perhaps you'd like to think about it."

"Perhaps," Amma said, bobbing her head from side to side in a way that indicated she would say neither yes nor no. When the door shut, she turned around and went back to sewing. The blank look on her face suggested that she had already put the couple out of her mind, although a small hook seemed to tug at the corner of her mouth, and I suspected that it was being pulled by thoughts of her meddling mother.

The next time she saw Nani, Amma likely said, "You have to stop this matchmaking. We're Sajida's parents. It's not up to you, it's up to us, and you're embarrassing the family."

Nani probably replied, "Far be it for me to embarrass you. I should think you'd be more embarrassed by your own behavior. I heard that you practically shoved those poor people out the door. Sajida is not getting younger. You should think about it."

Amma refused to rush this decision. Once Sajida graduated from high school and started college, Amma spent the next two years carefully looking around for a groom. She knew that there was little chance of finding a suitable match in Sialkot. There were a few marriages between Punjabis and Muhajir families, but she heard through the after-dark, rooftop grapevine that those marriages were filled with conflict that sent shock waves through both families. Not only did the couples have to overcome their cultural differences, so did the in-laws who perhaps shared the households or who lived with the complaints and the knowledge of their children's failure.

Amma was not about to let herself or her daughter fall victim to such prejudice or let herself become the butt of criticism. A year after my sister graduated from high school in 1958, Amma, Sajida, and I took a train to Karachi, where a majority of Urdu-speaking people lived. Education still came first in our family, so we went in the summer to ensure that we did not miss a single day of school. Abba stayed home to manage the store. Though we had many relatives in Karachi, including Amma's younger brother and several cousins, after nearly a decade in Pakistan, we had never visited Karachi.

The expense of buying tickets for the nine-hundred-mile train journey was one small reason for avoiding such a trip until necessary. The real expenses were the family obligations such a visit thrust upon us. We would need new clothes, and we would be expected to bring gifts for everyone, and our extended family was not small. I realized later that Amma must have saved for this matchmaking trip for some time.

I was stunned to discover how many relatives we had, and I was delighted to have another chance to see my older sister, Bilqees, who had moved to Karachi with her husband. I had a good time but once again found myself the butt of jokes over my accent. This time, it was my Urdu-speaking relatives who made fun of my Urdu accent. No one could tell that I came from an Urdu-speaking family. Anyone who didn't know our background would think we were Punjabis.

One day, I was arguing with my sister's kids, who were older than me. During the argument, I told them in Urdu that they were wrong, using the word *ghult*. My brother-in-law interjected, "Your ghult is ghlut." I turned to him with a puzzled frown. That night, lying in bed, I realized what he was saying: "You're pronouncing *wrong* wrong." It was a minor irritation in an otherwise enjoyable visit.

For the first time, I began to understand why extended family was so important to Amma. It gave me a sense of inclusion that I had never known. As for the accent, I began to realize that everywhere I went, I would always be different from somebody. I would always be an immigrant, because I had been born in a land to which I felt no connection and of which I had no memory.

For me, a teenage boy spending a hot summer among the combined familiarity and strangeness of cousins I barely knew, this was a vacation. For Amma, it was a mission. During our stay there, she took Sajida everywhere, giving all our relatives and their friends a chance to discover that the little girl they last saw when she was ten was now a beautiful, charming, smart young woman. It was not long before families began dropping hints.

Before we left Karachi, a family whose members happened to be distant relatives showed up at our doorstep. They stayed after dinner, laughing and talking far into the night. Afterward, Amma took Sajida into her room for a private talk. The marriage decision had been made.

Nani took the news gracefully. If she was offended that none of her choices had been considered, she never said so. Perhaps she was simply relieved, as Amma was, that the future for a daughter of our family was secure. She and Amma understood, as most men could not, that a woman without a husband was at risk of being tossed from household to household, with no assurance she would receive the same adoration that her parents had given her once they were gone. If Sajida never married, it was unlikely that she would end up on the streets, so long as she had brothers to care for her. Her education could help her find at least an office job, but marriage remained her safest path and her best hope of a life to call her own. Amma had given her daughter the most important thing a mother could give: a future.

Customarily, if the young people lived far apart, the groom's family went to the bride's hometown for the wedding. Amma offered to go to Karachi instead, which was a smart move on her part. The tickets to Karachi might be expensive, but if she and Abba held the wedding in Sialkot, they would be responsible for paying for the food and boarding all the guests from both families. It would be easier for most of the relatives from both families to attend a wedding in Karachi, and it would prevent Amma and Abba from spending every last penny they had.

In the summer of 1959, we went to Uncle Zaheer's house, where Amma took over the kitchen as well as all the expenses for the wedding. Amma was too proud to allow our family to become a burden on Uncle Zaheer or any of our relatives. I ran plenty of errands for the wedding, but I never considered it a burden. I was always aware of how much Amma sacrificed for all of us, and I adored my sister. I was happy and proud to do my part to add to the happy occasion.

Amma and Abba sent their daughter off to her future in a flurry of jewels and bangles, flowers and silk, music and laughter. I was not born when Bilqees was married, so, having nothing to compare Sajida's wedding to, I thought it was the most spectacular occasion my family had ever taken part in.

Though the wedding lasted just a few days, for Amma the aftermath went on for months. She funded much of her daughter's dowry and wedding expenses with years of savings, but it was not enough. She was forced to borrow, and in the coming months, she worked very hard to pay back the loans. One of the lenders was my brother, Mutahir.

Mutahir was still working for the settlement commissioner's office. As a settlement claims officer, his job was to determine the difference in value between the properties Muslim families left behind in India and the properties they took over in Pakistan. He lived comfortably, but he never offered any financial assistance to Amma and Abba. They never asked him to help until it came time for Sajida's wedding.

"I'm sorry, Amma, I'd love to help with my sister's wedding, but I can't spare anything right now."

"No, no, Mutahir, I don't expect you to give it to me. It would be a loan. Remember, we still have a land claim pending with the settlement claims department. You know that it is a legitimate claim, and it's only a matter of time before it's approved. Once it's approved, we can pay you back."

Mutahir agreed. A few months after the wedding, the claim was approved, and Amma signed the claim over to him.

With that, Sajida's wedding was over, and Amma's obligations to her children were at an end—except for me. I was the last child at home. Amma and Abba had done their best to care for eight children over four decades, losing two along the way. They had just sent a daughter off to her new life as a married woman. With that, a veil dropped on my family's collective past while a new one opened on my uncertain future.

My parents were entering their twilight years, and I knew that they had little energy or money left for our dwindling family circle. All my life, they had taken care of me. I now thought that it was my turn to take care of them, but Amma was a mother, and I did not understand that the vocation has no end.

-21-

ON MY OWN

I knew that Amma was proud that Mutahir was an excellent student, always among the top in his class. He never needed coaxing to study. When he moved to Pakistan with my oldest brother, Mutahir used to study late into the night by the light of an oil lamp. When Amma arrived in Sialkot, she saw him squinting and rubbing his eyes as he stared at his homework. She took him to an optometrist for an eye exam, and she bought him glasses and a better quality lamp.

Perhaps because Mutahir was ten years older, I rarely crossed paths with him in any way: physically, mentally, or emotionally. When he moved to Lahore to find a job and finish his degree, his absence did not affect me much.

During his early days in Lahore, Amma and Abba supported him financially, but when he went to work for the settlement commissioner's office, he stopped asking Amma and Abba for money. They were proud when he earned a four-year undergraduate degree and later a graduate degree from the University of Lahore. Looking back, I suppose it could not have been all that easy, but by the time I caught up with him, the hardest part was mostly behind him, and his life seemed like a lavish party.

I was in ninth grade when Amma, Abba, and I returned home from Sajida's wedding, the last remnant of our family life in Sialkot. Abba had seemed better at Sajida's wedding: happy, well, and younger. He had received treatment for his throat problem, and it had gone away, but it soon returned and worsened. He had trouble swallowing, his voice grew raspy, and he developed a persistent cough. He returned to the doctor for treatment a few more times. Each time, he felt better afterward, but each time, the problem returned. The times in between illnesses grew shorter, and my hours behind the store counter increased until I was almost running the place on my own.

The work grew easier, but that was not good news. We had fewer customers. The store was sliding down a steep, slick slope.

By 1960, my last semester of high school, I found myself trying to decide on my next move. I began to see that the town where I'd grown up—the city that had become my whole world—was actually a small, provincial place with limited opportunities. Mutahir's and Salim's experiences became my window to a different world.

Most of the people we knew in Sialkot owned their own small businesses, something I was not financially prepared to do. In those days, finding a job in the public sector was nearly impossible unless you knew someone with connections. It was not what you knew but who you knew.

My parents spent every last dime on their children's education, and still most of the children had to pay to finish their degrees. By the time it came down to me, our family fortune had dwindled to a few dusty cans on a shelf. There was no money left. Even though I had never been as good a student as Mutahir, I wanted nothing more than to continue my education. I tried to find a job to pay my expenses while I continued my studies, but there was nothing available except clerical work. The pay prospects were dismal, and it looked as if I would have to quit my studies so that I could work full time.

"No," Amma said, holding up a letter. "Mutahir has invited you to stay with him."

"You mean you've told Mutahir to take me in. Amma, no. I'm sure he has all he can handle with Salim, his own job, and school."

"Read it for yourself," Amma said. "It was his suggestion, not mine."

I suspected that Amma might have dropped a hint or two, but Mutahir's letter did contain a clear, direct invitation for me to live with him. I don't know the exact wording, but the letter was clear: It has been a pleasure having Salim here, and I'd be happy to help out my youngest brother, too, in any way I can. It will be much easier for him to find a job here, the schools are good, and he won't have to pay for housing. Tell him he is welcome to join us as soon as he graduates.

"Mutahir is a good student. Maybe he can help you with your studies," Amma said.

"And he got Salim a job. Maybe he could get you one, too," Abba said.

"That's a good point, Abba," I said.

"Of course it is," Amma said. "Your father and I have discussed this, and we agree that it would be best for you to live with Mutahir."

I laughed. "Well, I guess I'll go live with Mutahir."

Lahore is the second-largest city in Pakistan after Karachi. In the late 1950s, the city was a clash of old and new. The roaring engines of modern life cast a smoky veil over the ancient walls erected by centuries of foreign invaders: Persians, Mongols, Afghans, and more. According to legend, the son of the Hindu god Rama founded Lahore some four thousand years ago. Lahore once served as the capital of the Mongolian Empire, and, more recently, it played a key role in the Indian Independence Movement. The Pakistan Resolution, in which the Muslim League demanded a separate country based on the Two-Nation Theory, was passed in Lahore.

In such an atmosphere, I should have expected conflict.

Mutahir and Salim shared part of a house in a pleasant residential area close to the old Anarkali District. For hundreds of years, the Anarkali Bazaar has been a narrow, winding street where anything and everything is sold. This ancient marketplace is named after a famous dancer of the Emperor Akbar's court. Her enchanting beauty captivated the emperor's son, Salim. Emperor Akbar disapproved of their relationship, but Prince Salim and Anarkali rebelled against the emperor and pursued their love affair. As punishment, the emperor had Anarkali buried alive in a wall in the bazaar. When Prince Salim became Emperor Jahangir, he had this couplet engraved on Anarkali's wall:

Ah! Could I behold the face of my beloved once more, I would give thanks to my God until the day of resurrection.

Tomb of Anarkali

When I arrived in Lahore, my hopes were high. Both the modern bustle and the ancient history of this place grabbed hold of my senses and energized my dreams of a bright future. Meanwhile, Mutahir's home seemed like the right place to live while I pursued my goals of finding a good job and working my way through college. Though our shop back home was on the decline, Mutahir's and Salim's careers seemed to be off to a good start. They had an attractive house, a good standard of living, and they often went out on the town. I was glad to see Mutahir doing so well. Perhaps he really could help me find a good job.

I soon realized that I was living in an overpopulated bachelor's pad, or what today might be called an off-campus fraternity. Mutahir was the sheik of a 24/7 open house where friends, friends of friends, and hangers-on came and went at all hours. A never-ending card game was interrupted by trips to the movies and fine restaurants. It was such a popular hangout because Mutahir was the only one of his friends with an independent place—no parents, wives, or children attached.

I didn't enjoy the party atmosphere, because my brothers and their friends often kept me busy running back and forth to the store to buy food, beverages, cigarettes, and other supplies to keep their party going. They also had me take over more than my fair share of cooking and household chores.

Lahore was not for me. After a few months of waiting for the party to come to an end, I gave up. I was too independent to live like that, and though I was only sixteen, I had already learned how to survive in almost any circumstances. I had been earning my own money since I was ten, though I'd always given my profits to Amma. Growing up, I had watched Amma struggle to overcome one hurdle after another. I knew from her example that once I set a goal and applied myself to the steps required to attain it, I could achieve anything I chose. I returned home to explain to my parents why Lahore was not for me. We did not have much of an argument, they seem to understand..

I knew most of the storeowners in Sialkot's wholesale market. I had been buying from them to supply our store for quite some time, and I trusted my skills as an entrepreneur. I was prepared to become the man of our house and still make time for school. Unfortunately, even though I had been away from Sialkot for less than three months, when I returned, the family store was in considerably worse shape than when I left. I did not let this discourage me. In order to improve financial condition the first thing I did was to re-stock the store. To buy fresh inventory was not a problem since local vendors trusted us and extended credit without any hesitation. Though I was good at managing the store and dealing with the customers this was not something I wanted to do for the rest of my life. Besides, my parents made it clear that I was expected to continue my education.

The next thing I did was to enroll at Murray College, a junior college, which was established in 1889 by the Church of Scotland Mission in Sialkot.

The college was at least four to five miles from our house, and at the very least I needed a bike to get there and back each day, but I had no money to buy one, as I spent the last of my cash on the train ticket home. If my parents had the money for such things, they would not have sent me to Lahore in the first place. The store was bringing the family only enough money to survive. I wandered around the house, looking at our meager belongings, wondering what I could sell to make some extra cash. I spotted several household gadgets with bits of shiny, copper wiring peeking out from the mechanisms. Plenty of local factories had a use for copper.

I scavenged throughout the house, from top to bottom, pawing through every shelf and drawer for anything made of copper that we did not need. After selling the copper, I brought the money home and piled it on the table before Amma, just as Amma used to do with Abba a lifetime ago.

"I hope this is enough to buy a bike," I said.

"Of course it will be," she said. "Haven't I taught you how to bargain?"

I had just enough money to cajole the man at the bicycle shop out of a rusty bike with a slightly bent frame and a chain that occasionally slipped. That squealing, clattering junk pile on wheels worked well enough to solve my transportation needs for the next two years. Like Amma, the bike was aging and overworked with tired and aching joints, but it made sure that I got to school.

-22-

A NEW START

I believed what Amma always told me: education was the key to changing my life for the better. After two years in college, I realized that there was another key: location. In 1963, I finished the intermediate program at Murray College, but I knew that staying in Sialkot was not an option for any of us.

For me, the chances of educational growth or career opportunities were very limited in Sialkot. For Abba and Amma, the chances of making enough money to live on were decreasing. The family store was sinking fast, Abba's health on the decline, and the numbers of new neighborhood stores were on the rise. We had no reason to expect sales to improve. To meet living expenses for my parents and me, I needed to find a full-time job. This was not a problem in and of itself, but it meant I would have to discontinue my studies.

Most of our local acquaintances operated small businesses, and I could have gone to work for one of them, but it would have meant working long hours for low pay. Jobs in the public sector or at larger companies were few and hard to come by in Sialkot. I was young and unsure of how to go about looking for such a job. I only knew that without a four-year degree, I would likely be stuck with low-paying work for the rest of my life. It would defeat Amma's dream and mine, as I would spend my life struggling to pay bills, just as Amma and Abba had struggled for as long as I could remember. How would I be able to help them in their old age if I could not help myself?

My sister, Sajida, and her husband lived in Karachi, and she suggested that I live with them until I could find a job and a place of my own. Kalim had also moved to Karachi, and he was doing well, working by day and going to school by night. Karachi was Pakistan's largest city, main seaport, and financial center. At that time, it was still the nation's capital (the capital was later moved to Islamabad, a new city built outside Rawalpindi). Karachi had a sizable industrial base that included textiles, shipping, and automotive companies. Because Karachi was Pakistan's economic center, it would be much easier to find a job and colleges that offered evening programs there.

Amma and Abba liked the idea. There was not much left to attach them to Sialkot. Most of their relatives lived in Karachi, including both their daughters. Once I was fully settled in Karachi, they would be able to join me.

In the summer of 1963, I made the second migration of my life.

I was not sure what life with my sister and her husband, Ather, would be like, as I never got the chance to know her husband after their marriage. I was relieved to find Ather Bahi an easy-going guy and a gracious host. In fact, if I had taken him up on every offer to "Have some more, Zahir! Eat! Eat!" or "Sit! Sit! I was about to have a cup of chai, join me," I might have risked becoming fat and waterlogged. He was not a lazy sort, by any means. He worked in the training department of the United States Agency for International Development Aid, known as USAID.

Foreign assistance is a significant part of U.S. Foreign Policy and a significant component of the U.S. international affairs budget. USAID manages most of the United States' economic assistance programs. From my early discussions with Ather to my later observations over the years, I have long questioned the value of bilateral aid to underdeveloped countries like Pakistan. It seems likely that, under the disguise of aid, the United States sends CIA operatives to meddle in the internal affairs of those countries. Even if the CIA is not involved, there is still plenty of meddling. Though the touted purpose of foreign aid is humanitarian, but I am certain even the U.S. government would admit that offering such gifts to a country in need is one way to help the United States further its goals for foreign and national security.

As part of its aid package to Pakistan, the United States offered a training program for Pakistani government officials. Under the program, the United States invited senior government officials to America to attend educational courses and seminars in their areas of expertise. These all-expenses-paid trips included travel, lodging, and a generous food allowance. The program was popular among Pakistani officials who were eager to take what resembled a paid vacation to the exciting United States. My brother-in-law was in charge of coordinating the selection process and the placement of selected candidates in U.S. educational institutions.

It was not a bad thing as far as Ather was concerned. He was able to make friends with mid- to senior-level government officials, which made it a great networking opportunity. I suppose that I considered the possibility that I might meet some powerful people through my brother-in-law exciting, but it didn't happen often.

My destiny, it seemed, was still in my own hands. For the time being, networking would have to take a backseat to hard work.

My sister's firstborn child, a son, died as an infant, and Sajida and Ather treasured their daughter, Ghazala, all the more. When I met my niece, who was just eighteen months old, she instantly charmed me. She was the friendliest baby I had ever seen and was quite the attention-grabber. Sajida auditioned her for a baby formula advertisement, which she landed with ease. I had little experience around small children, and Ghazala was the first baby I ever befriended. Either I was a natural with young kids, or she was just that agreeable, and my sister found a willing babysitter in me. Whenever I was not busy, I loved to dandle Ghazala on my knees and sing songs or play hand games with her. When I think of my sister's house, the memory is suffused with the smell of baby powder and the sound of irrepressible giggles.

Though we all enjoyed each other's company, I had no intention of overstaying my welcome with Sajida's family. I wanted to become independent, so from the moment I arrived, seeking a job was my top priority. Even in Karachi, this was not easy.

At the age of nineteen, in the absence of any professional background, the only kind of office jobs I qualified for were clerical. The problem was that I did not know how to type, so before I applied for a job or enrolled myself in college, I took a typing class. Luckily, my brother-in-law owned a typewriter. I spent many hours practicing, much to the disappointment of little Ghazala, who wanted to sit on my lap and punch the funny little keys with me. A few times I gave in to her insistent charm until Sajida rescued me. "Okay, Ghazala, that's enough. Uncle Zahir needs to practice," she said as she picked her daughter up and carried her to the kitchen to play with something less interesting, such as a can and spoon.

I found my first job with Kalim's help. He worked at a company that was affiliated with a paint manufacturer. He recommended me, and I quickly landed a job as a clerk typist at United Paints. With that, I had my own income, and Kalim invited me to move in with him. He lived alone in a small portion of a single-family home. Kalim and I agreed to share expenses equally.

Kalim and I had no real problems at home, but I did have a problem at work. After six weeks of practicing on my brother-in-law's typewriter, I was still easily the slowest, most error-prone typist in Karachi. I wondered when I would be fired. One day the human resources manager called me in to talk. Here it comes, I thought.

"So how are you getting on?"

"Fine, fine."

"Are you feeling at home?"

"Oh yes. Everyone is very helpful, but I'm afraid, well, my typing isn't what it should be."

He smiled. "Don't worry, Zahir. There's no need to be nervous. I didn't call you in here to criticize, just to let you know that I'm here to help you. It takes a while to get used to a new job. You're doing better than you think you are."

I am certain I was almost visibly shaking with fear and nervousness, and there was a good reason for that. As nice as the human resources manager was, the opposite was true of the man I worked for. I was assigned as an assistant to one of the senior managers. Allow me to first say in his defense that he was right about one thing: I was the wrong person for this job. I was fresh out of a two-year college, with no experience, minimal typing skills, and little knowledge of English, the universal second-language of commerce in Karachi. He had almost bitten my head off the first time I typed a letter for him, shouting something like, "When I give you something to type, I expect you to do it yourself, not to hand it over to a monkey to type for you! Type it over!" From the comments that my neighbors in the office whispered, he seemed to be holding back because I was new. "Oh, he's in a good mood today. See that dent in the desk? He threw a stapler at the last guy."

Standing in the office of the human resources manager, I looked at the floor for a moment and then up again. His eyes were kind and patient. Was that a knowing look? I took a chance, "I'm a bit nervous, because I think my manager, well, I've heard that . . ."

"Yes, he does have a reputation for being somewhat unpleasant. Don't worry. You might have to answer to him on a daily basis, but remember one thing. I run this place. He can't fire you without my say-so. Don't let him frighten you."

"Yes, sir. Thank you, sir."

A few days later, my boss dictated another letter, and when I typed it, he once again caught a few errors. This time, he balled up the letter and threw it at me, shouting a long string of profanities.

I was nineteen years old. I had heard all those words before, but no one had ever talked to me like that. Without thinking, I reached for the first large object I could find, a small metal file organizer on his desk, picked it up, and threw it at him. It hit him in the shoulder with a light clang. Papers flew everywhere and floated down while I screamed, "You S.O.B.! Don't you ever call me that name again!"

"You insubordinate little prick! Who do you think you are?" He grabbed me by the collar.

I pushed him away. "Get your hands off me!"

"You're out of control!"

"You started it. You're an ass. You treat me like dirt. I won't tolerate it!"

"You pick up all these papers, right now!"

"You pick them up!"

"That's it! I'm having you fired."

He stalked past me, straight to the office of the kind HR manager, and demanded that he fire me immediately.

True to his word, the HR manager said he would simply transfer me to a different department. "Under no circumstances will I fire Zahir."

"He was insubordinate. He threw a metal file at me."

"He was the first person to stand up to your bullying. It's about time. He did nothing wrong. I would have reacted the same. In fact, I think you should apologize to him."

The man never did apologize, but the next day, I was transferred to another department.

I still wasn't happy at United Paints. I had to walk two miles to get to work. It might not sound like much, but during the summer, it was a miserable slog. Karachi was hot and muggy and, after walking two miles in 100 degree temperatures with 90 percent humidity, I would arrive at work soggy, miserable, and ready to nap instead of work. I did get better at typing, but by then it had become clear how mind-numbingly boring the job of a clerk typist was. How could I spend years doing nothing but punching out one word after another by day, while going to school by night? It threatened to drive me out of my mind or break my spirit. Even without the tyrannical boss, it might be only a matter of time before I threw something again.

I discovered another key to success in those years. Not only did I need a good education and a good location, I also needed good contacts. At first that realization scared me, because I did not know anyone, at least not anyone of obvious significance, except my Uncle Jamil, who took no interest in me. I was not going to let that stop me.

My mother had stressed to me the importance of education, and by her example, she had also shown me over the years that self-sufficient people know when to ask for help, and they never give up. So what if I did not know anyone? I would go out of my way to meet people, and I would seek friendships with educated, successful people who could mentor me. I would not befriend the devil just to get ahead, but I would pursue relationships with people I met along the way that I genuinely liked and trusted.

One of my brother-in-law's acquaintances had recently returned from Beirut after completing an MBA program sponsored by USAID. Aslam Khan was working for Karachi's Chamber of Commerce in a senior position. I met him one evening at my sister's house. In a short but productive conversation with him, I was able to get his contact information. Not wanting to look too eager, I waited a few days before

I went to see him at his office. When I did, I told him how unhappy I was at United Paints and asked him if he could help me make some contacts in search of a better job. He said he would keep his ears open for opportunities and drop my name with a few people. Over the next few months, he arranged a few interviews for me at several different companies.

From then on, every time I sat down to my typewriter, I told myself that it was only temporary, that better things were coming. That belief, plus the night-school classes that I knew would ultimately get me out of low-paying clerical work, kept me from becoming depressed.

Within a few months, thanks to my new friend Aslam, ATCO Industries hired me as an assistant to the sales manager. It was another clerical position, but it involved more than just typing. ATCO Industries owned a battery manufacturing plant and a pharmaceutical firm. The office was bigger and better organized, and the working environment was friendlier and more positive. Most important, my pay increased from Rs.150 to Rs.250 a month. I was on my way to the financial independence I craved, not only for myself but also for my parents. I wanted them to be proud, and I wanted to take care of them.

"It's so much better, Amma," I told my mother on the phone. "I can see myself growing here instead of just being an office robot for the rest of my life. The pay is almost double. Soon I can help you and Abba to move here."

"Don't worry about us. We'll come to Karachi one way or another, but I'm so proud of you, son." There they were, the words I loved to hear. Amma said them often, but she always made clear that I had earned them. "Your hard work will pay off, Zahir. You'll see. Just make sure that you're respectful to your boss."

"Yes, Amma. I always am." I never told her about throwing the file at my boss. She would not have understood, unless I told her the names he had called me, and I would never repeat that kind of language to my mother.

After a couple of months, my sales manager at ATCO resigned. The sales director who took his place was a kindly older fellow who seemed a bit lost in his new job. Mr. Iman Niazi had just retired as a commissioner at the government's income tax department, and it was soon clear that he had not been hired for his sales and marketing expertise. He had never worked in sales or marketing in his life. I am certain he was hired because of his connections within the inner circle of government. Mr. Niazi came from a very distinguished and reputable family. His uncle was Sardar Abdur Nishtar, a prominent leader from the independence movement. Mr. Niazi's easy-going personality, privileged family background, and public sector experience left him ill-prepared for his new assignment. He rarely came out of his office, and when he did, he seemed to have little idea of what everyone should be doing, though he treated everyone with respect and friendliness from the highest-paid manager to the lowliest clerk. Though he was the wrong person for the job, which called for a hungry, aggressive, hands-on leader, I immediately saw in the kindly Mr. Niazi another sort of mentor, one who would become invaluable.

He never called me by name, instead calling me Beta, which means "son" in Urdu. While he was not good at his duties, he was good at recognizing those who were and delegating accordingly. He was effective in spite of himself. Mr. Niazi saw that I was good at the balancing act of making both customers and branch managers happy. He also saw that though I was only twenty years old, I already knew more about sales and marketing than he did, and he began to rely on my judgment.

When someone asked Mr. Niazi to solve a problem that he did not understand, he smiled, patted them on the shoulder, and said, "I'll look into it and get back to you." He then called me into his office, explained the situation, and asked, "So, Zahir, what do you think we should do?" I gave him my take on the situation, and he grinned and nodded, saying, "Good, good. We'll go with your suggestion then." Each time my suggestions worked, he gave me more responsibilities. Pretty soon I was running the department.

While other young men in their late teens and early twenties gravitated toward coworkers their own age, I befriended several men who were twice my age or more. The gray hair either intimidated the younger set or reminded them of their parents. I suppose my contemporaries thought older guys would be dull, but they had interesting experiences to share, if you were willing to listen, and

I was. I knew their collective wisdom and the connections that they had spent years forging could help create a strong foundation for my future. I also genuinely liked them and felt comfortable with them. Maybe it was because I was the baby of my family and used to being surrounded by people older than me.

Amma used to tell me, "Remember, older people aren't much different from younger people except that they have more experience. They've already gone through many of the same things you'll go through in life, Zahir. It's not only respectful to listen to your elders, it's smart."

The men I met in my early years in business gave me valuable advice, but none could replace the wisest advisor I knew: Amma Ji. I was eager to have her near at hand again.

During my next visit to Sialkot, I asked, "Amma, Abba, I think it's time for you both to retire, don't you?"

Amma's smile was more serene than I'd seen it in years. She worked hard all her life, and I could see she would be perfectly content to leave that part of her life behind her. "Yes, Zahir, I think you're right. I've been preparing for this day. I've already given up sewing, and Abba, and I have already found someone to buy our place."

Abba's smile was knowing. "Amma is always one step ahead of us, son."

In late 1964, my Amma and Abba returned with me to Karachi. She was nearly sixty years old. For this migration, she did not wear a burqa. Amma had long ago dispensed with the tradition as impractical and now merely covered her head with a *chadar* (headscarf). "The Quran asks women to be modest in our behavior and appearance," she reasoned. "I've always been modest in my behavior. As for my appearance, I'm an old woman, and my head is covered. I think this is modest enough."

When we arrived in Karachi, at first we rented a house. We had a large extended family in Karachi, and now that Amma and Abba lived with me, frequent visitors became part of our routine. Many women in Karachi had it easy compared to their counterparts in smaller towns, because it was common for families in large cities to have a full-time cook as well as part-time help to clean the house and help serve guests. This was not true for Amma; my income was not enough to hire servants. When guests came over, I was the one who helped Amma serve them chai and food.

I was finally able to truly help my Amma, both with financial and personal support. It seemed a perfect situation. Amma was thrilled when Salim moved from Lahore to join our happy household. She always preferred to have her boys with her, a tradition that was not as common in Pakistan as it had been in India. Soon Amma and Abba suggested that we move out of the rental house and buy a house with the proceeds from the sale of their place in Sialkot. We decided to buy a place close to Sajida's house and found one within walking distance, approximately a quarter of a mile. This would bring our family even closer together, which pleased me almost as much as Amma. Before we closed the sale, something odd happened.

We made a verbal agreement with the seller and planned to return a couple of days later to seal the deal. When we went back, he told us that someone from our family had stopped by earlier to tell him that we had changed our minds. He had signed a contract with another interested party. We never found out who the mysterious relative was.

Amma was upset, and we were all angry at the faceless relative for ruining our chance at what seemed like the perfect house in the perfect location. As the saying goes, "Man proposes, and God disposes." Within days after the purchase was nixed, we found another place for sale just three houses away from our sister's home. We made an offer, which was promptly accepted. This time, we did not share the news with anyone until everything was in writing. The anonymous relative must have regretted canceling our agreement with the previous seller. The first house was at least a quarter of a mile away, and now we would practically be living next door to my sister.

Buying a house so close to Sajida turned out to be good for all of us. In 1964, my sister gave birth to her second daughter, Naila, followed by Sohila in 1965. My nieces spent most of their time at our house. I still remember Naila sitting in Abba's lap while he recited verses from the holy Quran. Sajida followed her children to our place several times a day. Amma and Abba were very happy spending time with their granddaughters, and so was I. Sajida enjoyed having a large, loving family support system around her. These were good times for all of us.

In the mid-1960s, Pakistan's government offices started moving to the new capital of Islamabad. All diplomatic missions and other foreign offices had to move. The USAID office temporarily moved to Lahore, which was closer to Islamabad. My brother-in-law had to relocate, and my sister's family was no longer a few doors away.

After moving to Karachi, I enrolled in Islamia College. I had to work full-time, so I did not attend classes but studied at home and took exams. The administration did not care if I showed up for classes or not, so long as I passed the tests.

In 1965, I graduated from college with a bachelor's degree in liberal arts, though most of my education had taken place at work. I was basically running the sales department and solving real-life business issues on a daily basis. This improved both my written and verbal communication skills. Because English was the common language of business, I had become an avid reader of English-language magazines and newspapers, which not only improved my language skills but also opened my eyes to a wider world. I remembered Amma staying up late at night to read our lesson books and to practice her letters and words on our spare sheets of school paper. This was how knowledge piled up in our family—with spare hours, spare cash, and spare paper.

Although I learned my most important lessons at work and at home, it was my liberal arts degree that qualified me to apply for better positions. In the spring of 1966, the Bankers Training Institute of The State Bank of Pakistan advertised banking trainee positions.

"I would sure love to try one of these banking jobs," I told my friend Syed Waqar, an assistant sales manager at ATCO, "but you know how it is, they only give those jobs to people with connections."

"Not always. I think you should apply. You have nothing to lose."

"Sure, I have nothing to lose, except the time it takes to fill out all those forms and go through the exams and interviews."

"That's nothing. Imagine getting the job" he said.

I smiled and nodded.

"Now imagine how you will feel if you don't try. You're smart, educated, and experienced, and you are probably more qualified than most of the applicants. Not everyone they pick knows somebody. I think you have a better chance than you realize."

I shrugged. He was right about one thing: I had nothing to lose. I took the written exam, which included an essay of fifteen hundred words. I knew I did well on the test, but I was still skeptical, certain the process was rigged to favor people with connections. I was surprised to receive a call inviting me to the second stage of the selection process.

The interview went well, and I was selected.

I pumped Syed's hand, saying, "I have to admit, I'm happy that I was wrong and you were right. I owe this to you. I wouldn't have even tried if you hadn't convinced me."

After our initial classes, successful candidates were assigned to commercial banks to finish their training. I was transferred to United Bank Limited, a job that sent me to Islamabad. I did not want to go, as I had developed a large network of friends in Karachi. More importantly, I did not want to leave Amma and Abba alone to fend for them. I had been taking care of many of their household needs, chores, and errands. I considered taking them with me, but realized that it made no sense. They were getting older and feeling settled in Karachi, surrounded by family and friends. Uprooting them again at this point in their lives would be too stressful for all of us. I told the bank administrators that I wanted to work in Karachi, and they promised to transfer me back as soon as they could. Since the opportunity would mean better prospects for the future and the sacrifice would be short term, it made no sense to turn it down.

I moved to Islamabad and visited Karachi on a regular basis to look after Amma and Abba. Although my parents had six grown children, I always thought of them as my responsibility. I felt guilty about leaving, and whenever I went home, I looked for ways to make it up to them. It did not take long for opportunities to present themselves. Amma still had an ambition or two in store, and she had a way of infecting people with her determination to achieve them.

❧

-23-

THE FAITH

My trips home from Islamabad to Karachi were usually happy occasions, but during one visit in 1969, I arrived at my parents' house to find it filled with gloom. I immediately wondered if Abba was ill.

"What's going on, Amma?"

"Nothing much. A few of your cousins have visited, and Bilqees brings the younger children over sometimes. Other than that, I keep busy around the house, cleaning, making dinner. Abba reads the paper. Sometimes we watch TV. We don't do too much these days." Her voice strained on that last sentence. Her eyes, filled with some guilty knowledge, moved to Abba's and then away.

"Is Abba sick?"

"No, no. We're fine," Abba said. He gave Amma a stern glance, not an angry look but a silencing one.

"You realize that I'll keep pestering you both until I find out what's going on, so you might as well tell me why you both keep giving each other funny looks."

Amma turned to me, her mouth set in a decisive line. "Your Abba and I applied to go on a *hajj*, but our applications were denied."

Abba tipped his head from side to side, resigned to this obstacle as if it were God's will and there was no point fighting it. "Because of the shortage of foreign exchange these days, the government has limited the number of people who can go."

There were always more people who wanted to go on the pilgrimage to Makkah than there were available applications. Pilgrims in Pakistan had to submit to a drawing to determine who would go. Abba was content that Allah had spoken on the matter. To console Amma, Abba said, "Besides, we're a little old for such a demanding trip."

"Most people have to save for a long time to go to hajj," Amma said. "So many of them are older people like us. That's no excuse."

"I'm not making excuses," Abba said. "It's just not up to us. We'll go to hajj when Allah invites us to go and not before. Maybe we'll have better luck next year."

"By next year, I might be dead. I don't want to die without ever going to hajj."

"If you die next year, you have nothing to worry about. You'll see Allah soon enough."

Amma chuckled, and tried to stuff her laughter back into her mouth, like a letter into an envelope. "That's not funny," she said.

"My point is that Allah knows our intentions. That's what's important."

"I know you're right," she said, "but Allah also knows when I really plan to do something, I don't just give up."

This was true. Amma never simply accepted whatever came her way; all her life she had made things happen. Her mother had given up on almost everything the moment her husband died, so Amma took over the job of raising her younger brothers. Amma had lost standing in the community after her father died and after she married a man with few prospects, but through her efforts to create strong relationships with her relatives and her neighbors she helped our family gain respect in the community. She and her husband had started out penniless, but she carved out goals and plans and pushed her husband to help her bring those dreams to fruition. When the family businesses went under, she did not give up, but committed to educating herself and her children in hopes of a better future.

During all these struggles, she had never forgotten her duty to Allah. She might have given up the burqa because she did not see the necessity, but she wholeheartedly believed in the teachings and traditions of Islam. She approached her faith with the same determination she gave to all other aspects of her life. "The world is temporary," she always told me. "Here, we have a chance to show Allah our love for each other and for him, but in the end, we must all die, and the way we live on this earth will help prepare us for the hereafter."

Amma believed that to show God her devotion, she had to adhere to Islamic teachings in her daily life and also fulfill the five duties of every Muslim, the Five Pillars of Islam. These are four of those pillars:

- *Shahada*: The Shahada is a pronouncement of faith in the unity of one and only one God (Allah) and accepting the prophet Mohammed as the last messenger of Allah.

- *Salat*: Salat is Islamic prayers consisting of five prayers: *Fajr* is performed at dawn, *Zuhar* is at noon, *Asr* is performed in the afternoon, *Magrib* at sunset, and *Isha* is evening prayer.

- *Zakat*: Zakat is the practice of charitable giving. It is obligatory for every Muslim who can afford to give 2.5 percent of one's accumulated wealth each year. It is considered a personal responsibility to ease the economic hardship of others and eliminate inequality.

- *Sawm* (Fasting): Every Muslim must fast during the month of Ramadan. While fasting, Muslims must abstain from food, drink, and sexual intercourse from dawn to dusk. The fast is meant to allow Muslims to seek closeness to God and to express their gratitude.

Amma always complied with these four Pillars of Islam. Even when we faced extreme financial setbacks, she never missed giving zakat from whatever meager savings she had. She had yet to fulfill the fifth and last pillar: the hajj.

The Hajj is a pilgrimage to the holy city of Makkah during the Islamic month of Dhu-al-Hijjah. Every Muslim must travel to Makkah at least once in their lifetime, so long as he is physically fit and financially can afford it. Amma believed she was both physically and financially capable of making the journey. To her, it would be wrong to stop trying as long as she had enough strength in mind and body to deal with whatever obstacles got in her way. I realized that she would never give up, even if it killed her.

This last possibility was what worried me. I did not want to see Amma work herself into an early grave. I remembered how we had walked in the heat for hours, and then days, to sit in front of the mansion of the Indian High Commissioner, waiting to beg him to let Amma go to India to bring her husband home. How much further might she push herself to fulfill her obligation to God? With that thought in mind, I made a decision.

I returned her look of determination with one of my own. "I'll see if I can get you permission to go to hajj."

"How?" Abba looked even more skeptical than usual.

"I have no idea, but I'll check with some friends."

"I know you can do it, with Allah's help," Amma said.

She disappeared into her bedroom and returned to the kitchen carrying a small package wrapped in a piece of cloth. She put it in my hand without saying a word.

"What is this, Amma?"

"Open it."

I unwound the cloth to find a small stack of cash in different denominations. "What's this for?" I asked.

"When you get our applications for hajj approved, you must use this money, and only this money, to buy our tickets."

I wrapped the cloth back around the money again and tried to hand it back to her. "No, no, Amma, just let me take care of it. It's no trouble. I want to do this for you."

She crossed her arms over her chest, refusing to take back the bundle. "I know you always do, son, and I appreciate it, but that's not what I want. It is very important to me that you use this money to buy our tickets. You must promise me."

"I'll promise, if you'll tell me what's so special about this particular money."

"Why can't you just do what I ask, like you usually do?"

"Why can't you just answer my question, like you usually do?"

"All right, all right. I've been saving for my hajj even before you were born from the money I earned when I had my small business in India and later when I was sewing clothes in Sialkot."

"That must have been hard. I know sometimes we didn't have enough to pay the bills."

She gave me a small, guilty smile, but whether her guilt was for her family or for God, I don't know. "During those months, I didn't save anything, but the money I saved for hajj? Once I promised it to Allah, it wasn't mine to spend anymore on my family or myself. Any money that went into this fund, I didn't touch. It wasn't easy, but I knew my reward would be in heaven."

I carefully placed the package on the table in front of me, staring at it with the wonder some people must feel when seeing Makkah itself. "Did you know about this, Abba?"

"No, but I'm not surprised. Your mother was always good at saving money. Every time I told her something couldn't be done, she would pull out the cash. I don't know how we would have made it all these years without her clever planning. I never begrudged her those little piles of money, which always went to something worthwhile. She's right, hajj is important. I'm glad she saved the money. Even if you can't help us this time, son, I'm sure we'll make use of that fund someday. If Allah smiles on anyone's faithfulness, surely he'll smile on Amma's."

I wiped the tears from my face. "I'll do my best."

"You're your mother's son," Abba said.

I had my doubts that I was as resourceful as my mother. If I had been in her shoes, all those years ago when she had struggled to get a visa so that she could return to India for Abba, I don't think I would have gone back to the Commissioner's house a second day, much less a third.

I honestly did not believe I could do anything to help my mother get to Makkah. The names of would-be pilgrims were picked by lottery. I had no power to interfere with that. Even if I had, time was against me. The hajj does not take place at just any time of the year. To fulfill her obligation to God, Amma had to travel at the same time as millions of other Muslims from all over the world, from the eighth to the thirteenth day of the twelfth month of the Islamic calendar, known as Dhu al-Hijjah. The last ship of intended Hajjis was set to sail for Saudi Arabia within the next few days. This was not going to happen. I felt certain of it, but because I had made a promise to Amma, I had to try. Amma's persistence became mine. I started first thing in the next morning. There was no time to lose.

During my bank training, I had developed personal relationships with a few officers of the State Bank of Pakistan. One of them was Amin-Ul-Haque Chaudry, former principal of the Bankers Training Institute and one of the nicest men I had ever come across. By this time, Mr. Chaudry was the director of Pakistan's Foreign Exchange Department. He was the only contact I knew who might be able to open the right door to make my mother's long-awaited hajj a reality.

When I went to see Mr. Chaudry, he was clearly delighted to see me, which gave me hope. When I explained my parents' dilemma, he called the director of the Karachi Port Trust, who was also in charge of the Hajj Department, and asked him to please make room for two more people on the last ship out. "I'll see what I can do," was the reply.

I also spoke with a friend in the State Department, who promised to help expedite the application process for my parents. I began to believe that Amma and Abba might go on their hajj after all, but before they could help me, I had to overcome a major hurdle. I needed to find Amma's and Abba's original, rejected hajj applications, just two pieces of paper among thousands, representing all the people of Karachi whose dreams of going on that year's hajj had been dashed.

A friend and I found the storage building where all the rejected applications were stored, only to discover that the offices had closed early to observe Friday prayers. We were running out of time. The last hajj ship was set to sail on Saturday evening, but I was not ready to give up, not after all I had been through to get this far.

I knew that all government offices had security guards. My friend and I located the one on duty and explained to him why I needed to find my parents' applications. The guard knew which storage room I was talking about, but he had no authority to open it.

"I'm sorry, you'll have to come back on Monday."

"But the last ship sets sail tomorrow night."

"Some people might be here on Saturday," he said.

"Isn't there a strike tomorrow?" my friend asked.

"That's right. I doubt anyone will be here," I said. "Even if there were, the ship sets sail tomorrow night, and I have to take the application to the Karachi Port Trust no later than nine o'clock tomorrow morning. Look, you can go in with us and watch what we do. We are not trying to steal anything. We just want to find my parent's rejected applications, which will become nothing more than trash in twenty-four hours."

"You don't understand. I'd like to help you, and in this case I wouldn't mind bending the rules, but I don't have the keys for that room."

"Can we try prying open a window?" my friend asked.

"I don't know," the guard hesitated.

"I wouldn't ask, but my mother has been saving for this trip since before I was born, and she's worried that she might not live long enough to go to another hajj." I knew this was stretching the truth a bit, but I saw no harm in it. "I wouldn't ask for myself. It's for my mother."

The guard smiled. "Okay, okay. I hate letting my mother down, too."

He tried to pry open the window, but the fittings were too tight. "Hold on," he said and ran off. He came back carrying a metal bar and a towel. He wrapped the towel around his hand and said, "Stand back." We stepped back and watched as he hauled his arm back and slammed the metal bar into the window, shattering it. He brushed away the shards, climbed through the hole into the room, and let us in through the door.

"I hope you don't get in trouble," I said.

"Don't worry. I'll tell my boss that I heard a crash and arrived just in time to chase a couple of kids away. He'll see that nothing's missing and think I saved the day."

"I can't thank you enough."

"Don't thank me yet. You still have to find the applications."

That wasn't easy. We didn't find a coherent filing system, just a big pile of paper. My friend and I each took a stack and began searching through it. The guard went back to strolling the grounds and left us to sort through the mound. If Amma had seen us find the two applications in that pile, she would have declared it a miracle. I am not sure I believe in miracles, but we were certainly surprised to find the two names we were looking for after only an hour or so of searching.

We rushed the documents back to the Foreign Exchange Department for processing. This was only a formality, because Mr. Chaudry was in charge of the department and had promised his approval. However, success was not yet assured.

After the applications were processed, we needed final approval from the director of the Karachi Port Trust, who had only promised Mr. Chaudry, "I'll see what I can do." The boat was leaving in less than twenty-four hours, and my parents' fate now rested with him. We would have to wait until morning for our answer.

When I returned home that night, I told my parents about my adventure. I said, "You should pack your bags. If he approves your application, we'll barely have enough time to get you on the ship."

"We're already packed," Amma said and pointed to the doorway, where two pieces of luggage sat waiting for a trip that might or might not happen.

As if our mission was not uncertain enough, the nation of Pakistan had selected the next day to protest against the rule of General Ayub Khan. All parties opposing Ayub's rule demanded an open and independent election. To turn up the pressure, they had called for a general strike. Known as "Stop the Wheel," the strike would possibly be the most successful strike in the history of Pakistan. Having to cross the city during a strike made it even more likely that our quest would fail. We had no transportation of our own, and there would be no public transport of any kind the next day. We asked a family friend, Maroof Ahmad, if he would drive us in his car. He agreed, but driving a car through the middle of a strike was not something any of us looked forward to.

Maroof, Salim, Kalim, and I loaded the car early the next morning, still unsure whether we would make it across the city in time or at all. We first had to get to the Hajj Office to find out whether Amma and Abba were going or not. We decided to take my parents with us, so if their application was approved, we could take them directly to the boat for boarding.

We knew that there was a chance of violence on the streets but tried not to think about it. We were more worried about delays. We made a big cardboard banner to post atop the car. We scribbled some words in support of the strike and wrote below that in big, bold letters, GOING FOR HAJJ. We placed the banner on the roof and tied it upright with a string. Amma and Abba stepped into the back seat, and the rest of us piled in. Amma looked surprisingly serene, given the circumstances.

Maroof pulled out onto the streets, and it was not long before we saw the protestors swarming at every turn. The country had come to a standstill. Nothing was moving. Our car crawled through the crowds. It was the only vehicle on the road, but that was the problem. Protestors stopped us a number of times, challenging us for trying to break the strike. Each time, we introduced them to my parents and explained that they were going for hajj, and the people immediately let us go, even helping to push back the crowd for us. "Let them through! Let them through! Their parents are going for hajj!" People who had been shouting and waving fists moments before smiled and waved as they let us go by. It was like being in the world's slowest parade, with our car as the only float. We were touched by everyone's kindness, but it seemed less and less likely that we would make it.

We arrived at the Hajj Office with time to spare. Inside, more smiling faces greeted us. The office was mostly empty because of the strike, but the director of the Karachi Port Trust had called earlier that day, and the few people on hand knew to expect two more intended hajjis. He had approved their request. All that was left was to put my parents on the boat. The Hajj Office was at the port, and the boat was just a short walk away.

When we reached the ship, our goodbyes seemed stilted and drawn out, after all the tension leading up to that moment. When Amma turned to smile at me, I could see by the look in her eyes that I had become the heroic son I had tried so hard to be since my days as a small boy. Those eyes also held a knowing look, as if all her panic a few days ago had been a pose, and she had known she would make her hajj all along. She had wanted to serve Allah and had counted on him to help her. I wondered if I had done anything at all—after all, it was Amma's determination that had set everything in motion.

"Have a safe journey!" I said.

"Allah will protect us," she said.

As Amma walked up the gangplank, she held onto Abba's arm for support, but it was clear that she was holding him up more than he was holding her. In that moment, I knew Amma truly was the strongest person in our family. Although she had never traveled so far before in her life, I knew I did not need to worry about her. Even if stormy seas tossed the ship, my Amma Ji would find her way to Makkah. I was sure of it.

-24-

THE HAJJIS

The hajj is the largest annual pilgrimage in the world. Prior to the founding of Islam, tribes from all over the Arabian Peninsula—people of many different faiths, including Christians and pagans—gathered in Makkah for an annual pilgrimage. The Kaaba, the sacred, cube-shaped building that believers consider to be the center of the world, was filled with many different idols representing many different visions of God to the different believers. The followers of different faiths made the trip at different times, according to their traditions.

Muslims believe that the pilgrimage they call Hajj has its roots in the story of the Prophet Ibrahim. One day, Allah ordered Ibrahim to take his wife, Hazarat Hajra, and his infant child, prophet Ismail (Ishmael), to the place now known as Makkah. When Ibrahim reached Makkah, God ordered him to leave his wife and son alone there and return to Egypt. After Ibrahim left, Hazarat Hajra went in search of water for her baby. She laid her son on the ground and ran between the hills known as Saf-e-Marrwah, frantically searching the dry, rocky desert for water. While she was gone, the thirsty Ismail began kicking the ground with his feet. When his mother returned to check on him for the seventh time, a spring had appeared where his feet had scratched the ground. The miraculous spring, known as Zam-Zam, remains there to this day.

Zam-Zam has an important place in the hearts of all Muslims. Any Muslim who goes to Makkah always brings back a bottle or two of its water to give as presents.

The foundation of the Kaaba was placed next to that spring. Muslim tradition holds that the original Kaaba was the first building built by the first man, Adam. Later, after Ibrahim obeyed Allah's command to sacrifice his son, Ishmael, and Allah spared Ishmael, Ibrahim rebuilt the Kaaba to thank Allah for his mercy. In 632 AD, the prophet Mohammad led his followers from Medina to Makkah to perform the first Muslim hajj in honor of Ibrahim, Hajra, and Ismail. With that, the hajj became the Fifth Pillar of Islam.

I never saw Amma and Abba at Makkah, and they never took pictures, but when I heard their stories later, I often imagined them there. Over time I came to believe that the purpose of hajj is for God to bring people together from different walks of life, different cultures, different races, and show them that they're all one. No matter if we are kings or peons, in the end, we all return to the earth. Amid the buildings, hills, intense sun, and dry desert air of Makkah, our equal standing before God is made manifest.

At Makkah, all people wrap themselves in a similar version of a plain, white cotton sheet—men and women, young and old. It's the same way their bodies will someday be wrapped for burial, because they'll face God as equals. At Makkah, no one receives better or worse accommodations than anyone else. Everyone is treated the same. Everyone spends their stay under the same roofs in the same tents. No matter who you are, famous or infamous, leader or follower, rich or poor, you sleep on the ground, and you fight to use the limited resources just like every one of the other million people there.

Makkah is the one place where, even among fundamentalists, women are forbidden to cover their face or follow the rules of *hijab* (a head covering used by Muslim women to cover their head and face). Everyone is reduced to nothing but a face, a white cotton sheet, and bare feet—no shoes, no makeup, no jewelry, no burqa, no scarf, and no colorful materials. At Makkah, men and women are equal before God.

I still like to imagine Amma's broad smile of devotion as she walked barefoot at Suff-e-Mural, Mara's Hills, scurrying across the same ground where Hajra once ran back and forth looking for water. I imagine the soreness of Amma's feet as she tried not to hobble, though her cracked and calloused feet must have been blistered and sore from walking on the floor made of tiny stone chips. I can see Amma counting relatives on her fingers so that she could buy everyone a small bottle of *abe-zam-zam* (holy water from the spring Ismail created when he kicked the ground).

I can see my parents performing the tawaf side by side, circumambulating the black-and-gold curtain draping the Kaaba, built of granite atop marble, hiding within it a sacred stone Muslims that believe God sent from heaven.

Each night, approximately two million people move from one place to another, constantly progressing through the stages of their pilgrimage, spending their nights on the open ground under the stars. No beds, no cots, no tents, just an occasional mat or sleeping bag. It is a mass of white-clad, blank-faced humanity, lying in the place where one day God will hold court and pass judgment on the human race.

I can easily picture my parents losing their sense of direction. You see, when you're in Pakistan and you turn toward Makkah to pray, you face west. When you're in America, you face northeast, but when you're at Khana Kaaba, everyone is turned toward the center, circling. My mother and father had reached what was, for them and millions of other believers, the center of the universe. If they died at that moment, or even if they died later, their soul would fly from there to the eternal world.

Among such a mass of people, in such a place, it was only a matter of time before my mother confronted the same sudden horrifying moment that comes to many at Makkah: she was separated from her spouse. One moment he was walking next to her, and the next time she turned, was gone. She was terrified. She turned this way and that, her eyes skipping from person to person as she called out in panicky bursts. "Zahir's Father! Zahir's Father! Did you see the man I was walking with? Um, did you see my husband? Abba!" A Muslim woman of my mother's generation would never call out her husband's given name in public.

Finally she stopped, took a deep breath, and stood still. As she looked around her, it struck her how everyone looked the same; it was a sea of blank, undecorated souls wrapped in white. This made it even harder to find him, but the sea of white sheets also reminded her that she was in Allah's place, among Allah's people, on Allah's mission. She told herself that God would help her find her way back to her mate, though a part of her devout soul was not convinced.

With her usual determination, she quietly asked Allah to tell her what to do and spun slowly in place until she caught site of a hill known as Jab-Lul-Rahmat, a place where our Prophet used to go to pray and meditate. Rahmat means "God's blessing" or "God's mercy," and it is said that if you pray to God on that hill, he will respond. Amma decided to head for the hill and talk to Allah there.

It took her several hours to get there. Occasionally, she looked back down the hill to survey the hordes of humanity shifting this way and that below. Humanity all being the same before God had seemed a beautiful thing before, but now it was terrifying. She clung to faith like a seamstress holding a delicate thread, though panic threatened to tear the thread apart.

Maybe Allah would help her find her husband. Why had he separated them in the first place? Amma was one of those who believed that everything happens for a good reason. Perhaps she was wondering how losing her ailing husband fit into this plan. Abba was sick, and it was likely that he could not make the hajj had they waited another year.

Nonetheless, until Allah gave her some sort of answer, there was nothing to do but keep putting one foot ahead of the other as she made her way up the rocky hill. Several people kindly parted to make way for her or took her hand to give her a boost up this or that rock. ("How kind everyone was," she later told me.)

When she reached the top, she prayed aloud. "Allah, as you know, I can't find my husband. Please, if it's your will, please help me find him." Even when she talked to God, Amma remained straightforward and practical. She prayed a little longer in the same vein, and then she rose and turned to look downhill again.

When she described it later, I tried to see it through her eyes. There were waves of heat shimmering, making the crowd bend and elongate before her eyes, her body seeming to bend and fold with them. The sun was intense, and her cotton wrapping clung to her body, making it wet and sticky. She wiped a hand across her forehead and pushed sweaty strands of hair behind her ears. She swayed slightly, wishing that she had thought to bring some water up the hill with her.

As if reading her thought, a nearby voice offered help: "Would you like a drink of water?" She turned to see a young woman offering her water from a canteen or thermos.

"You're so kind," she said. "Thank you, yes."

She took the offered water, tipped her head back, and sipped. She was careful not to drink too much, lest the woman not have enough left for herself.

Allah had provided water. That was a start. She surveyed the crowd again.

Everyone still looked the same. No one stood out. Have faith, she told herself as she walked down the hill to where she had last seen Abba.

After praying atop Jab-Lul-Rahmat, Amma felt fortified by faith. Allah would help her find her husband. She returned to the campsite where she had spent the previous night with Abba and sat down to wait. As she listened to the buzzing human hive layered with accents from all over the world, she finally heard a familiar soft-but-firm tenor, speaking in Urdu, "Yes, yes, there she is." She turned to see Abba walking toward her in the company of a young man.

"Ah, there you are," Abba said. "I got turned around, and this young man helped me find my way back. All the camps look the same to me. What happened to you?"

"What happened to *me*?" Amma said. "I was looking for you."

"Yes. I was worried, too, but I knew if I kept trying, I'd find you sooner or later."

"With a little help from Allah. I didn't find you until I went up to Jab-Lul-Rahmat and prayed. I think God returned you to me."

"Perhaps," Abba said. "However it happened, I'm glad we did find each other." From the fond looks that passed between them through the years, I gathered that he often considered himself lucky to have such a spouse. Perhaps those few hours of loss and rediscovery at Makkah reminded him again of what a treasure he had in his wife.

When my mother came home, she told the story of getting separated, and it was as if the young man who helped Abba find his way back to her was a guardian angel, or at least sent by a guardian angel, as an answer to her prayer.

When Amma and Abba returned to Karachi, they received an energetic reception from neighbors and a surprised reception from family. My parents had not considered how their sudden absence might raise a stir among those who knew them. Abba's daily routine included sitting in the courtyard outside his home's main door for hours at a time, reading his newspaper and accepting visits from neighborhood retirees like a humble king holding court. Sometimes Amma would send tea out to them. Because Amma and Abba didn't know until the last minute that their hajj request would be approved, they hadn't told anyone that they were going.

Their neighbors had spent days speculating about what happened to them, and they were relieved and excited when we explained the reason for their absence. Meanwhile, our relatives were stunned when we called to invite them over to welcome the returning pilgrims. This was and is a common practice after a hajj, but they had no idea that Amma and Abba had even left. My brothers and sisters and most of my relatives were full of praise for the faithfulness and devotion of my parents, and everyone was excited that Amma had brought them souvenirs of the journey, especially the little bottles of abe-zam-zam, the blessed water from the holy spring that was sure to bring good luck.

-25-

ARRANGED MARRIAGE

I t seemed that Amma had brought home a bit of good luck for me, too. Right after she and Abba returned from their hajj, I got my wish, and the bank transferred me from Islamabad to Karachi, where I moved back in with my parents. By then, Salim and Kalim had both married and moved out.

In Karachi, the bank promoted me to branch manager. I was earning a good income for the first time in my life, and I was having a blast, meeting other young professionals, doing lunch and going to parties.

Because I had a good job, Amma decided that it was high time for me to get married, and she thought it was her obligation to find a mate for me, just as she had for my siblings.

I was not excited about the prospect of marriage; I was too busy having a good time. I said, "I'm not quite ready for a wife, Amma. I'd like to be single and just enjoy life for a while before I settle down."

She looked at me as if I were speaking a foreign language. "What do you mean, not ready? Nonsense. You have a good job, good money. What sensible young man wants to live alone when you can have a wife to take care of you? Why work so hard only for you? A man wants children, so he can pass on what God gives him. Family is most important, Zahir. I want to see my grandchildren before I die. Who doesn't want to get married? What kind of person prefers to be alone?"

"I'm not alone, Amma."

"You know what I mean." She gave me a knowing smile, as if she had figured me out. "Don't worry, Zahir. I know you better than you think. I'll find you a good wife."

I shrugged. I knew her search would take some time, and perhaps by the time she found this wife, I would be ready.

In Amma's mind, finding the right bride for me was not only her duty to me as a parent, it was her duty to our family. Marriage was not just between two people but between two families. In considering her choice, Amma was not just thinking about the bride who would come into our family but also of that bride's siblings, my siblings, her parents, my parents, and even our cousins, aunts and uncles, nieces, nephews, and everyone who would be spending a lot of time in the family sphere. The compatibility of families was her first consideration, and the compatibility of the couple was often assumed from there.

Amma's choice of my bride would affect everyone in our family. Except for me, it stood to affect Amma most of all, because we would all be living together in the same house. This was a recipe for family conflict. The saying among Pakistani women goes something like this: *"Jub main bahoo thee too sas buri meli and main jub sas bani too bahoo buri meli."* (When I got married, my mother-in-law was such a bad-natured woman, and when I became a mother-in-law, my daughter-in-law was such a bad-natured woman.)

The system worked when my mother lived in India; family members were tied to each other economically, because economics were tied to family lands or family businesses that passed from one generation to the next. Families had no choice but to put up with each other. When people moved from India to Pakistan, many had to give up the idea of owning land and find white-collar or blue-collar jobs. Many people who came from small towns found themselves in big metropolises. These changes began to break up the joint family system.

My mother was not a fan of the joint family system. Her experience with her own husband's family was not good, but in her mind, the system was still the one we had to live by. As a woman in Muslim society, she had little access to the world outside her home, and she could not see the changes that were making the old system obsolete. Certainly, other parents on the cusp of this societal shift were still doing as she was doing. As she considered options, she applied her life experiences to the process she knew, even though some forty years separated us. The partition of the old India and the creation of Pakistan had separated us further.

It was not that young people didn't respect family traditions; it was that we were not the same kind of people once served by those traditions. Arranged marriages did not fit the growing trend toward independent living and thinking, personal choice, and personal freedom. We did not know how to explain to our parents that as well-intentioned as their efforts were, they were putting us at risk for unhappy, unfulfilled lives, the opposite of what they were trying to achieve.

I could not blame my mother for acting against my wishes. I could have participated in the bridal search if I wanted to. Several families who knew me from work or from my social circles in the city approached me, telling me that they had marriageable daughters who would be perfect for me and that they wanted to meet my parents. As an educated man from a good family, with a good job and good pay, I was an eligible bachelor. I knew some of these young women had relatively liberal parents. I might have done well marrying one of them.

I decided it was pointless to participate in the search for my own bride. Because tradition did not allow me to date my bride or get to know her before our engagement, I figured that I had as good a chance of a happy life with one choice as the next. Amma and Abba had done okay, hadn't they?

The biggest problem with letting my mother choose my bride was that she thought she knew who I was, but in many ways she did not. She had observed me as a son and a brother, but she did not know what kind of man I had become. Part of this was because of my own good intentions; I tried to protect my parents from worry or disappointment by keeping my social life private. Though I was twenty-seven, something as innocent as staying at a party until midnight was not something they could have understood. Because neither of my parents had ever been to school, worked in an office, or read many books, they would have understood little about the life I led outside our house. My parents used their sharp minds to plan and achieve goals, but to them, the mind was a tool, not a place to live. Finding me a bride full of social liveliness and skilled at intellectual conversation did not occur to my mother.

My mother found me a bride who she thought would make me happy. She was a simple, old-fashioned girl who knew nothing of modern social changes or the wider world. We had nothing in common. I tried to explain this to my mother, but she did not understand, and I gave up trying to convince her.

I was not interested in marriage, but I wanted to avoid confronting my mother. I did not like her choice, but I wanted to please her. I thought it might be helpful to my parents to have a young woman in the house who could help them and keep them company, and for that reason, the fact that mother thought she could get along with her seemed like the most important criterion.

On April 30, 1972, I married the woman that my mother chose for me, a young woman I had met only in passing at a few family gatherings. Zaiba Usmani was the niece of my sister Sajida's husband, Ather. Zaiba was young, and I hoped that she would become more of a real companion to me over time.

Zaiba had no idea what I did at work and never asked. She had no idea how I spent my off-hours in the city and only asked why I came home so late. She had no interest in meeting my friends and seemed bored by my stories of the hilarious things they did and the insightful things they said. She never spent time in a social circle like mine—the new yuppie class of Karachi society. She was a conservative Muslim, attached to the hearth, and I was a liberal creature who wanted to move out into the world, make connections, and be part of change.

I did not know how to discuss those things with her, so instead we argued about household issues. Sometimes we argued late into the night. We did not raise our voices, but the tension in our voices seemed designed to slip through the cracks, roll across the floors, and drift out the windows. She began spending most of her time at her parents' house. They did not approve of me, which gave us something else to argue about.

One day, we paid a visit to her parents. While we were talking about an unrelated subject, her father brought up my mother.

"Your mother needs to understand that the house is not only hers now, and she must learn to share it with her new daughter-in-law." He made some choice comments about my mother, though he had never witnessed an exchange between her and Zaiba.

We had only been married a few months, and I did not want to get into an argument with my father-in-law, but I was outraged that he was interfering like this without first asking my mother for her side of the story. I stood up without saying a word and walked out.

In our bedroom that night, I told Zaiba, "The next time you run to your father, tell him this: today he opened his mouth and I walked out quietly, but the next time he opens his mouth, I won't walk out quietly."

Within six months, we were barely speaking. She told me she was pregnant and was angry that I did not act happy about it.

"Why should I be happy about bringing a baby into such an unhappy household?"

"How can you say that?"

"It's the truth."

That's how the argument began. It ended with her declaring that she was going to move out and stay with her parents.

"That's not a bad idea. You're happier there. I'll stay here where I'm happy."

She packed her bags and left. I heard through mutual cousins that she was hoping that I would go to her and ask her to come home. I told another cousin who I was confident would carry word back to her, "I didn't kick her out of the house. She left on her own. If she wants to come back, she'll have to do that on her own, too."

Her pride was at stake. She would not come home.

I did not miss her.

It seemed that life was much more peaceful for both of us. I began to realize that this was as it should be and that I had made a mistake in letting my mother make this choice for me. I knew there was only one way to correct my mistake. I had to do the unthinkable: get a divorce.

It was the right thing to do, but I knew it would make life hard for all of us. Just as an old-fashioned arranged marriage was designed to bring two extended families together, a divorce was sure to rip two families apart. This decision would impact my whole family as well as Zaiba's, and it would devastate my amma, who had chosen my wife with only good intentions. Amma wanted only to make sure that I was happy before she parted this world, and I did not want her to feel that she had failed.

Farhan with Imran

-26-

DIVORCE

My marriage to Zaiba was my mother's decision—getting out of the marriage was mine. Lying alone in bed, night after night for several weeks, I tried to figure out how I could make this decision work without destroying two families deeply bound by tradition.

I never doubted my decision. I had watched unhappy couples stay together for years, trying to make the impossible work, each waiting for the other to change. These couples not only made each other unhappy, they spread gloom throughout their families like a disease. Their children suffered from living in an environment filled with conflict, resentment, and depression, even more than they might have suffered from the conflict of a divorce. Our child was not born yet, so I could spare my child, as well as everyone else in our families, if I acted quickly.

Although the decision itself was easy, telling my parents was not. After Zaiba had been gone for a few months, I knew that I could not wait any longer. On the surface, our house was more peaceful, but tension gripped us all. Her long absence made it obvious that my marriage was in trouble. I knew that my parents would worry about me until I resolved my issues with Zaiba, so one night after dinner, I sat down with my parents to discuss my decision with them.

"Amma and Abba, I know you'll be disappointed by what I'm about to say, and I'm sorry for that, but I want you to know my mind is made up. As you know, Zaiba and I have many problems."

"Of course you do. You haven't been married long, and you're still getting used to each other," Amma said.

"Marriage requires compromise," Abba said.

"No, Amma. No, Abba. I'm sorry, but it's much more than that. I know you did your best to find a compatible partner for me, but I think you both know that Zaiba and I are completely unsuited for each other, in fundamental ways that go to the roots of our characters and values. It's pointless for either of us to expect the other to change. We cannot just make adjustments to get along. We have to become completely different people. I am sorry, but there is only one solution. I am getting a divorce."

"Divorce should only be a last resort," Abba said.

"You should first try to work things out," Amma said.

"That might be true if we ever had a relationship in the first place, but we didn't. From the beginning, we were a mismatch. There's nothing to work out, because there was never anything between us. There is no relationship to repair. I should never have married her in the first place. You can't turn a bad decision into a good one just because you decide to stick with it."

"He has a point," Abba said.

"This is my fault," Amma said.

"It's no one's fault," I said, "or it's my fault, for letting you choose a wife for me without my input. You were only doing what you thought was right. If I thought it was wrong for me, I shouldn't have agreed to it. Anyway, there's no point in assigning blame. I've identified the problem, and now I know what I must do to fix it. I realize this is going to cause big problems for you."

"Don't worry about us. You do what you need to do. We are your parents, and we will support you," Amma said.

"You are my parents, so of course I'll worry about you. I know her father will resist this decision, to protect his daughter. You know his family will put pressure on our family, hoping that my family will put pressure on me."

This was more of a cultural issue than a religious issue. Islam permits divorce, but in Pakistan, many people considered it socially unacceptable. I would be painted as a bad guy for leaving my wife. That was one reason so many Pakistanis stayed in unhappy relationships, and another reason is one known in many countries: "for the sake of the children."

In my case, our many family entanglements complicated the social pressures even further. Zaiba was my brother-in-law's niece. I knew that if I divorced her, her family would try to retaliate by threatening to cut off all relations between our families. I suspected that when I started divorce proceedings, they would press Ather to divorce my sister. Tit for tat. My sister had been happily married for fifteen years, and she had four beautiful kids. To me, it was clear that my sister and her family had nothing to do with all this, but I knew that my brother-in-law's extended family would see it differently. To them, family was family, and an injury to one member of their family was an injury to all. I deeply loved my sister and her family, and I knew if things started down that path, I would feel pressured into giving up on a divorce.

I explained all this to my father, and he told me he would talk to Zaiba's father and try to smooth the way. Abba was often tired in those days, his throat pained him more than usual, and he had developed a persistent cough. He was often in bed as soon as night fell, and he rarely ventured beyond the courtyard in front of our house, but within a few days of our talk, he put on his best clothes and made the trip across the city to my father-in-law's house to explain the situation.

Abba suggested to Zaiba's father that if my relationship with his daughter didn't work out, perhaps they should solve any remaining family issues amicably between the two of them and leave the rest of the family out of it. Her father was outraged at the suggestion. Without directly saying so, he made it clear to my father that if I divorced his daughter, he would consider it our family's declaration of war against his.

When my father returned home with his shoulders more slumped than usual, I was not surprised. I had already decided what to do. I knew there was only one way to keep my family out of this: self-imposed exile. I would have to leave the country. I was nervous about leaving and resentful about the necessity, but I knew that it would mean a fresh start for me. A clean break. In all honesty, I was excited about the prospect of relocating.

In my job as a bank manager, I had made friends with a lot of people who traveled or had international connections. The country they all talked about, the place where everyone who dreamed of a different life dreamed of going, the place that was all about future and freedom and opportunity, was the United States.

It was not easy for my parents to give my decision their blessing. They had always opposed any of my suggestions that involved leaving the country to further my studies or pursue employment opportunities, but talking to Zaiba's father had convinced Abba that my divorce was going to be harder than he and Amma had imagined. This time, when I presented my arguments, they were prepared to accept my reasoning. I felt a twinge of guilt over leaving my parents in a lurch, and I worried about what would happen to them without me.

My father had not worked for more than thirteen years, and they had no savings. As in most Pakistani families that weren't wealthy, my elderly parents relied on their children as their social security. As the youngest child, I had become their sole provider, but not once during our discussion of my plans to move to America did they ever bring up the subject of their own finances. Instead, they expressed their concern about my financial security.

"What will you live on?" Amma asked.

"I have a small amount of savings, and I have a friend in Chicago who I can stay with until I get on my feet. I've been planning this for a while, and a few of my connections have been helping me. I'll be fine. I promise to help take care of you, too, no matter what."

"Don't worry about us. We will be fine."

"I just want you to know that I'll always be there for you, even if I'm thousands of miles away."

"We know that, Zahir. We've always known that," Amma said.

Before I left, I visited my sister Sajida in Islamabad. We had never before talked about my marriage problems, but she had heard through the family grapevine that things weren't going well. I told her I was getting a divorce. When I told her my plans to leave the country and why, she laughed.

"Zahir, you're being too dramatic. Ather and I are fine. Your problems won't affect us. Please don't leave on account of me. There's no need."

She had no idea how wrong she was. "It's not just for you," I said. "It will be good for me to get away and make a new start. Anyway, I always wanted to see America."

"Ah, so that's what this is about," she teased.

There were tears in her eyes when I left. I wondered when I would see her again, and I could tell that she was wondering the same thing, though neither of us mentioned it.

On June 21, 1973, I left Pakistan for the United States on a student visa. In the 1970s, it was easy for a Pakistani to get a student visa to the United States. All you needed was to gain admission to an accredited college or university and to pass an English test. A friend helped me find a program that had an easy enrollment process. The YMCA Community College in Chicago quickly accepted me, and the entire process took only a couple of months. I was already accepted before I told my parents that I was leaving for America.

Leaving the country started a chapter of ugliness for my family members who stayed behind. For the next couple of years, Zaiba's family did their worst, even beyond what I had feared. Amma and Abba, the dearest people to me in the world, were left to deal with threats, intimidation, and gossip from my ex-wife's family. Although these hurt my parents, most of our family, friends, and acquaintances knew Amma and Abba too well to believe any of the gossip that drifted their way. Many of them grew angry with Zaiba's family and defended my family and me.

Just as I predicted, the members of my ex's family did their best to break up Sajida and Ather, but as Sajida told me, her marriage was strong enough to withstand it. Even still, they paid a high price. Though most of Ather's family stood by him, his older brother and a few other family members disowned him. He showed his character and resolve by doing the right thing and standing by the woman he loved, no matter the price.

After a couple of years, things quieted down. Ultimately, I felt that all the harassment proved I had done the right thing. I believe to this day that had I not left the country, things would have been even uglier. If I had stayed, I might never have escaped that terrible marriage.

The worst thing was hearing how many people believed I was a terrible father that had abandoned his son. I stayed until our baby was born, but Zaiba's family treated this as an empty gesture. In their eyes, I was leaving just as my responsibility arrived. How could a decent man do such a thing?

I did not want to leave my child, but I believed that he would be better off with one loving parent than with two parents at each other's throats. If I had stayed, Zaiba's family would never have allowed me to see him anyway unless I stayed married to her. I vowed to visit my son as often as possible and to someday explain to him why I left, but Zaiba's family would make that difficult, too. They ultimately relented when it came to the rest of my family: they never forgave me. No one ever told my son Farhan about his father until the boy began asking questions, and then they told him only that his father had abandoned him and his mother. Whenever I came home and asked to see my son, they denied my requests. Writing to him wasn't an option. His family wouldn't let me have anything to do with him. That was their final, ongoing punishment to me.

I still believe Farhan was better off than he would have been if his mother and I had stayed married. In spite of my problems with his mother as a wife, I did not fear that she would be a terrible mother— maybe not perfect but an upright woman who would love her son. He could do worse. I was sorry to be separated from my son, but I did not worry about him. I knew that he would be cared for, even if I did not care for the people who cared for him. Later, when Farhan was in his twenties, I was able to make contact with him. He understood the circumstances and my predicament. Today he not only has a good relationship with me but also with the rest of my family.

The only people I really worried about were Amma and Abba. I sent money home regularly, but they still had no one to watch over them. I knew that my father was not well, and I thought that taking care of him would put a strain on my mother. Mostly I worried because there was nothing more important to Amma than being surrounded by family, and now her family was scattered. I imagined that she might grow depressed with only her quiet, ailing husband for company.

In 1974, after a short bout with cancer, my oldest sister passed away. Bilqees was in her early fifties, and although the bloom of youth had long since left her, her face still held traces of the attractive girl for whom Amma and Abba had once thrown the most beautiful Muslim wedding in Pur Qazi. Seeing a third child go before her was another cruel blow to my mother.

There was an unexpected bright side to this sudden loss. Because Bilqees' second husband had already passed, and her children were still teenagers at the time of her death, both she and her kids asked Amma and Abba if they would live with the kids until they were grown. My parents moved in with my teenage nieces and nephews. From Amma's letters, I could tell that this living arrangement once again filled her and Abba with a sense of purpose. Being surrounded by children gave her new energy, and I no longer worried that there was no one around to look out for my aging parents. Grandparents and grandchildren watched over each other. For Amma, it was further proof of the importance of family and a reliable refuge in the midst of trouble.

Meanwhile, I was discovering for the first time what a hole the absence of family could create. Though I missed my parents terribly, I was far from unhappy with my situation. The excitement of an American city was everything I had dreamed it would be.

Me, Farhan, Imran and Bernard

-27-

CABBIE

For me, living in Chicago was like living in a movie about utopia. The city seemed so clean, the life so uncomplicated, the people so interesting. I made many new friends, and it was much easier here to find people with open minds and a desire to improve the world. Chicago's many different ethnic foods were an entertainment in and of themselves. There was Chinese, Mexican, Greek, Italian, French and I could still get Pakistani/Indian food when I wanted a taste of home.

After I registered at the YMCA Community College, my next priority was finding a job to sustain myself in America and take care of my parents back home. I left them with enough money to take care of their needs for a few months, but I arrived in the United States with just $200. Because I had a student visa, I was not allowed to seek the kind of jobs that made use of the business experience I had gained in Pakistan. I would have to rely on odd jobs and slowly work my way back into the corporate world.

One week after I arrived in Chicago, I went to work in a factory as a machine operator. The job was messy, but what was worse was that I got stuck with a graveyard shift: 10:00 p.m. to 6:00 a.m. After a month, I quit and went to work for an office supplies manufacturer. Once again, it was not my business experience they were after; I worked as a packer in the shipping department. Even though it was a blue-collar job, the working conditions were better and so were the hours: 4:00 p.m. to midnight. For the next six months, my routine left little room for a private life. I went to school at six o'clock in the morning, finished classes just in time to hit the factory at four in the afternoon, and arrived back at my shared apartment at one in the morning, which gave me less than five hours of sleep before I headed out for school again. This routine lasted until the office supply company closed the second shift due to lack of business. They gave me the option to move to the day shift, but that would mean quitting school. I quit the job instead.

All my new friends thought I was foolish to leave my job. Finding work in 1974 was not easy. In a soft market, most foreigners could not expect to find jobs when Americans were going without. I knew that my friends were probably right, and I had no idea what I would do next. It seemed to me that if I quit school, my future would be even more limited than it had been in Pakistan. Why would anyone come to America to limit his life and give up on his dreams?

School was not going to pay the rent, and I still had to eat. After applying for several jobs and repeatedly hearing no, I began to despair. I watched for years as Amma turned despair into opportunity. Now it was my turn to prove that my mentor had taught me well by creating my own unexpected opportunity.

One evening, I was riding a bus home, staring out the window, letting my mind wander. The wheels turning beneath me and around me must have sent my mind spinning on the idea of the many kinds of transportation in Chicago. I thought of a conversation I had a few days after I arrived in the city.

That day, I had been waiting for a train and started chatting with a fellow passenger. I asked him for a few pointers on navigating my way through the city. He explained that Chicago is laid out on a grid, with the zero point downtown. Addresses are identified by south, north, east, and west, and the numbers indicate how many blocks a particular address is from the zero point. It seemed a simple layout and was easy to understand.

As I was staring out the window of the bus, a cab passed by, and I thought, "That's it. I'll be a cab driver. This is an easy city to navigate, and I have a driver's license. How hard could it be?"

When I told my new friends about my plan, they laughed and tried to discourage me. "You know nothing about the city. You haven't lived here long enough. No one will hire you. Even if they did, you wouldn't be able to find your way around, customers would yell at you, no one would tip you, and they'd fire you in a week. Don't waste your time."

"Maybe you're right," I said. "I still have trouble finding my way to any place besides school and destinations near my apartment."

I sat on a sagging second-hand couch in a sparsely furnished bachelor apartment and let my shoulders sink into the shape of the couch, but I wasn't ready for defeat. I sat up, thinking, it doesn't matter. I can't get any other job, so I have nothing to lose.

The next day, I went to the office of a Checker Cab Company to apply for a job. With an ongoing recession, most places would not give an interview on the spot, but I supposed that driving a taxi is a job of last resort for a lot of people. The manager agreed to come out to the outer office to talk to me. During our brief interview, he asked if I had a license.

"Yes, I have it right here." I pulled my driver's license out of my wallet and held it out to him.

He did not take it from me and barely glanced at it before he gave me a pitying smile. "That's not what I meant. You need a chauffeur's license to drive a cab."

"Where do I go to get a chauffeur's license?"

He raised an eyebrow. "Are you sure this is what you want to do? It doesn't sound like you've thought much about it."

"Yes, absolutely. I'm sure."

"Okay, here's what you do." He gave me the details on where I needed to go to apply and warned me that I would have to take a test.

"Thank you. I'll be back as soon as I get my license." I started to leave.

He called me back, "Hey, um, Zahir? How long have you lived in the city?"

"Six months."

He laughed even harder this time. "Do you even have a car?"

"No, but I've seen quite a bit of the city."

"So you say, but seeing it and driving it are two different things. You're from India?"

"Pakistan, actually."

"Right, Pakistan. So you're from Pakistan, you never lived in America until six months ago, and you've never driven a car in Chicago, America's number two city. What makes you think you'll be able to find your way to all the nooks and crannies of the two hundred square miles of this metropolis, plus the suburbs?"

I explained to him what I had learned about the city's grid-like layout. "I know if I'm ten blocks south of zero and five blocks east of zero, and someone wants me to take them to an address ten blocks north of zero and five blocks west of zero, I know I need to head twenty blocks north and ten blocks west."

He stared at me with his mouth open. "You seriously think you're going to be able to use your little mathematical formula to find your way around?"

"Well, I know it's not that simple, but I think it will help, and I'm a fast learner."

"Okay, okay. You seem like a smart guy, and I bet you probably could find your way around easily with just a little experience, but I can tell you right now, you're not going to be able to just walk out of here and get a chauffeur's license."

"Well, I have to try. I really need this job."

"I can see that. Just wait a minute, I'll be right back." He walked into his office and came back out with a handful of papers. "Go study this before you take that test. If you pass, come back and I'll give you a cab."

"Thank you," I said and pumped his hand. "Thank you very much, sir."

He chuckled. "Don't thank me yet."

As I left the building, I flipped through the papers he'd given me. It was an information packet that included addresses for various landmarks and popular spots around Chicago. Back at the apartment, I spent a couple of hours studying the list.

The next day, I went to the vehicle commissioner's office and took the test. As I started the exam, I instantly recognized the questions. I realized that the "information packet" the cab company manager had given me was actually a copy of the test with all the correct answers. I still happened to have those papers with me, so I took them out of my pocket and copied all the answers, while the young woman who had handed me the test watched. She could see exactly what I was doing but did not say a word until I handed her the completed exam.

She smiled and asked, "Do I need to check the answers?"

I simply smiled.

I passed the test.

A few days later, I returned to the Checker Cab Company to talk to the manager. He waved me into his office and asked, "So how'd you do on the test?"

I grinned. "I did great, thanks for your help." If he hadn't helped me, I never would have passed. I showed him my new chauffeur's license, and a short time later, he handed me the keys to a cab, just like that.

I quickly learned why my boss had said, "Don't thank me yet." He was not just referring to the fact that I had to pass the test. I had to experience driving complete strangers around a strange city. I spent much of my first few days on the road lost and disoriented, and a number of customers rolled their eyes or reacted with angry impatience. One or two raised their voices. At first, I did not know which areas were safe to cruise for fares or which drop-off points I should avoid.

The worst moment came quickly. I was robbed at gunpoint on the south side of Chicago. This was about as terrifying as I had imagined, yet there was not much to it. A passenger pulled out a gun, pointed it at the back of my head, and demanded all my money. I gave it to him without hesitation and said, "No problem. It's all yours." He hopped out of the cab and ran off.

When I told another cabbie what had happened to me, he did not look surprised. "Oh yeah, I don't take passengers in that area. I don't know anyone who does," he said.

"I wish someone had told me before."

"They probably figured you knew. Most drivers do."

Such was my introduction to "watching your back" in America. On the other hand, driving a cab taught me that most Americans really were as friendly and open as I had heard. Most of my passengers were polite and kind, and when I told them that I was new on the job, they were more than happy to give me directions to their destinations if they knew where to go, which most of them did. When I got lost, I took a few dollars off the fare, which helped to smooth over a few ruffled nerves.

Meanwhile, other cab drivers were nice enough to show me how to find addresses more quickly. As I had promised my boss, I quickly learned my way around the city and became an accomplished cab driver. In fact, it was a great way to immerse myself in the city of Chicago. Later, when I stopped driving a cab, I remained the person that friends turned to when they wanted the best, fastest, safest, or most scenic way to get somewhere.

I not only learned my way around the physical city but learned the culture. Some passengers liked to talk, and we often had conversations about the weather, sports, music, movies, politics, even relationships and family issues. It was as if I had added a class to my school schedule: American and Chicago Culture 101.

I got a lot of questions about my home country and culture, too. This was in the early days of the influx of Indian and Pakistani immigrants in America, so I was probably one of the first few people of Indian or Pakistani origin to drive a cab in Chicago. Many people enjoyed telling me about a local father-son cab driving team from India and asked if I knew them. I did not. Most people did not have any prejudice against me as a foreigner, and if they did, they kept those thoughts to themselves. America was a melting pot, and I was welcome as a guest, as a fellow human, or occasionally as a novelty.

I drove a cab for three years. In spite of my rocky start, it was a perfect job, as I was able to set my own hours to accommodate my school schedule. It provided me with almost twice the income I'd earned throwing office supply boxes around and for half the hours.

I soon realized that the YMCA Community College did not offer the level of education I was seeking or the prestige that was likely to help me find the best job offers in the future. Luckily, the classes were easy enough that I could earn top grades, which made it possible for me to transfer to the University of Illinois at Chicago. When I stepped into my first class at the UIC, I realized that all the colleges I had attended before and thought of as institutions of higher learning really were not. For the first time, my mind was not just challenged to pass tests but to think critically and to share my thoughts and questions with others.

There was still a lot of memorizing and regurgitating information, and I often sat in large classes where I felt like an insignificant drop of water in a giant pool, but I had a glimpse of higher thought, and it made me almost dizzy with excitement. This was the America that I had dreamed of, where I could live a life of the mind, and where I could at least hope to go as far as my effort could take me.

With my income from driving a cab, I was able to save enough money for the first semester's tuition at the UIC. After that, the university granted me a tuition waiver, which took a lot of pressure off. Though I was making more money as a cabbie than I had in my warehouse job, it was still a working-class income, and I was still sending money home to support my parents.

In the spring of 1975, my roommate, Maj went to Karachi to visit his family. I asked him to stop by and say hello to my folks. I still worried about them and was glad to know that my friend was going to look in on them, but most of the time, I was too busy with work, school, and my new social life to linger on my worries about family. Life was good.

The call of family became too loud to ignore. After Maj visited my parents and gave them news of me, he flew home with news of them.

I had known that my father was sick, so I should not have been surprised at what Maj told me. I rarely considered my parents' aging in terms of death, only in terms of loneliness, frailty, and illness. From what my friend told me, I could no longer avoid the specter of mortality. With one look at my father, Maj did not believe my father would last long.

In spite of all that my amma had suffered back when Abba was living alone in India and keeping his illness a secret from us, she had chosen a similar course. She had not wanted to worry me, believing that I had enough to worry about as I tried to forge a new life in America. In her letters, she carefully kept from me the news that Abba's health was rapidly failing.

I returned to Pakistan in June 1975, unsure whether I would make it home in time to say goodbye to my father.

-28-
ALVIDA ABBA JI

Amma Ji did not look surprised when I showed up unannounced. She said she had been expecting me. She knew that once my roommate returned from Pakistan and told me about my father's condition, it would not be long before I jumped on a plane bound for home. Maj had tried to prepare me with explanations of my father's weakened condition and how shrunken and dried-up he looked, closer to death than life. When Amma took me to his bedside, the sight of his sickly skin lying like a shroud over his bones, his eyes dulled, and his throat an open wound shocked me. His body looked lost under the sheets. He appeared both as ancient as something resurrected from a tomb and as tiny and vulnerable as a child.

Abba was suffering from throat cancer, also known as pharyngeal cancer. It can develop in the lower part of the throat, the back of the mouth and the tonsils, the middle of the throat, and the part of the throat behind the nose that leads to the lungs. Wherever his cancer had started, it was now in all those areas. Smoking, chewing tobacco, and drinking alcohol increase the chances of developing throat cancer, and he never did any of these. As a devout Muslim, he never touched a drop of alcohol, not even for medicinal purposes. His lifestyle carried no risk factors for throat cancer: he just had bad luck. After a lifetime of hard work and ill health, his body had succumbed to a shocking enemy.

When I arrived in Karachi, Abba had just finished another course of chemotherapy. At that point, the doctors were just going through the motions. After I saw him, I discussed his case with his specialist.

There was not much left to do. The doctor did not expect him to live long. The cancer had spread throughout his body, and even the chances of getting him well enough to live comfortably were not good. The chemotherapy was effectively killing the cancer at that point, only poisoning him. In his weakened condition, the treatment was prolonging and increasing his suffering.

I spoke to Amma. "I'm sorry, but I think we have to stop thinking about curing Abba and start thinking about how we can make him as comfortable as possible."

"Yes, I know," Amma said. "I only had to look at him to know, but it's good to hear you say it. I was afraid of making the wrong decision. Will you talk to his doctors for me? I know it's the right thing. I know we've done everything we can. I just don't think I can say the words."

I spoke with his medical team, and we all agreed to abandon the treatment so that Abba could pass on to the next world with as much peace and as little struggle as possible. We wanted him to feel embraced by the love of his family in his final hours instead of buried in a sick chemical haze.

Like many Indian couples of their generation—remember, Amma and Abba grew up in India—they had never publicly displayed their affection, even in front of their children. You had to look closely to see their love for each other, to see it in their shared glances, their light-hearted teasing, and how they consulted and supported each other in every decision. During those final days, as Amma and Abba prepared to say goodbye, it was if they had taken the clothes off of their deep love for each other and allowed me to see it naked. It was not that they hugged and kissed in front of me, but every gesture was heightened: every look, every glass of water, every sponge bath, and every word, which were few of those on Abba's part.

As weak as Abba was, it was difficult for him to talk, and with cancer taking over his throat, the painful growths made it almost impossible. He rarely said more than two words, but he never uttered a single complaint. Instead, he smiled—not the strained smile of someone trying to convince you that he is okay but a smile of genuine contentment. Whenever I asked him how he was feeling, he raised his finger and pointed toward the sky. I knew that he was thinking something he had often said to me: "It's all from Allah." Abba knew he didn't have much longer to live, but his faith told him that this world was just a transition and the pain he was experiencing would be worth it when he found what was waiting for him on the other side.

One day, he was feeling slightly better, or maybe he found enough courage to deal with the pain of saying a few words. As I sat next to him, he told me that he was worried about Amma.

"Zahir, you know I'll be leaving this world very soon. I'm ready to meet Allah, so I'm not worried for myself, but I am concerned about your mother. You know how Amma always tried so hard all our working lives to save and plan ahead, but I was never that way. Now Amma will be alone, and I'm leaving her with no saving on which to live on. What will happen to her?"

I could not believe it. Perhaps the disease had robbed him of his power of reasoning. If he had been able to think rationally, he would have realized that they did not have any financial problem while he had not earned any money for at least fifteen years. I was not as stunned by that as I was by the power of his love for Amma. Whatever strength he had left, he spent on his wife and was concerned on her well being while he is gone. They shared a strong bond of love, even if it was mostly unspoken, and he believed as a man it was his duty to care for the woman he loved, his wife, my mother.

I took his thin hand in mine and said, "Abba Ji, don't worry, Amma has a lot of money." This wasn't strictly true. "A lot" was an exaggeration, but seeing his confused state, I knew it would be too complicated to explain that I had been taking care of them for years and would continue to do so for Amma. I did not want to destroy his illusion that he had been the one taking care of her until now.

Though he had forgotten many things, some stubborn part of his brain had not forgotten that Amma had no savings. Weak as it was, his voice had the strength of adamant conviction. "No, Zahir, you don't understand: Amma has no money."

I did not want to upset him with an argument. I called my mother into the room to join us and explained Abba's concern.

Amma laughed, sat on the edge of the bed, and put a hand on his shoulder. "Abba, I do have money. Remember, I was always good about setting some money aside. I have continued to do this. I have more than you think. Do not worry about me. Rest now, okay?"

Amma and I understood each other. We told Abba the part of the truth he needed to know and let go of the rest. This was how Amma and I gave him our final gifts of love, by letting him know he had done his best and it had been good enough, and that thanks to him, we had nothing to worry about. This was truer than we could express. Abba's years of gentle patience, hard work, and attention to family life had contributed to making me the man I was: the kind of man who could and would now take care of Amma.

Amma and Abba had always shown real devotion to each other, in good times and bad, as all young brides and grooms promise, but nobody really knows what bad times will be like until they happen. I was impressed to see Amma's love and care for my father during the hardest times of all, those days of his slow slide out of this world. She was by his side twenty-four hours a day and spent most of the time sitting next to his bed with the holy Quran and a box of tissue. The seeping wound that his throat had become required constant cleaning; in between, she recited verses to him from the Quran, trying to make him feel peaceful as he journeyed to the next world. When they were first married she had not been able to read the holy book that meant so much to her, not with any understanding. She had learned much since then, and though conservative Muslims feared that educating women could lead them off the righteous path, knowledge had only clarified her belief. She understood the wisdom in the book she read and was happy to be able to share it with her husband as a true partner.

After three weeks, I had to leave my mother alone with her nursing task. I could not afford to take more time from school and work, or I could lose my visa and slide down the ladder I had worked so hard to climb. My parents understood. As I took my father's hand and kissed him goodbye, I knew it was for the last time, and so did he. He smiled and told me he was glad that I came.

"You're a good son. You've made me proud. I'm glad we had a chance to say goodbye. Someday we'll be together again, you'll see." His breathing was ragged, his voice raspy, and it hurt me to see him suffer with the effort to share this loving blessing with me. Before I left him, I bowed my head and silently prayed to God to take mercy on him and end his misery soon. I did not want my father to die, and I was not a very religious Muslim, but my parents' deepest beliefs were ingrained in me. I knew without a doubt that death would take Abba Ji to a better place, free of suffering and pain.

I was the only one of my parents' children who did not live in Pakistan. Sajida spent a lot of time with Abba at the end, and although Tayab and Mutahir had never been as close to our parents as Sajida and me, they were good sons and they visited often. Tayab traveled from not too far across town; Mutahir traveled 125 miles every other week. Salim and Kalim still thought of Abba as the only father they'd ever known, and they spent as much time as they could by his bedside. Before Abba died, we all showed him how deeply he was loved.

Abba passed away on August 25, 1975, six weeks after my departure. I never got over the nagging guilt that I should have been there, but Amma insisted, "You were. You were here when he needed you here. You were here to say goodbye when he could still tell you goodbye. He knew you loved him."

When he was young, Mohammad Hanif Kazmi had sometimes exasperated Jamila Kazmi with his lengthy, lazy visits to the mango groves, leaving her alone with her children and her schemes to advance her family's standing in the world. At the age of seventy-five, he left her alone again with her family and whatever schemes she might yet have up her sleeves. This time she was not exasperated at him for being absent, only sad at the prospect of spending the rest of her life without the man who had balanced her energy and determination with his quiet, unassuming nature. His had been a generous love. In a world where women were often been devalued, he had supported her efforts to blossom into the full person she was born to be. He had been a good husband, a good father, and a dear friend.

Two people who live in sync with each other cannot avoid growing together, and though Amma remained fully herself her whole life, Abba must have left some piece of himself with her after he died. She was as feisty as ever, but there now was also a quiet and reflective quality about her that felt like Abba. Perhaps it was a gift he left behind for her as a reminder not to forget him until they meet again.

In 1976, Mutahir moved to Dubai. When Amma mentioned this news in a letter, I was surprised. He had what appeared to be a good-paying job with Pakistan's Water and Power Development Authority, and though he was not rich, he and his family lived in comfortable style in Karachi. "Foreign fever" was running through Pakistan, and many people were seduced by the promise of better economic opportunities in other countries. It was trendy to leave the country in search of a better dream.

The younger generation often headed to Western Europe and America to pursue higher education and careers in health care. Meanwhile, the Middle East was experiencing a boom in good-paying jobs, both skilled and unskilled, and many Pakistanis employed in the private sector were seeking better jobs there. The advantage of going to the Middle East was its proximity to Pakistan, which was just two hours away by air.

Amma was living by herself and, in the end, was forced to sell the house. The tenants who lived on the second floor refused to move, and Pakistan has property rules similar to Manhattan's rent control. Once you rent out any portion of your house, it is almost impossible to raise the rent to receive fair market value. It was not worth it for Amma to hold onto the house. She finally sold it for less than market value and moved into a smaller place. She gave most of the proceeds from the house sale to charity, with the exception of a small portion she set aside to go on another hajj.

I wrote Amma regularly and phoned when I could. Every time she wrote or spoke to me, she asked the same question. "When are you coming home, Zahir? You know there's no need to stay away anymore. All that old trouble is over with." She did not understand that I had learned to enjoy the freedom and excitement, the education and like-minded friends, the modern ideas and sense of being part of something I had discovered in America. She did not know that America had become my home. She only knew that she was lonely and assumed I must be, too, being so far from family and from what she now thought of as home.

I would have liked to at least visit more often, but my student visa made it hard for me to leave the country, even for a short visit.

I graduated from the University of Illinois in 1977 and soon became a Certified Public Accountant. My new employers, Philip Stone and Howard Shapiro, were impressed with my work abilities and my enthusiasm for America, and they agreed to sponsor me in applying for a permanent visa. By December 1980, my application was approved, and my status in America changed from "student" to "permanent resident."

Amma Ji did not understand why I would want to live away from home permanently. She was sure that as soon as I found the right girl and got married, I would want to settle down and have a family—back home. She knew she had made a mistake in choosing a wife for me the first time, but she thought she understood me better now and would do a better job the second time.

"Amma, I don't need you to find a wife for me."

"Have you already had luck in finding one yourself?"

"No, not yet, but when I'm ready . . ."

"When it's the right girl, you'll be ready. I understand that you're an intelligent, educated young man, and I've found a woman who will be a much better match for you. Look, I won't try to tell you who to marry this time, I promise. I am only asking that you meet her. If you don't like her, you don't have to marry her."

I continued trying to discourage her, but I knew that Amma would not take no for an answer. "Okay, next time I come home for a visit I'll meet her, but I'm not promising anything."

I was determined that this time I would not let Amma persuade me.

-29-

SECOND ARRANGED MARRIAGE

In 1981, when I flew to Pakistan to see my mother, Amma saw it as my journey from lonely exile to marital bliss. Like me, my mother was determined not to make the same mistake twice, but her idea of correcting the past was different from mine. I had promised myself never to agree to an arranged marriage again and to instead allow my love life to take a natural course. Amma had promised herself to research my future bride more carefully so that my happiness wouldn't be left to chance.

When I arrived, Amma asked me to take her on a string of family visits. I couldn't say no. Family was always her top priority, and now that she lived alone, she had fewer opportunities to visit relatives. I would have preferred to just quietly visit with Amma, Sajida, Ather, and their children. It was not that I hated visiting our relatives, I just found it exhausting.

I noticed that Kalim, my nephew/brother, could not resist teasing me over and over again, saying, "You're becoming such an American."

"What makes you say that? I'm still the same person."

"No. You've changed."

"In what way?"

"Whenever you talk about America, you brag about it as if it's your own country. You talk about how great the conveniences are, how great the people are, how exciting the city is, how comfortable your lifestyle is."

"I'm sorry. I hope it doesn't sound like I'm bragging. I just like it a lot. Americans work hard, and most of them seem honest and helpful. So many people I meet care about what's happening in their government or in their community. They seem to have a strong sense of justice, of treating each other fairly."

"You see! That's what I mean. It's like you think these Americans can do no wrong. They're not so perfect, you know? They just think they are."

"You've never been there. What makes you so eager to find fault with them?"

"Maybe I've never been there, but I know enough to think Pakistani society is much better than American society."

"Why?"

"In America, everyone drinks alcohol, and I know that alcohol is evil. If you look closely, you'll see how alcohol and drugs are the root of all problems in society."

"Even worse than the corruption that pervades Pakistan, without any help from alcohol?"

"Corruption is a small problem compared to alcohol."

"I'm sorry, Kalim, but I think your views are naïve, but, if that's the basis of your judgment, then I guess you're right. I have become an American. I don't think alcohol is the root cause of social problems. It's a personal decision. The people in the countries that dominate the world, lead in education, and take care of their people all consume alcohol openly. You assume it is bad not from personal experience but because our religion bans it, and you accept it, but corruption is a disease that eats up a society. It has become so entrenched in the Pakistani way of doing things that everyone accepts it as normal. You cannot see that? Pakistanis believe that as long as they blindly follow religious rules that make them good people. They have forgotten the difference between right and wrong."

Many other relatives were curious about America, and answering their questions could be exhausting. Aside from Kalim, most of them did not challenge me so seriously.

One day, Amma asked me to take her to visit some distant cousins, but she did not warn me that I would face an audience with an agenda.

Despite my repeated admonitions not to do so, Amma set up this visit because she met the cousin's daughter at a few family gatherings, inquired about her, and was convinced that she was perfect for me.

Shahana seemed to be nice and tried to ask intelligent questions about America in an effort to engage me in conversation. Even so, her parents did most of the talking, as was expected on a visit like this. They wanted to know about U.S. politics, whether I knew a lot of Americans, and whether I knew a Pakistani friend of theirs who had also moved to Chicago. Of course, they were curious about my job.

They were nice people, although not very educated. Their daughter seemed pleasant and sociable. She had a bachelor's degree and was working as a teacher. She did not seem overly conservative, but beyond that, I knew nothing about her, and there was little chance of finding anything out. I did not try to learn much. I was not going to let Amma convince me to accept another arranged bride.

On the ride home in the cab, Amma could barely contain her excitement as she smiled up into my face. "So, Zahir, what did you think of Shahana?"

I compressed my lips in frustration. "I don't know, Amma. There wasn't much chance for us to talk or for me to get to know her. She seemed nice enough."

"She's not so formal, did you notice? She seems more relaxed, more open, more smiling and friendly."

"Yes, Amma she seemed to be outgoing and less conservative, but that alone isn't enough on which to base a whole relationship. I've already told you that I don't want to marry."

"Zahir, be realistic. You must marry sooner or later. You can't stay alone forever. How will I die with any peace if I know you're alone?"

"Amma, in America people don't all get married so young."

"You're not so young, Zahir. You're already thirty-six. Many men your age have grownup children."

"I don't want to marry the wrong person again just because of some idea that I have to get married. I think it's important to know a person before marrying."

"Yes, and don't they have a high divorce rate in America?"

"That's my point Amma. They have the freedom not to be stuck in a bad relationship."

"But you're not American, Zahir. How will you find a wife there who will understand you the way a Pakistani woman can? And Shahana is not just anyone. I really spent some time getting to know her, Zahir. She is a sweet girl. I know you better now, and I know she's the right girl for you . . ."

On and on she went until something else occurred to me. Amma worried about me being alone, but as I listened to her voice in the quiet of her house, I realized that I was worried about her being alone. She was almost seventy-six years old, and I did not want her to spend her later years by herself. She would need care and companionship in her declining years, and by unspoken agreement, I had become the family member who watched out for her. I had changed too much and became too westernized to ever consider returning to Pakistan. That meant that Amma would have to come to America to live with me.

I knew that she would not agree to make the trip and stay with me unless I had a family; she was too traditional to accept any less, and I felt certain that if I took an American wife, Amma would be very unhappy living with us. My mother spoke no English, had no interest in learning English, and was unlikely to change her mind about that at this late stage. She would be appalled at the casual ways of American women and might even consider them disrespectful. I could imagine how unhappy she would be living with an American daughter-in-law.

I convinced myself that the only way I was going to be able to properly care for Amma and make her comfortable in her old age was to marry a Pakistani girl. Although I had a few Pakistani friends, I did not run in Pakistani circles in Chicago, so there was little chance of my finding a Pakistani bride except in Pakistan, and there was little chance of meeting an eligible Pakistani woman without Amma's help. If the purpose was to make my mother happy, what better choice than the woman for whom my mother had already shown a preference?

I had stopped listening to Amma, who was still extolling the virtues of marriage. Without preamble, I interrupted. "You're right, Amma. It's time I got married. There's no reason to wait. If you like Shahana, I'm sure I will, too. I'll be happy to marry her."

Maybe I really believed my rationale, or maybe I just convinced myself because I was tired of resisting my mother's wishes. Whatever the reason, I was committed and that was that. Once I gave my approval, Amma wasted no time in contacting the girl's family with a marriage proposal, and they accepted our proposal without delay. After that, everything happened very quickly. I had to return to America to get back to work, so the wedding would have to be soon. I called my employers and extended my stay for another two weeks. Shahana and I were married a week later. We had only a few days together as a married couple before I returned to America alone.

It would take another six months to finalize her paperwork to come to the United States. I would have six months among my friends to realize that somewhere along the way I had become as American as I was Pakistani. Like any American, I wanted to wait to find the right woman on my own, and getting married just to please my mother was the stupidest thing I'd ever done. Twice.

I knew that if I had held my ground and refused to marry, my mother would have ultimately accepted my decision, just as she had accepted my decision to divorce Zaiba and move to America. As I prepared my apartment for the arrival of the stranger who was now my wife and contemplated another loveless marriage, I knew that I had only myself to blame. At the same time, I was determined to sincerely give my best to make this marriage work.

When I had left Pakistan in 1973, the commotion over my divorce from my first wife, the death of my sister Bilqees, which left her children orphans, and Abba's failing health had kept Amma occupied for a few years. After Abba passed away, she was alone for the first time in her life. She had lots of time to spare, which was probably why she worked so hard to find me a bride. Family had always been her priority, and without someone to take care of, some tie to strengthen, or some broken family bond to mend, Amma did not know what to do with herself.

After she found me a bride, the problem of what she could do grew worse. Amma might not be as physically strong as she once was, but she was still in vigorous health for a woman of her age, and she thrived on activity. After Abba's death, she became more involved in religious activities, helping at the community center, joining women's prayer groups, and attending meetings of Jamat-e-Islami. Jamat-e-Islami was a political party, but the group was actively involved in religious and social activities. Amma attended meetings about improving social welfare in Karachi.

She took almost no interest in politics anymore and had not since the days of the national partition. Seeing India's struggle for freedom devolve into a religious civil war may have soured her on politics, or maybe being closer to life's end, when she would be rewarded for her good deeds, had increased her religious fervor.

Amma had always been devout, but even Allah could not fill the hole in her life left by all the children and grandchildren who were now grown and gone. She did not complain often, but occasionally she told me of her surprise at finding herself alone in her house. In the culture she grew up in, living alone in one's old age was unheard of. She was used to the joint family system, which was still common in Pakistan but not practiced uniformly.

Tayab and his family lived in the same city as Amma, but she had no relationship with his wife and therefore did not know their children very well. Tayab visited her whenever he found time, but the rest of his family rarely came. Since Mutahir and his family had lived in a distant city even before they moved to Dubai, she had never gotten to know those grandchildren well, either. Amma was never with them for more than couple of days. The only grandkids who spent much time with her—with the exception of Kalim and Salim, who were more like her own sons—were Sajida's children. Amma adored them, and they loved spending time with her. Unfortunately, Sajida's husband Ather was transferred to Islamabad. With that, Amma was effectively alone.

When Shahana moved to Chicago in late 1981, my sister Sajida and her family had already started the process of moving from Islamabad. The USAID department, where Sajida's husband worked, was leaving Pakistan. As part of the severance packages, USAID offered immigrant visas to all employees who wished to migrate to America. Ather knew that he would never find another job in Pakistan that paid nearly as well.

He called and asked me for my opinion. Did I think that he would be able to find work in America? Ather Bahi, as I affectionately called him, was already in his fifties and had never worked in the private sector, so I warned him that the chances of finding a high-paying job weren't good.

"You won't be able to maintain as comfortable a lifestyle as you had in Pakistan. You'll probably have to struggle, but your children will get one of the finest educations in the world, and their future opportunities will be wide open."

"That's important to consider," Ather said.

My sister and her kids moved to America first, and Ather stayed at Islamabad's USAID office until the last possible moment. Most of his colleagues went to New York, but Ather Bahi and Sajida chose Chicago.

I expected that Amma would inevitably come to America, but it was almost uncanny how all the pieces began falling into place to drive her in that direction. It felt like destiny. When I called and wrote to my mother, the inevitable conversation asserted itself—we no longer spoke about *if* she would move to the United States but when we should start the process of moving her to the United States.

"Apparently it's part of Allah's plan for my life," she said on the phone. "I've known for a long time that I would come to America to live with you, sooner or later."

"You never mentioned that before," I said.

"I didn't think I needed to. Didn't you know it?"

"Yeah, I guess I did. You'll like America, Amma. You'll see."

"Hmm." She sounded skeptical. "I'll let you know how I like it when I get there. Anyway, now that Sajida will be there, I can live with her."

"You're welcome to live with Shahana and me."

"Yes, I know, but you're newlyweds, and Sajida will be all alone until Ather leaves his job. It will be better this way. Anyway, Sajida has already invited me."

Though it made sense, I wondered how much of her decision was based on the fact that, like me, she was not sure Shahana would be the right fit for her.

Sajida moved to Chicago in late 1982, and Amma arrived around the same time. Ather Bahi came to visit a couple of times, but it took another year before USAID in Islamabad finally shut down, allowing him to join his family. His family had tucked away as much savings as they could, and now they would just have to do their best and hope that they invested wisely in the future of their children simply by being in America.

We were all excited at the prospect of living near each other again. We had always been the closest members of the family. I had the best of both worlds: living in my home of choice with my favorite people from my home of origin.

If Amma felt culture shock on her arrival in America, she did not show it. She looked around with curiosity and kept an open mind, waiting to develop an impression.

"What do you think of Chicago, Amma?" I asked.

"Don't rush me," she said. "I have to get used to it."

This was the third migration of her life: first from India to Pakistan with five young kids, then from Sialkot to Karachi to follow me, and now a real sea change. Once again, she left behind her country, her culture, and the people she had known all her life, but this change was even greater than those before. The language was different, the culture was different, and the religion was different. She had never been any place as foreign as the United States.

I watched Amma for signs of stress or depression but saw nothing but calm serenity. She spent hours reading the Quran, and once she found that spiritual center, she seemed fine. She went about her business within the family sphere and didn't venture far from home without us.

Watching Amma's adjustability through a lifetime of turmoil, I should not have been surprised, but she always impressed me. I was now old enough to understand how stressful the moves from India to Pakistan must have been. Now she was nearly eighty years old. I knew that even I had become comfortable living in my bubble of Chicago life. Even in the jungle, animals stay in their own territories and rarely venture outside those habitats. When they do, they undoubtedly sense that it will not be easy to survive.

Amma did it willingly, because her children had and because family came first. Amma understood that putting family first didn't always come easy. This was a lesson I would have to learn the hard way as I adjusted to my Pakistani family, old and new, that now surrounded me in the territory I previously had all to myself in Chicago.

Bilal

-30-

BILAL

A mma liked living in Chicago, but it's not as if she explored the city. As always, her life was family life. She lived with my sister Sajida and her family and came to stay with Shahana and me for short visits. She liked to come with us whenever we got together with friends who had someone around who was close to her age, especially if they were Pakistani. Amma was comfortable as long as she was with somebody from her generation, someone who was familiar with her time, if not her home, or someone who also lived with the changes of dislocation.

As she had when she moved from India to Pakistan, Amma took notice of those new ideas that seemed sensible to her and embraced them. When we took her into the city for shopping or lunch, she nodded and smiled at the young people who waited on her. "These Americans are so friendly, even though I'm a foreigner."

"So you like Americans, Amma Ji?" I asked.

She nodded slowly, thinking. "You know what I like about Americans? They work hard, and they're so honest. Their government and their businesses don't have the corruption that we have in Pakistan, do they?"

"They still have it, Amma Ji, but no, not as much."

"I wonder how they manage it."

Amma arrived with an open mind, prepared to observe first and judge later. She watched, read, and asked questions, and in the end, she developed a reasonably informed opinion of America. She did not judge people based on religion, race, or culture, and she remained more open to new ideas than many younger Pakistanis who had lived in America for a long time. They took advantage of all the opportunities of freedom, equality, and economic opportunity that America offered, but complained about the free-thinking, aggressive, individualistic attitudes, and beliefs of Americans. They complained that Americans put themselves first and God and family second.

Amma did not see it that way. She did not think that Americans were worshipping themselves but simply approaching the means to their ends in a different way. "I see why you wanted to stay here, Zahir," she once told me. "This really is a land of opportunity. In India and Pakistan, even with hard work, it was difficult to get ahead, but here, if you're willing to work hard, no one will try to stand in your way."

She loved her religion and her relationship with God, but it never occurred to her to think that other people were wrong for not believing as she believed. "They're just different people. If they had grown up in India, they might think more like me, but they grew up in America, so they think like Americans."

Though she never commingled with ordinary Americans, it was not because of prejudice. A woman of her age was unprepared to absorb or participate in a new culture. Language was the biggest barrier of all.

Amma's family circle was enough to absorb her attention. By the standards of the world she came from, she was an intellectually liberated woman, but God, family, and home still came first for her. She kept herself busy by reciting from the holy Quran twice a day, studying other books about Islam, watching Indian movies with her daughter and son-in-law, and doting on her grandkids when they came home from school.

If anything in America shocked her, it was the sexual openness she saw on TV. Someone once asked Amma what she thought about her new adoptive country, and she said, "America is a very nice country. The only part I do not like is the nudity. It certainly not a country based on the values God has given us in the holy Quran." The subject didn't come up often, and usually Amma simply changed the channel.

Unfortunately, she could not change the channel when it came to witnessing my marriage, which had already started to deteriorate before she arrived on the scene. My relationship with Shahana had become a checkered pattern of arguments and silences. Amma visited us often enough that she could not help noticing. It is possible that my second marriage finally changed her mind about arranged marriages. After she came to America, she conceded, "I suppose there are advantages to doing your own choosing."

As two Pakistani women, it would seem that Amma and Shahana would have common interests to tie them together, but cultural and family ties did not dictate the course of their relationship. Shahana's extreme moods did. Shahana could be loving and welcoming but could quickly turn into a block of ice. Unwilling to ride the tides of her daughter-in-law's ever-changing emotions, Amma Ji spent most of her time at Sajida's house. When she visited us, she and Shahana did not argue but barely acknowledged each other. Amma never seemed to relax into the furniture at my house but remained rigid and tense, as if ready for a fight at any moment. Shahana did not have a job, so when I went to work for the day, Amma spent most of the day in her room until I returned from the office.

The tension did not lift when I came home. The uncomfortable atmosphere was not because Amma was there. Shahana carried negativity with her wherever she went, like a disease. It seemed to me that this woman could not stand happiness.

I should have seen the signs before she came to America. For the first several months of our marriage, she lived in Pakistan, and I had hoped that the tension that emanated from her resulted from being newlyweds, forced to live thousands of miles apart.

When she came to America, I had my first inkling that the physical distance that separated us was not our only problem. I tried to shrug off her moods, thinking that she was just nervous about leaving behind her life in Pakistan, but over time, her moods only grew worse. When we went out, she was excited, dressing up, putting on makeup, and talking a mile a minute about what a great time we were going to have. She laughed and had a good time. Suddenly, as if someone turned a switch, something I said or did would set her off. She would start poking at me with angry comments. I never let her provoke me into arguing in public, but when we got home, we had it out.

I think she liked these fights, though she would not admit it. They seemed to release the tension that I had seen churn inside her. After the arguments, she was so relaxed and calm. It was like the way a drug addict might act after going through withdrawal and then getting a hit of their drug of choice.

She got pregnant. This made her unhappy, as children were not on her agenda. Some Pakistani people thought Americans were all about "me, me, me," but Shahana really was all about her. She did not try to hide her frustration that having a child would make life difficult. She'd get fat, she already had enough to do taking care of the house, it was hard enough dealing with a husband, and now she would have to deal with a child.

After my son, Bilal, was born on February 22, 1983, Shahana showed no interest in motherhood.

In Pakistan, when a child is born, the parents perform a ritual called *aqiqa*, in which they sacrifice a goat, give away the meat to the poor, and turn the whole thing into a party for family and friends. On the day of Bilal's *aqiqa*, Sajida, her family, and my mother came over to pick Shahana and me up for the party, but while they were waiting for us in the car, Shahana decided that she could not bear seeing a lot of people.

"I'm not going," she said.

I'd seen her like this before, and I knew that if I got angry, it would only make things worse. I tried to speak calmly. "Shahana, there are over more than hundred guests waiting for us."

"I know. That's the problem. I can't face them. I'm tired, I'm depressed. I don't want to go."

"I'm sorry you're tired, Shahana. I'm sorry you're depressed, but we have guests waiting for us. You and I both planned this party and invited everyone. We have to go. If you won't do it for me, do it for Bilal."

"No. I won't do it, I tell you, not for anyone."

I gave up. I was tired, tired of going through this. "Okay, you're not going to go, but one of us has to, so I'm going. I have no choice." I went downstairs to the car.

"Where's Shahana?" my sister asked.

"She's not coming. Let's go."

"What do you mean, she's not coming?"

"I mean just what I said. She doesn't want to come. She's not feeling well, so we'll have to go without her."

Sajida turned to Ather. "Wait here. You wait here, too, Zahir. I'll talk to her."

I sighed. "Forget it, Sajida. It won't help. You'll only make her angry."

Sajida was gone several minutes before she came back to the car with her lips pursed. "Let's wait fifteen minutes."

Later, Sajida told me what she had said to Shahana: "Let me tell you something. If you want your marriage to last, you better get up and come to the party. If you want to insult your husband inside the privacy of your home, that's your business, but do not insult him in front of all his friends. If you don't go and you let him be humiliated, do not expect him to come back the same person. After that, you can be sure that he won't care anymore. If you want this marriage to last, you better get up from that chair and come downstairs in the next five minutes."

After a few minutes, Shahana joined us in the car. She smiled, laughed, and played the part of the perfect hostess. Her cheerfulness was unnerving.

She never did bond with Bilal. When he was barely a month old, I saw her spank him because he would not eat, and we had an argument over it. Another time, I saw her shake him because she could no longer stand his crying. I took Bilal away from her, comforting him until he calmed down.

After I put him in his crib, I came back into the living room. "What's wrong with you?!" I said angrily. "You never, ever shake a small baby like that!"

"You don't know how hard it is! You're not here with him all the time!"

"That's no excuse. You cannot shake or hit a baby."

"If you think it's so easy, then you take care of him."

"I don't think it's so easy, but I think you're right. He's not safe with you. From now on, you don't touch our baby. I'll take care of him. From today, he's not your responsibility."

"How will you do that, when you're working all day?"

"I'll ask my mother to come live with us. She'll take care of the baby when I'm not here."

"Great. Yet another person in the house."

"Don't worry. You won't have to take care of anyone. Amma will take care of Bilal, and I'll take care of Amma."

That night, I called Amma and asked her to come live with us. I explained to her that I needed her help. She did not ask any questions, only said, "Of course, Zahir. I'd love to help take care of that sweet little boy."

Amma Ji and I became a team again. We took over raising Bilal. Shahana and Amma lived in the same house but barely interacted with each other. When I was not there, Amma took care of Bilal. The rest of the time, whenever he was wet or hungry, or whenever he was curious or wanted something, he came to me first. When we visited friends, and he needed to go to the washroom or was hungry, he always came to me. He had become used to that routine at home. There were times his mother seemed embarrassed by this, loudly telling Bilal that she would take care of whatever he needed, but Bilal told her, "No, my Daddy will do it."

The closest thing my son had to a mother was my mother. Amma shared a bedroom with Bilal. She rocked him when he woke from bad dreams. She fed him in the wee hours after her dawn prayers with one of the bottles I had prepared the night before. Before I went to work, I bathed him and gave him breakfast, and Amma assumed responsibility for Bilal the rest of the day while Shahana took care of the house, shopped, went out with friends, or watched TV. When Bilal was old enough to talk, he would lift his hands toward Amma, grinning with anticipation, saying, "Amma, Amma."

Bilal became the center of Amma's world, and he responded in kind. As he grew older, whenever we were around other people, in parks, restaurants, or department stores, he always gravitated toward grandmotherly women, surely because they reminded him of Amma. When he was two, I started taking him to day care, and on the way, we stopped at McDonalds for breakfast. We almost always saw the same small group of elderly women gathered at a table. Every day, he walked to their table and greeted them with a smile.

"Hi Grandma!" he said to them.

"Hello, Bilal!" they said back.

Everyone loved Bilal. Maybe his mother did, too, but she never showed it.

That was the beginning of the end for Shahana and me. Seeing her neglect Bilal only made me feel more distant. Now that Amma was living with us, she could also see that my marriage to Shahana was a disaster. When we argued, Amma gave us a sad look, picked up Bilal, and carried him to another room.

In 1984, Shahana found an ally when Mutahir and his family followed the rest of our extended family to Chicago. Mutahir's wife, Huma, immediately hit it off with Shahana. Until Huma arrived, though Amma and Shahana did not have much of a relationship, they tolerated each other without incident. The sisters-in-law started confiding in each other. I am not sure what they talked about, but within weeks of Huma's arrival, Shahana's attitude towards Amma changed.

One day, she told me that she wanted Amma out of the house.

"I feel like I have no place of my own, Zahir. She runs everything. I have no privacy, and you have more of a relationship with her than with me. It's her or me!"

"Who will take care of Bilal?"

"He's in day care now when you're at work, so we don't need her anymore."

I was angry, but I seemed to have no choice. I knew Shahana would push until she got her way. It was just how she was built. For Amma's sake as much as mine, I knew that my mother had to go. I thanked her for her help with Bilal but told her I thought it would be easier for everyone if she moved back in with Sajida.

When Amma left, my relationship with Shahana grew worse, and in the fall of 1984, she filed for divorce.

As a father I knew that I had very little chance of gaining sole custody of Bilal. I offered Shahana a generous settlement in exchange for liberal visitation rights, but she refused to settle out of court. As it turned out, Bilal and I were lucky that she turned down the settlement offer, because I had no idea of the extent that Shahana would go to until we separated. Once she turned down my settlement offer, I decided to fight for custody of Bilal. I was convinced my son was not safe with her.

At first, the court awarded us joint custody, but Shahana made it difficult for me to see Bilal. I was not able to pick up my son because she was never home at the agreed-upon, court-ordered time. Shahana often stayed away from the house for extended periods, leaving me with no idea where she and Bilal had gone.

Amma became sad and fretful. She often had tears in her eyes when we talked. "How can that woman use her own child as a weapon? If she keeps this up, she's going to ruin Bilal's life. Anyone can see that you're a good father, Zahir, and that this woman is not fit to take care of a child. How can the court let this happen?"

One day, Shahana disappeared with Bilal, and I could not trace them for days. I lost many hours of work and sleep. I called around and drove around, searching for them. I knew Shahana and Huma were friends and co-conspirators, and I had a gut feeling that Shahana was at Mutahir's house. I asked Amma to call Mutahir and ask if he knew the whereabouts of Bilal and his mother.

I sat at Sajida's kitchen table and watched Amma make the call. As she talked to Mutahir, she shook her head at me. "He says he has no idea where Shahana is. He says he hasn't seen or spoken to her or Bilal in a long time."

I called all of Shahana's friends. Nothing.

My mind kept returning to Huma. I did not trust her. I knew that Shahana had convinced everyone, including herself, that I was the bad guy in our relationship, and I believed that Huma was a crafty manipulator. I imagined that Shahana might have convinced Huma to hide her, and in turn, Huma might have convinced Mutahir to help conceal Shahana's whereabouts.

After a week, I decided to go to Mutahir's house unannounced. When Mutahir opened the door, I saw Bilal running around behind him. Even though I had had my suspicions, I was still shocked and disappointed, saddened to know that my own brother would lie to our mother about something like this. The moment Bilal saw me, his face lit up, and he ran toward me, calling, "Daddy!" He leapt into my arms. I cradled him, turned around, and left.

I renewed my fight for full custody of Bilal. It was expensive and time-consuming, but in the end, the court decided in my favor. Although Amma did not move back in with me, Bilal spent every weekend with her and Sajida at Sajida's home. Sajida's children—Naila, Sohaila, and Ahsan—adored Bilal. They never tired of entertaining him and taking care of him. Meanwhile, Bilal's grandmother and aunt became the most important female forces in his life. With them, he found the love and affection he never received from his mother.

One day as Bilal stood in Sajida's kitchen, he asked her, "Can I call you mom instead of *phooppo* (aunt)?"

Sajida smiled and hugged him. "It's okay with me, but let's ask your father."

Part of me didn't mind, but I told Bilal. "No, Bilal, you have your mother. You should call your phooppo Phooppo." I was grateful to my sister for showing my son the generous affection of a mother.

Meanwhile, Bilal and Amma developed a bond much closer than she had with her other grandchildren, who had more-attentive mothers and did not need as much from her. Whenever I went to Sajida's house with Bilal, I saw how Amma's eyes followed him everywhere. When Amma visited people, I often saw her pull out the picture of Bilal she had tucked into whatever book she was reading and show it to them.

One day, when Bilal was four, we were driving to a picnic with friends when Bilal said, "Abboo "(Dad), can I ask you a question?"

"Go ahead, Bilal."

"Why did you marry my mother?"

The question caught me off guard.

I was still trying to think of the best way to answer when he said, "Abboo, I think you made a mistake."

"You don't think I should have married her?"

"No."

"Why do you think that?"

"Abboo, you and my mother are too different."

I nodded. "You're right, Bilal. You're very smart."

I sometimes wondered if I'd ever find the right woman, but as I drove in the car with my son that day, I considered how lucky I was to have Bilal. I thought about Amma and Sajida. I knew how incredibly fortunate I was, even if I never married again, to have two good women in my life.

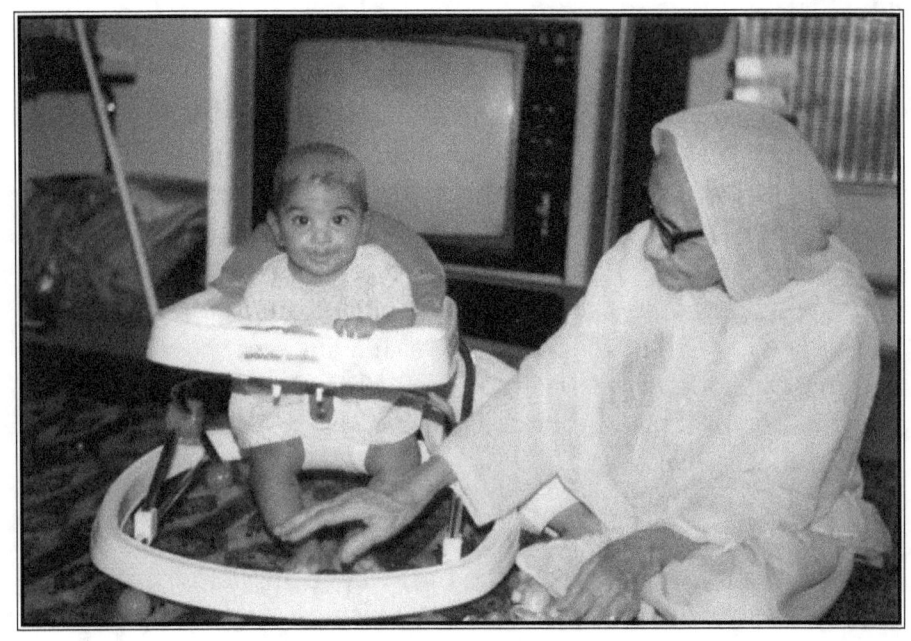

Amma Ji with Bilal

-31-

STROKE

O
ne day in late 1988, I received a call from Sajida. She sounded panicked. "Amma isn't responding to me. I called 911."

"I'll be right there!"

I hung up the phone, grabbed Bilal, and rushed to the car. Sajida didn't live far, and I got there within minutes. The ambulance was still there, and paramedics were trying to stabilize Amma. She was breathing, but she was not speaking or looking at them, and her body was as lifeless as a rag doll.

The medics rushed her to Ravenswood hospital, where she was diagnosed as having suffered a stroke. The doctors told us that hardening of the arteries had likely precipitated the stroke. In the days that followed, Amma couldn't speak or move, and she seemed confused. The doctors told us that the chances of her recovering her speech, mobility, and mental faculties depended partly on her age and partly on her determination. Sajida and I exchanged looks. We knew that determination would not be a problem.

"I can tell Amma hates the hospital," Sajida said. "You know Amma will be more comfortable at home."

"I agree. I think she'll have a better chance to recover at home."

We discussed this with her doctors, and they agreed. Amma went home with Sajida, where she began an extensive rehabilitation regimen with supervision from several therapists: a physical therapist to help her regain strength and mobility, an occupational therapist to help her relearn daily tasks, and a speech therapist to help her learn to talk again. We had to find a speech therapist that spoke Urdu.

She became fully alert and was able to think rationally. Her eyes became shining and fierce with determination. She was determined to talk to her family again, determined to resume her religious studies, and most of all, she was dead set on taking care of herself. Amma had no problem with accepting help from her family. She believed that families were meant to rely on one another, but she also believed that it was important to be a contributing member of her family. She was not about to let a stroke prevent that. As with everything else, Amma drew her strength from family, and in so doing, let us draw inspiration and strength from her.

I watched her work to regain as much as she could of what she had lost. With this, she became my teacher again. She was a study in human resilience. At first, Amma could not form words or sit up unassisted. Her right side was the most affected. Instead of feeling sorry for herself, she did what she had to do to recover. She listened to her therapists and followed their suggestions with concentration and discipline. No one had to urge her to cooperate with the therapists or to do the exercises that they assigned her. She knew her therapy schedule by heart. When it was time for her physical therapist to arrive, she sat in the living room, waiting for him. If he was even a few minutes late, she asked us to call him to remind him of their appointment.

She often asked one of us to help her through her exercise routine, but what she practiced the most was speaking. She couldn't tolerate not being able to communicate with us. With practice, her speech improved until soon she was conversing with us without much problem. Within a couple of months, she could sit up by herself without help, and soon after that, she could stand unassisted. It took some six months for her to learn to walk with the aid of a walker.

After that, Amma exercised on her own intermittently throughout the day, determined to do as much as possible without our help. Sajida and I both begged her not to go to the washroom alone, afraid that she might lose her balance and hurt herself. She tried to comply, but she was impatient. She would call out, "Sajida!" or "Zahir!" and we would head down the hall right away, only to find that she was already heading into or out of the bathroom.

"Amma, why didn't you wait? It's not safe."

"I can't wait all day for you to show up!"

Even when she did not need to use the toilet, brush her teeth, or bathe, she sometimes walked to the washroom to keep up on her exercise or simply stood up and walked around her bedroom.

We all knew it was too much to hope for her to ever return to her full, prestroke abilities, given her advanced age and physical condition. She was never again able to walk without the help of a walker, and her speech was never as clear as it had once been, but as soon as she mastered that walker, she was back to taking care of herself. She learned to live with her physical limitations and never once complained.

After all the times Amma had been there to help Bilal when he could not do everything for himself, Bilal finally had his chance to return the favor. He had exceptional patience, perhaps because he spent so much time around this older woman. He loved going to get her a glass of water, a tissue, or a book.

Amma taught me how to grow old—not with physical grace, perhaps, as her gait was too uneven for that—but with strength, perseverance, and unflagging love. She never stopped being who she was, and she never gave up on herself or the people she loved. We did our best to pass that gift on in our own lives.

Bernie and me on our wedding day

-32-

BERNIE

After seventeen years in the United States, I decided to apply for American citizenship. In January 1990, I went to the U.S. Immigration Office in downtown Chicago to take the oath of citizenship. I arrived early so that I would have time to complete the paperwork required for the swearing-in ceremony. The waiting room was almost full, so I sat in one of the few seats left in the front row. I removed the forms from my bag to begin filling them out, and then reached back into the bag for a pen. A typical accountant bag, it held several pencils but no pen. I looked around for someone that I might ask to borrow one. A petite, attractive young woman who appeared to be Southeast Asian sat to my right. She seemed friendly and approachable.

"May I borrow a pen?"

"Sure." She handed me her pen, peered over my shoulder for a moment, and frowned. "You're just filling those out now?"

"Yes. That's why I came early."

She looked at her watch. "Aren't you worried that you might not finish on time?"

I looked at her and smiled. She was so earnest and so attractive. I looked back down at the papers and furrowed my brow to imply that I did not see the big deal. "I don't know. It seems pretty straightforward to me."

She shrugged and turned away, looking as if it were none of her business. I got the impression that she did not think much of someone who took such things so casually, but when I returned her pen, she gave me a beaming smile. I took a chance.

"Oh, wait, would you give me your telephone number again?" I asked, as if she had already given her number to me before.

I don't know if I fooled her, or if she simply made up her mind that she wanted me to call her, but she gave me her number without blinking an eye. I wrote it down in my notebook, along with her name: Bernadette Turqueza Mariano.

I shook her hand. "Nice to meet you, Bernadette. My name is Zahir, Zahir Kazmi. May I ask you, what kind of name is Mariano?"

"Filipino. What kind of name is Kazmi? Indian?"

"Sort of. I'm from Pakistan."

We spent the next few minutes talking about our countries of origin and what had brought us to America. Bernadette was visibly excited to become a U.S. citizen. We stood next to each other during the ceremony, and I believe I caught her wiping a tear from her eye after she recited the oath of citizenship, though I said nothing.

Afterward, she asked if I knew where to find the U.S. Passport Office. I did not know, but I suggested that she try the information desk and offered to go with her. It was so easy talking to her, and it felt natural being with her. We discovered that the office was actually across the street, and we walked there together.

She had a few questions for the clerk at the passport office, and normally I might have left, but for some reason, waiting for her felt like the right thing to do, as if we were longtime friends. When she finished, we walked outside together into a cold and windy winter day. There was no excuse to linger, and we finally said our goodbyes. Before I left, I asked, "Can I call and take you out to dinner later this week?"

"I'd like that."

"I'll call you later to get your address and make plans. Goodbye, Bernadette."

At dinner a few nights later, she confessed that she had indeed been shocked at my casual attitude about my citizenship paperwork. "I completed mine days ahead of time, just in case there might be a problem." She said this with good humor and honesty, which made me like her even more. She was level-headed, hardworking, and smart, and this new American citizen also had that other American trait I loved so much: honesty. She told me that she was married and had a one-year-old child, and that her husband had left her just one week after her baby was born.

"I had to take my son to the Philippines to live with my parents, because I had no one to help me. I have to work full-time. I miss him so much, but by staying here, I can take better care of him. Most of my pay goes home to the Philippines, not just for him but also for my parents, brother, and sisters. They're all counting on me, so I'm glad I'm a citizen now. That way I'm sure I can stay and keep taking care of them."

I could not believe how much we had in common, not the least of which was a determination to improve our lives while still taking care of the families we loved. By the time the waiter served dessert, I was falling in love.

I brought Bernadette home to meet Bilal on our second date, and I cooked dinner for all of us. Bernadette was one of those people with such self-confidence that she made everyone around her comfortable, much like Amma and Sajida. I was not surprised when she and Bilal hit it off immediately.

Bernadette soon became a regular fixture in our lives. We spent every weekend together, and anyone who saw the three of us would have assumed that we were a long-time family. I began calling her Bernie, and soon everyone knew her by that name.

A few months later, we began talking about marriage. By then, Bernie had filed for and been granted a divorce. Each Thanksgiving, I invited my sister Sajida's family and a few of my closest friends to my home for a traditional American Thanksgiving dinner. That year, I invited Bernie to introduce her to my family, especially to Amma.

Bernie was not at all shy or nervous around Amma, showing great interest in her and asking her a lot of questions. This was not exactly easy. Amma did not understand English, and Bernie had to rely on Sajida and me to translate, but Amma seemed happy with the attention. Even if they were not learning much about each other because of the slow communication process, I was thrilled to see them getting along. As the night progressed, anticipation grew. I could not wait any longer to tell my family our news. I stood up at dinner and announced that

Bernie and I were getting married. Everyone was surprised, especially Amma, though she immediately gave us her blessing.

Amma did share a concern. "Aren't you worried your children will look Chinese instead of Pakistani?"

"Amma, Bernie is not Chinese, she is Filipino."

"I don't care. They all look Chinese to me." With that, we all laughed.

Amma just shrugged and said, "I don't care if she's Filipino, or Chinese, or African. So long as you love her, I will love her."

We translated for Bernie, toning down Amma's bluntness in the process.

Bernie laughed. Amma smiled and nodded. Considering the language and cultural barriers, it was not exactly an auspicious start, but I was happy that Amma and a bride I had chosen for myself seemed to accept each other! It looked like I was finally going to be happy.

On April 20, 1991, Bernie and I were married in a simple family ceremony in my sister's living room. With that, Bernie became Amma's fifth daughter-in-law, counting my two ex-wives.

Amma's relationship with Bernie developed slowly. They had to work their way around the language barrier. Bernie never did learn to speak more than a few polite words of Urdu, and Amma spoke no English at all, butt through hand signals, unspoken gestures of kindness, and mutual acceptance, they began to understand each other and grew closer.

Of all her daughter-in-laws, Amma had the best relationship with Bernie. Her relationship with Tayab's wife was never pleasant. Though she got along well with Mutahir's wife in the beginning, their relationship deteriorated over time. She had chosen each of my ex-wives, and in the end, she had regretted her choices. Amma never spent any time with her other daughters-in-law, who avoided her even when she was around.

The stereotype of the daughter-in-law/mother-in-law relationship in India and Pakistan is that of a domineering mother, with complete control over her son, and a soft-spoken bride who is completely submissive to both of them. Though Amma Ji was not a domineering mother-in-law, her daughters-in-law entered relationships with her with that stereotype engrained in their minds. Their relationships started in a spirit of suspicion and mistrust, which led to misinterpretation of actions, which led to more suspicion and mistrust until the spiral led to distance and even enmity.

A Pakistani friend of mine put it best when she said, "Kazmi Bahi, it does not matter whether my mother-in-law is good or bad, the problem is that she is my mother-in-law."

Looking at the facts alone, Amma should have found it easy to have good relationships with all her sons' wives; she never lived in their homes, never had a say in running their households, and made sure never to depend on them financially. Old stereotypes die hard. I am convinced it was the fear those stereotypes stirred up that doomed her relationships with her Pakistani daughters-in-law.

Amma's relationship with Bernie came with no preconceived expectations. They had no shared cultural expectations that might shape their relationship. They were strangers to each other in every respect, and they were free to make up their relationship as they went along. When Bernie treated Amma with respect and kindness, Amma did not take it as her due; she treated it as a gift and reacted with appreciation. When Amma behaved appreciatively, Bernie also treated it as a gift. Their relationship was one of mutual respect.

Other facts helped as well. Bernie was the only one of my three wives who married me for love, and that was an enormously important factor. Bernie realized how important Amma was in my life, so she made sure that Amma was always welcome in our house. She realized that I loved my mother, so she was determined to love her if she could, and the reverse was true. Amma knew how much I loved Bernie and saw how well she treated me, so she was eager to love Bernie. They made it easy for each other.

Bernie looked after Amma's every need. After her stroke, Amma could not bathe herself and needed someone to help her. When Amma visited us, Bernie took on this task with good cheer, setting a lawn chair in the bathtub to bathe her and carefully oiling and combing her hair afterward. Even though they did not speak each other's language, I could hear them chattering away in the bathroom. Amma talked to Bernie in Urdu, and Bernie replied in English, sometimes in Pilipino. I knew that neither of them understood a word the other was saying, but they never missed a beat. Sometimes, Amma would ask for something, and Bernie would say, "'Yes, Amma. *Theek hay, theek hay.*" (You're right.) This was followed by good-natured chuckling. At times I could hear Amma's voice rising in mild complaint. Bernie remained patient, even when she could tell that Amma was scolding her.

"I asked her to do something, and she did another," Amma said to me.

"Amma, you have to be more patient. She doesn't understand what you're saying," I replied.

"Don't be silly, of course she does. Bernie and I understand each other perfectly."

To some extent, that was true. Theirs was the unspoken communication of caring. Amma always included Bernie in her prayers, asking Allah to give her a happy life.

Bernie also got along very well with Sajida. I never heard her make a single statement critical of my sister. Sajida later moved to California, and whenever she came to visit us, Bernie never failed to take her out for a manicure and pedicure. They would go shopping and have lunch at their favorite Chinese restaurant. They enjoyed each other's company and always came back giggling like schoolgirls. Sajida had never been so close to one of her sisters-in-law.

In late 1992, Bernie discovered that she was pregnant. Bernie was born a Roman Catholic, and before she met me, she never met a Muslim, even though Islam is the oldest recorded religion in the Philippines. It is believed that Islam was introduced in the southern part of the country, known as Mindanao, between the twelfth and the fourteenth century, but today, the Philippines is the only Christian country in Asia. The population consist of 85 percent Christians, 10 percent Muslims, and 5 percent other religions.

Bernie was born in the northern part of the country and grew up and went to school in Manila. She had heard only negative stereotypes about radical, militant Muslims all her life, but when we married, Bernie learned more about Islamic beliefs and teachings through my family and friends. While she was pregnant, Bernie came to me with her decision to make a change. "I want to convert to Islam," she said.

"That's not necessary, Bernie. I don't care what religion you are."

"But I do. I don't want our son to grow up in a religiously divided household."

"You shouldn't convert to a religion you don't believe in just for our son or for me. You should do it only if you have faith in Islamic teachings."

"That's not the only reason I have started believing in Islam and its teachings. I plan to learn more. I am sure I want to convert."

She began studying many books and taking religious instruction. She asked Amma many questions about the Quran, which Amma was thrilled to answer. In early 1993, Bernie converted to Islam. Although Amma never mentioned wanting her daughter-in-law to convert, she grinned from ear to ear on the day that Bernie became a Muslim, and I knew she was pleased that the woman who had long been so kind to her now shared her religion.

One day, Amma took her last set of gold bangles—the only thing she had of any value—out of her jewelry box and gave them to Bernie as a gift. I knew that she had planned to give those bangles to Bilal's future wife; she had given me instructions to do so if she passed away before he married. Bilal had a special place in Amma's heart, and I understood that changing her mind and giving the bangles to Bernie was no small gesture. Bernie understood this, too. She resolved that she would ultimately follow Amma's initial wish, giving one bangle each to the future wives of all four of our sons: Farhan, Bilal, Bernard, and Imran.

Bernie treasures those bangles more than any other piece of jewelry she has ever owned.

Amma's gift to her was a testament to how close they had become and how much love and respect Amma had for the daughter-in law she did not choose. Amma could have simply told me to pass them on to Bernie after she passed away, but she did not want to wait until she was dead to let Bernie know her true feelings.

Bernie, me, Bilal and Sohaila

-33-

IMRAN ZAHIR

Me, my sister Sajida and Imran at his first birthday.

Throughout Bernie's pregnancy, she drove all over the city searching for food to fill her cravings, and only Filipino food would do. I believe she found every Filipino restaurant and grocery store in Chicago and became a regular customer of each one. I like to think that I'm open to new and exotic delicacies, but it seemed that Bernie had latched onto a category of food that I can only describe as spicy, stinky, and strange. I tried not to be annoyed, but as the air in our house thickened, I sometimes begged for mercy.

Our son was born on August 14, 1993. As I stood in the hospital room with my glowing wife and our beautiful newborn boy, I knew that the perfect family had fallen my way by pure chance, and it came after all my mother's old-fashioned, optimistic scheming and arranging. Maybe it was fate. I could not help but realize that my third son's birthday coincided with the date of Pakistan's independence from British rule. This was the date when my life moved away the path of rural tradition and onto the path of the sojourner, a path that prepared me for embracing the unknown. If not for this, I might never have come to America.

Although all of our friends thought it was an auspicious date for a birthday, I disagreed. I still believed that the decision to split India up to create a separate country for Muslims was a bad idea that had led to resentment, mistrust, and conflict. I always wondered if my mother's life, my family's life, my own life, and lives of millions of Muslims in the Indian Subcontinent might have been happier and better if India had not divided. It might have been quieter, simpler, and easier in some ways.

Bernie and I asked members of our close family for suggestions for the name of our new son. I entrusted the list to Bernie. "You choose," I said. The day our son was born, I asked her, "What name did you decide on?"

"Imran Zahir."

The name was Amma's choice. She had tried for a long time to get one of her children to name one of her grandsons Imran. Mutahir and his wife had at first agreed to the name for their first son but changed their minds. When my sister Sajida's son was born, she decided to let Abba and Amma name him. Amma chose Imran, but Abba suggested Ahsan. They decided to write the names on two sheets of paper and draw one: Ahsan it was.

Amma finally got her wish with my third son, the only son born of a love marriage, and Bernie chose Imran not knowing the emotional story behind it.

That same year, Sajida's youngest daughter, Sohaila, got engaged. Sajida and Ather, who had had better luck than I had with arranged marriages, had chosen their daughter's husband. Alamgir and his parents lived in Los Angeles, and the two families decided that the wedding should take place there. This was a happy opportunity for my sister, because her middle daughter, Naila, also lived there.

Our family flew to California to attend my niece's wedding and made a side-trip to the Grand Canyon. The Grand Canyon was the most astonishing sight I had seen in America. Bilal was impressed with how high up we were. He was old enough that he would probably remember the experience, but it would take years before the memory would take on the kind of significance that only comes with time. I will never forget that first train ride to Pakistan with my mother; though I knew it was important, I was too young to understand how it would change my destiny.

After Sohaila's wedding, my sister decided to move to California for the same reason that my mother had once moved to Pakistan. She wanted to stay close to her children or at least to Naila and Sohaila. Ahsan was about to start medical school in Central America. None of her children lived in the Chicago area anymore, so there was nothing in particular to hold her there. She and her husband said they were tired of the Chicago weather and would like to grow old someplace sunny and warm. After Sohaila's wedding, they sold their boutique shop and moved to Los Angeles. Amma was living with Sajida, and so it made sense for her to pick up yet again and go with them.

Amma and I were sad to part ways. I spent so much of my life near her, and she and Sajida had become Bilal's surrogate mothers. Amma was disappointed that she would be living so far from her youngest grandson. "There's no telling when Allah will call me home. Imran may never get to know me," Amma said.

All of us, even Amma, couldn't argue that the warm weather of sunny southern California would be easier on her aging body.

I missed her so much, and I worried that her time was growing shorter since her stroke. At first, I flew to California almost monthly, and Amma insisted that I could not come without bringing Imran. My son became a frequent flyer before he was even a year old.

The next few years passed quietly. Amma spent most of her days sitting in her chair at Sajida's, reciting from the holy Quran and studying other religious books. She also read as many Urdu-language newspapers and magazines as she could get her hands on. My brother-in-law, Ather Bahi, was retired, and he spent considerable time listening to Amma's stories of the past. Ather Bahi is one of the best listeners I have ever known; he listened with great attention and never interrupted except to ask questions or offer encouragement, so long as you kept the tea coming. Because the closest members of my family were so far away, I was often comforted by the image of Ather Bahi and Amma Ji sitting across from each other, sipping from their ever-present cups of tea, while Amma brought to life Pur Qazi, the mango groves, and her beloved father, now gone some eighty years.

After she moved to California, Amma did return to Chicago few times to stay with us for a couple of months. My oldest brother, Tayab, and I had become closer over the years, and I invited him to visit America a few times. Whenever he did, Amma and he spent considerable time together discussing politics and religion. As Tayab grew older, he developed an interest in religious studies, and he and Amma often discussed questions of Islamic theology. I could tell that Amma was very proud that her son had taken such a strong interest in his faith. She had followed him to Pakistan, hoping to be close to her son, but it was not until he visited her to America, in her advancing years, that they finally returned to the closeness she had missed since they walked hand in hand through the village.

The sight of them sitting together, sometimes nodding and agreeing, sometimes locked in intense debate, made me smile. It was the first time the three of us had been so happy together.

- 3 4 -

A HEARTBEAT OF 250

Not long after Amma and Tayab's visit to Chicago, in the summer of 1997, she developed chest pains. The paramedics rushed her to the hospital. It was a heart attack. Even Amma, who had been preparing us for the possibility of her demise for some thirty years, was taken by surprise. Sajida called to deliver the news. "Amma is in critical condition."

I caught the next possible flight to Los Angeles. This time, I did not bring Imran.

While the doctors were trying to stabilize Amma, my niece Naila was holding her hand. "Amma Ji," she said, "you're not going to leave us. *Mamoon* (uncle) Zahir isn't even here yet, so you can't leave us."

Amma waved a single, reassuring finger in the air, indicating that she was not going anywhere just yet.

By the time I arrived at the hospital, Amma was stable and breathing normally. This had her attending physician flabbergasted. He told me he could not explain it. "This was a massive heart attack," he said. "Her heart rate reached a high of 250. I have never seen a patient in her condition survive such an assault on the body, at any age. The only explanation I can come up with is that she was determined not to leave right then." As she continued to recuperate, he said, "She must have incredible willpower."

As worried as we all were, the family members smiled at each other, and my sister and I chuckled softly, thinking, You do not know the half of it!

That evening, after Amma was stable, my niece Sohaila's father-in-law came to visit Amma. *"Bahi Sahib, Aaj Meana Moot Ke Frishta Ko Shkisat Dade."* (Bahi Sahib, today I defeated the angel of death.)

Soon Amma was moved to a nursing home for a few weeks of rehabilitation, and we were all amazed when she improved enough to come home to Sajida's. I returned to visit her there and stayed for some time. I had always known that my sister was a good mother to her children and a good daughter to Amma Ji. During those visits, as I watched her spend countless hours by Amma's bedside, attending to her every need, I realized that my sister was an extraordinary woman. She did everything with matter-of-fact grace, never once hinting by gesture, tone, or look that any of it was an inconvenience. Sajida saw Amma as the source of all she had and all she was. What else would Sajida do besides care for that source with every last ounce of her strength?

Though Amma survived the heart attack, she was not in good shape. Her heart had been severely damaged, and at her age, in her weakened condition, the doctors did not dare do anything to repair it. Surgery was too big a risk.

We brought up the possibility that if she got stronger, she might consider an operation. Amma shook her head. "I've had a long, healthy, happy life. My family has all made me very proud, and I know you'll all be fine without me. I know it will soon be time for me to leave this world. If Allah is ready for me, then no operation will help. It's okay, I know where I'm going, and I'm ready."

In the weeks that followed, she was rushed to the hospital several more times. Each time, the attending physicians expressed their astonishment upon reading Amma's case file, shaking their heads in disbelief. "This must be a typo," one of them said. It wasn't.

I found myself splitting my time between California and Chicago. Bernie never suggested that I was overdoing it, though I repeatedly skipped work and then doubled up when I came back, suffered jet lag, missed sleep, and fretted constantly. She understood how much Amma meant to me and that it would be too difficult to risk not being there at the end.

In August 1998, paramedics once again took Amma to the emergency room at Brea Community Hospital. Her pulse throbbed in slow motion. Her heart was giving up, but as her body grew weaker, she remained mentally alert. From the moment we arrived, Amma seemed to understand that her worldly life was coming to a close. She was determined to do so on her own terms. She made every decision herself. She made it clear to us that she did not want to be kept on life support.

"When my time comes, you must respect my wishes and the wish of Allah and let me go peacefully."

"Okay, Amma Ji," I said.

"Whatever you say, Amma," Sajida said.

When Amma had little strength to eat, the doctors wanted to start feeding her intravenously. They discussed the idea with us, but Amma was still awake, so she was still the one making the decisions, just as she always had in this family. When we asked her about the feeding tube, she firmly rejected it. The doctors understood that she did not want medical personnel to take heroic measures when her systems stopped, but this was different. Without inserting the feeding tube, it would be tantamount to starving her. We understood the doctors' dilemma, so we told them to try it and see how she responded.

Amma was sedated, and the tube was put into place. She was still under the anesthesia when an orderly wheeled her out of the operating room, and we heard her murmuring in Urdu.

The doctor and nurse walking with her looked at her in surprise. The nurse turned and asked, "What's she saying?"

"'My God, help me,'" Sajida translated.

The nurses looked even more surprised, saying it was not often that a woman of Amma's age under heavy sedation had the presence of mind to ask God for help. The doctor entered this unusual development into Amma's medical record.

The following morning, we discovered that Amma's feeding tubes had been removed. Sometime during the night, she regained consciousness and pulled them out.

"Why, Amma?" Sajida asked. "This is the only way for you to get enough food."

"I told you I don't want any life support. I'm still your mother, and you don't get to decide things for me. This is my life, and I'll decide how I want to die."

Sajida and I looked at each other and nodded in surrender.

"Okay, Amma," I said. "We understand. We won't let the doctors do anything like that again."

We all knew it was only a matter of hours or days until Amma passed away. Bernie was still back in Chicago with the kids, and I telephoned to ask her to join me in Los Angeles. I did not ask her to bring the children, but I smiled when I saw Imran, Bilal, and Bernard walk into the hospital with her.

"I knew Amma would want to see them," Bernie said, "and they really wanted to say goodbye to their grandmother."

I gave my wife a hug. "Thank you, Bernie. You're so right. I don't know why I didn't think to ask you. I guess I just didn't think that children and hospitals went together, but you did exactly the right thing."

As the hospital filled with more than a dozen members of our extended family, I thought the staff might lose patience with such a large crowd, but they went out of their way to make us comfortable, giving us a large, three-bed room with no other patients. They brought us extra rollaway beds and chairs so that we could hold vigil day and night. This was definitely not the hospital's usual policy, but Amma's amazing case of spiritual mind over matter had captured their hearts. For a week, the hospital became our temporary home, and management bent the rules to let us say a long farewell.

Although Sajida's home was only ten minutes away, and we could easily have gone there to sleep and come back at a moment's notice, none of us left Amma's side any longer than necessary to shower, change clothes, or buy food.

Amma wore a smile that told us she was strengthened to have us all by her side. Her physical heart was weakening, but her heart of hearts, her soul, was strong.

In late August, Amma's final struggle began. She was having more difficulty breathing. I moved to her bedside, took hold of her hand,

and leaned close to her ear to speak, my voice as soft as it was when I sang a lullaby to Imran.

"Probably the time has come for you to leave us. I know how much you love us and how much you must be worrying about our well-being, but you know that you've raised us well and taught us to be strong, and you can trust us to carry on in this journey of life."

Amma fell into a comma. We took turns reciting Amma's favorite verses from the holy Quran. On the morning of August 31, most of us except my sister left the room for one reason or another—to go to the restroom, grab something to eat, or stretch our legs. Without consulting each other or finishing whatever we were doing, everyone returned from different parts of the hospital as if something had called us. We would later stare at each other in wonder, all believing that Amma needed us right at that moment.

On the surface, there appeared to be no change in Amma's condition, yet we all experienced a shift. I always thought that my niece Naila had the sweetest voice, and I suggested she alone stand close to Amma's bedside and recite Surah-e-Yaseen from the holy Quran. The passage of Surah-e-Yaseen is traditionally thought to ease one's passing from worldly life to eternal life.

No one left the room, and no one tried to shield even our youngest children from this final moment with Amma Ji, which was not tense or frightening but relaxed and peaceful. Three generations encircled Amma's bed with warmth and love as we watched her take her last breath. I heard the final inhalation. It slowly blew out of her in a soft, inaudible puff. Her spirit left with it.

Amma had often talked of how she envisioned the end, how she would leave this earth. She wanted to be surrounded by her family, while one person recited the Surah-e-Yaseen. Amma had inspired all of us to work hard to make our lives even better than we had hoped. The least we could do was give her the death she wished for, and the peace I felt in the room at that moment told us that we had.

After a doctor confirmed that Amma had passed away, and the nurses and technicians separated her from the equipment, we all gradually returned to practical considerations. Sajida's face developed a determined expression. She said she was going to remove Amma's hospital gown and put on her usual clothes. Amma had always been modest and religious, and Sajida did not want to see her carried out in the hospital gown with the undignified opening in the back. "Amma would have thought it improper," she said.

She asked the nurse to help her. The nurse said, "I don't think you'll be able to do it. It's been a while, and her body must be stiff already."

"Please, can we just try?"

The nurse reluctantly agreed and looked surprised as she shifted Amma's body out of the gown. "That's odd. Her body is as flexible as ever. I've never felt anything like it."

"Amma was always different," Sajida said.

"She must have been a very pious woman," the nurse said as she and Sajida put on Amma's traditional tunic and pants.

I did not witness this moment, but I did see Amma again after she died, and I too was taken aback. As Amma had grown older, she had developed pimples on her face, but within a few hours after her death, they all vanished. Her face looked soft and smooth, her skin almost dewy. She looked the way I remembered her when I was a boy and one of the lucky few allowed to see the sweet face under the burqa.

"She looks like Aunt Dollat," Sajida said.

"You're right, I see it," I said. Not only was Aunt Dollat a very pretty woman, she was one of Amma's closest family members. In fact, Amma was so close to her aunt that her mother used to say that sometimes she seemed more like Dollat's daughter than hers. I could not help but wonder if Aunt Dollat had come back for a moment to take Amma with her to heaven.

I had experienced Amma's last breath leaving her with sureness, gentleness, and grace. It was her spirit brushing past, and it knew exactly where it was going.

-35-

SUITE 115

Amma Ji's last breath still lingered in the air, whispering some final wisdom I could not hear but could feel. In Islam, it is important to bury the dead as soon as possible. Muslims do not embalm their loved ones, do not try to keep them preserved for a drawn-out goodbye or try to save the corpse as a keepsake of what is no longer here. Amma Ji's spirit had departed. We did not need her body to remember her, as the spirit that filled her body was too great for us to ever forget. It made sense to let her beautiful shell become part of the earth again, the dust from which God had made an extraordinary woman.

Ather and I left to make arrangements at the cemetery. The cemetery's grass and trees were an unfailing green; Los Angeles was perpetually hot, though rarely as hot as Amma Ji's childhood home in India. Transplanting her life to America had allowed her to grow more fully into who she was, like the strong old trees around us. Her body would rest easy here. The graves were well maintained and clean, which would suit her sense of order. I could easily imagine her putting a hand on my shoulder and saying, "This is a perfect place for me to begin my final hajj, just so long as it is not too expensive."

In spite of my sadness, I smiled as I turned to Ather Bahi and nodded. This would do nicely.

We went back to the office to take care of the paperwork. After I wrote the funeral director a check, as he began to attach it to the other documents, he glanced down and did a double take. He checked the paperwork again, looking back and forth from the forms to the check. He shook his head with astonishment and said, "What are the chances?"

"What is it?" we asked, puzzled.

He placed the check and the cemetery documents in front of us. "Take a look at this."

He pointed to the number of my office suite in Chicago and then to the number of the lot for my mother's gravesite: suite 115 and burial lot 115. My eyes grew round with wonder. Amma Ji had been my greatest teacher, and I could not help but wonder if she was she still trying to tell me something. Later, my sister would say, "Amma just wanted to make sure that you'll never forget her." I see that number every day when I open my office door; it is imprinted right above the door lock. It is fitting, as she made my career possible, first with her dreams, then with her very real sacrifices.

We instructed the funeral home not to touch my mother's body. My sister would come to the funeral home the next day to give Amma her final bath. Sajida arrived in the morning, carrying the rusty, old blue bag in which our mother had already placed all she would need for the final ritual. A funeral home employee kindly offered Sajida some soap and shampoo, but Sajida said, "I don't think I need it." Amma always took care of everything in life and was no different in death. Just to be sure, Sajida looked in the bag and saw that she was right. She saw soap and shampoo, as well as itar (scent) to sprinkle over her kafan—the white cotton burial shroud in which Sajida would wrap her sat neatly folded inside the bag.

Amma bought her kafan in 1971, the first time she went to Makkah for her hajj. There, she had her shroud dipped in abe-zam-zam. On that same trip, Amma bought the simple bag that her daughter now carried. From that day on, for the next twenty-seven years, Amma brought that bag wherever she went. No matter if the trip was far or near, long or short, she always took the bag of her favorite color, blue, with her. Everyone in the family knew what was in it and what to do with its contents when the time came.

As is customary, only people of the same sex are present at the final bath of the woman who was both head and heart of our family. Only women of Amma's family, young and old, watched as Sajida lovingly rubbed soap over our mother's body, massaged her hair in luxurious lather, and slowly rinsed her. They all worked together to gently wrap her in the *kafan*, leaving only her well-loved face showing. Every woman present remarked that Amma's body still had not stiffened. As resilient as she had been in life, part of her strength had always been her softness and pliability. That part continued in death, making things easier for us, as always.

Once Amma's body was sprinkled with sweet-smelling *itar*, we placed her in the hall for viewing. Her soft face resembled that of an angel, still faintly glowing with the inner light she always had. The children refused to be held back from Amma but surrounded her closely, giving her kisses and gently stroking her face. They were not afraid to touch her dead body. Amma had never been anything but loving and compassionate with all of them, and nothing about her body could be frightening.

We took her to the mosque for the final prayer before burial at Zuhar prayer time and then on to her final resting place. In Islam, burial is very simple, and the body of every Muslim is prepared and buried in the same way. There is no distinction between rich and poor, because in the eye of our maker we are all equal. We all come empty-handed into this world, and we all return the same way. Even for Amma Ji, greatness came not from what filled her hands but from the way she chose to fill her heart and mind.

I watched as her body, enveloped in the layers of her pure white *kafan*, was lowered into her lot, number 115. I said my final prayers, said farewell to Amma Ji, and left her side for the last time. I knew she would never leave mine.

In the evening, we sat and reflected over Amma's life. Ather Bhai told us that two weeks prior to her passing, Amma told him she felt sorry that we were all worrying for nothing. She said that all the arrangements for her leaving this life were complete and that she would be leaving very soon. "This time I'm not staying," she said, referring to her previous brushes with death. She asked Ather not to tell anyone about their conversation. She would tell everyone when she was ready to leave. True to her word, Amma announced her departure two days before she passed away.

We buried her in Los Angeles, eight thousand miles from the village where she was born, but I sometimes imagine her spirit traveling from heaven to the homes of all her children and grandchildren. I suspect Amma sometimes returns to Pur Qazi to visit the mango groves, the memories of her father, and the family life she began there. After all, Amma was never afraid of a long journey, especially one that promised to take her closer to those she loved.

GLOSSARY

- Amma – Mother
- Amma Ji – Dear Mother
- Abba – Father (Amma's husband)
- Abba Ji – Dear Father
- Jamil-un-Nisa(Jamila) Usmani – Amma's maiden name
- Mohammad Hanif Kazmi – Abba's Name
- Family Members:
  o Bilqees – Oldest Daughter
  o Tayab – Oldest son
  o Sayeeda – Daughter
  o Tahir – Son
  o Zubaida – Daughter
  o Mutahir – Son
  o Zahir – Youngest son
  o Farhan – Grandson
  o Salim – Grandson
  o Kalim – Grandson
  o Ghazala – Granddaughter
  o Naila – Granddaughter
  o Sohaila – Granddaughter
  o Ahsan – Grandson
  o Bernadette – Amma's daughter-in-law and writer's wife
  o Bilal – Grandson
  o Imran (ImranZahir) – Grandson
  o Bernard - Grandson

- o Sajida – Youngest daughter
- o Taqi Ahmad – Older step brother
- o Nani – Maternal grandmother
- o Abdul Hai – Abba's cousin, a feudal land lord in Pur Qazi
- o Jamil – Younger brother
- o Zaheer – Younger brother
- o Rauf Ahmed – Bilqees first husband
- o Yahya Rizvi – Bilqees's second husband
- o Syed Murtaza – Cousin
- Makkah – City of Makkah in Saudi Arabia. A holiest place for Muslims
- Alvida – Good By
- Allah Hafiz – Good be with you
- Pur Qazi – A small rural town in Northern India, where Amma was born
- Burqa – A piece of garment used by women for Hijab
- Angun – Court Yard
- Appa – Older sister
- Tanga – A horse driven carriage
- Chai – Tea
- Bahi – Brother
- Biryani – An Indian/Pakistani dish, rice cooked with spicy meat.
- Paratha – Hand made bread fried with oil
- Mangni – Engagement
- Mayun – A period of seclusion (for bride) before marriage.
- Uptan – A paste of turmeric, sandalwood powder, herbs and aromatic oil – used by women to clean and beautify their skin.
- Sadka – An offering to ward off evil
- Behshti Zevar – An instructional book for women to make their married life successful.
- Barat – A procession composed of bridegroom, his family and friends leading to Bride's place for marriage.
- Nikah – Marriage ceremony
- Maulana – A spiritual leader
- Sureh – Verse

- Liaquat Ali Khan – First Prime Minister of Pakistan and second most influential leader in Pakistan's Independence movement.
- Maulana Abdul Kalam Azad – A Muslim Leader against dividing India on the basis of religion
- Maulana Shabbir Ahmed Usmani – A Muslim Leader
- Gurdaspur – An Indian City
- Muzaffarnagar – A City in Northern India
- Sialkot – A city of Pakistan
- Mohammad Allama Iqbal – A poet and philosopher
- Faiz Ahmed and Faiz – A Poet
- Dadu – A city in Pakistan
- Naan – baked bread
- Dari – A throwaway carpet made out of cotton
- Bibi – Sister
- Baji – Older sister
- Aabdul Ghani – A neighbor
- Mahmooda – A neighbor
- Muhajir – A term used for people who migrated from India to Pakistan after creation of Pakistan.
- Lahore - An historical city in Pakistan
- Anarkali – A famous business district in Lahore, Pakistan
- Chaddar – A headscarf.
- Aqiqa – A party to celebrate a new born.
- Phooppo – Paternal aunt
- Moomani – Maternal aunt
- Mammon – Maternal uncle
- Abboo – Dad